Hans Zimmer and James Newton Howard's *The Dark Knight*

Film Score Guides
Series Editor: Kate Daubney

1. *Gabriel Yared's* The English Patient: *A Film Score Guide*, by Heather Laing. 2004.
2. *Danny Elfman's* Batman: *A Film Score Guide*, by Janet K. Halfyard. 2004.
3. *Ennio Morricone's* The Good, the Bad and the Ugly: *A Film Score Guide*, by Charles Leinberger. 2004.
4. *Louis and Bebe Barron's* Forbidden Planet: *A Film Score Guide*, by James Wierzbicki. 2005.
5. *Bernard Herrmann's* The Ghost and Mrs. Muir: *A Film Score Guide*, by David Cooper. 2005.
6. *Erich Wolfgang Korngold's* The Adventures of Robin Hood: *A Film Score Guide*, by Ben Winters. 2007.
7. *Mychael Danna's* The Ice Storm: *A Film Score Guide*, by Miguel Mera. 2007.
8. *Alex North's* A Streetcar Named Desire: *A Film Score Guide*, by Annette Davison. 2009.
9. *Nino Rota's* The Godfather Trilogy: *A Film Score Guide*, by Franco Sciannameo. 2010.
10. *Miklós Rózsa's* Ben-Hur: *A Film Score Guide*, by Roger Hickman. 2011.
11. *Zbigniew Preisner's* Three Colors *Trilogy: Blue, White, Red: A Film Score Guide*, by Nicholas W. Reyland. 2012.
12. *Franz Waxman's* Rebecca: *A Film Score Guide*, by David Neumeyer and Nathan Platte. 2012.
13. *Jerome Moross's* The Big Country: *A Film Score Guide*, by Mariana Whitmer. 2012.
14. *Leonard Bernstein's* On the Waterfront: *A Film Score Guide*, by Anthony Bushard. 2013.
15. *Ilan Eshkeri's* Stardust: *A Film Score Guide*, by Ian Sapiro. 2013.
16. *David Shire's* The Conversation: *A Film Score Guide*, by Juan Chattah. 2015.
17. *James Newton Howard's* Signs: *A Film Score Guide*, by Erik Heine. 2016.
18. *Hans Zimmer and James Newton Howard's* The Dark Knight: *A Film Score Guide*, by Vasco Hexel. 2016.

Hans Zimmer and James Newton Howard's *The Dark Knight*

A Film Score Guide

Vasco Hexel

ROWMAN & LITTLEFIELD
Lanham • Boulder • New York • London

Published by Rowman & Littlefield
A wholly owned subsidiary of The Rowman & Littlefield Publishing Group, Inc.
4501 Forbes Boulevard, Suite 200, Lanham, Maryland 20706
www.rowman.com

Unit A, Whitacre Mews, 26-34 Stannary Street, London SE11 4AB

Copyright © 2016 by Rowman & Littlefield

All rights reserved. No part of this book may be reproduced in any form or by any electronic or mechanical means, including information storage and retrieval systems, without written permission from the publisher, except by a reviewer who may quote passages in a review.

British Library Cataloguing in Publication Information Available

Library of Congress Cataloging-in-Publication Data
Names: Hexel, Vasco, 1980- author.
Title: Hans Zimmer and James Newton Howard's The dark knight : a film score guide / Vasco Hexel.
Description: Lanham, MD : Rowman & Littlefield, 2016. | Series: Film score guides ; 18 | Includes bibliographical references and index.
Identifiers: LCCN 2016002714 (print) | LCCN 2016005181 (ebook) | ISBN 9781442266728 (pbk. : alk. paper) | ISBN 9781442266735 (electronic)
Subjects: LCSH: Zimmer, Hans. Dark knight. | Howard, James Newton. Dark knight.
Classification: LCC ML410.Z557 H49 2016 (print) | LCC ML410.Z557 (ebook) | DDC 781.5/42—dc23
LC record available at http://lccn.loc.gov/2016002714

♾ The paper used in this publication meets the minimum requirements of American National Standard for Information Sciences—Permanence of Paper for Printed Library Materials, ANSI/NISO Z39.48-1992.

Printed in the United States of America

To my students

CONTENTS

List of Figures		ix
List of Tables		xi
Editor's Foreword		xiii
Acknowledgments		xvii
Introduction		xix
Chapter 1	Musical Background of the Composers	1
Chapter 2	Critical, Textual, and Historical Context of *The Dark Knight*	13
Chapter 3	The Technical Approach of the Composers	31
Chapter 4	Analysis of the Score as Musical Text	53
Chapter 5	Analysis of the Score as Part of the Soundscape	111
Conclusion		133
Notes		135
Appendix I: Spotting		149
Appendix II: Orchestrations		173
Bibliography		195
Index		197
About the Author		211

FIGURES

3.1	Collaborators getting and staying involved in *TDK*	42
4.1	Helmholtz nomenclature	53
4.2	Joker Theme splits and rises	74
4.3	Joker Triumphant	78
5.1	Shared sonic territory and conceptual overlaps between music and sound design	114

TABLES

2.1. Comparison of Batman and the Joker   28
4.1 Cue numbering in the orchestrators' scores   56

EDITOR'S FOREWORD

I observed in the Editor's Foreword to Erik Heine's Scarecrow Guide about James Newton Howard's score for M. Night Shyamalan's film *Signs*, that Howard's way of being in the world rather subverted the contemporary dominance of the cult of personality. In this volume, Vasco Hexel explores the idea of personality through two rather contrasting lenses: the thesis on identity that is Christopher Nolan's movie *The Dark Knight*; and Howard's co-authorship of the score with Hans Zimmer, one of the most dynamic individuals to have influenced film scoring in several decades. As Ben Winters discussed in his Scarecrow Guide on Erich Korngold's score for *The Adventures of Robin Hood*, notions of authorship in film music have been neither straightforward nor easily defined since the 1930s. But Dr. Hexel's study explores just how complex both the practice and the relationships can be. As if the dialogue between composer and director is not nuanced and dynamic enough, affected by production logistics as much as artistic sensibilities, introducing two composers with very contrasting musical styles and technical approaches to the process surely generates creative energy which must be absorbed by the score.

Dr. Hexel takes us through the processes and techniques used by each composer and for those interested in Howard's method, Dr. Heine's book makes a good companion read. But what will strike even the most casual reader is the distinctive resonance between the two composers, for all their differences. As Dr. Hexel demonstrates, both have adapted readily to the opportunities provided by technology to build up sounds and music beyond what is possible with a live orchestra. The suffusion of the final score with samples and textures, both purely musical and artificially generated, shows how diversely the same creative tools can be employed. Indeed, perhaps the dynamic of Howard's and Zimmer's similarities and differences finds its metaphor in the dynamic of Batman and the Joker; both creative and powerful influences on the world they define, using similar forces to rather different yet equally impactful outcomes.

On a similarly metaphorical note, Dr. Hexel explores the evolution of the so-called Batflaps element of the soundscape, a sonic effect that ambient music designer Mel Wesson originally created to meet the absence of Batman until one hour into the film. Zimmer had suggested that Wesson try to create the sound of wings flapping, even though Batman's suit does not have wings and he glides rather than flies. In many ways, the Batflaps are an excellent analogy for the way in which this score has been constructed for, as Dr. Hexel ably demonstrates elsewhere in the same chapter, both Zimmer and Howard have sampled live performance and used it in conjunction with the original performance. This evolution of layers of texture from the actual—removed yet connected, recognizable yet not visible, synergistic yet not the same—is a metaphor for the expectation of continuity and coherence in the soundscape that is very much a feature of the modern science fiction epic. The boundary between music and sound is, for Zimmer and supervising sound editor Richard King, utterly irrelevant: "all sound is music."

The Series of Film Score Guides was established to promote score-focused scholarship but that simple aim has long since been outstripped by the achievements of the Series' authors. They have divulged such great variety in what the analysis and scrutiny of content and production of film music reveals that I sometimes feel that composers will now have to keep up with what the discipline is able to explain and interpret. Indeed, fans of Zimmer, Howard, Batman, and Nolan will thoroughly enjoy this book for its minute and precise unpicking of the aural experience, no matter their level of musical knowledge.

It is therefore all the more disappointing that, for the first time in the almost twenty years that this series has been running, the rights holders for the music copyright have refused to grant permission for musical examples to be reproduced in this scholarly text. They have not given a reason for refusing this permission. It could be one of any number of reasons–concern about lost revenue, anxiety about musical texts being lifted and reproduced elsewhere without authorization or payment, or perhaps something more artistic around protecting the right of the composer to keep their tools hidden from view–but without explanation it seems little more than sadly short-sighted. Dr. Hexel has therefore used a notation system which circumvents the need for this permission, is illuminating nonetheless, and which still complements Zimmer's own thoughts on his work, thoughts that any film fan will find fascinating.

Editor's Foreword

Audiences may be more sophisticated these days, composers' tools more complex, directors more imaginative and receptive to production discussions about music, and films about so much more than just story. But these aspects are all an indication of how integral music has become to the immersive experience that is contemporary cinema. A few years ago, at a conference, an academic from my own discipline suggested to me that score-based scholarship as found in the Scarecrow Guides was largely pointless, now that such complicated soundscapes are so common. Vasco Hexel's book on what is really Zimmer, Howard, Wesson, and King's *The Dark Knight* shows us instead to be wary of using such limited definitions of what "score" actually is.

Dr. Kate Daubney
Series Editor

ACKNOWLEDGMENTS

I am deeply grateful to a number of people who encouraged me to complete this book despite tremendous obstacles posed by the music copyright holders.

Hans Zimmer welcomed me to his London apartment and studio in the summer of 2013 and then visited the Royal College of Music the following October. Few composers have had a greater impact on the evolving craft of recent Hollywood film music composition, and even fewer speak of their work with Hans's candor.

Mel Wesson was most generous with his time, sharing insights on his work on *The Dark Knight*.

My colleague Matthias Kapohl, one of the organizers of the SoundTrack_Cologne festival in Germany, personifies focus and professionalism in bringing together doers and thinkers in our field.

The University of Southern California Library, including its James Newton Howard Collection, is an invaluable resource for the study of film music.

Dr. Kate Daubney, series editor of these film score guides, recognized the importance of *The Dark Knight* as a recent commercial success whose groundbreaking score deserved academic scrutiny.

In the months I was researching for and writing this book, the students on the Masters Programme in Composition for Screen at the Royal College of Music continued to inspire me with their passion, energy, and wonderfully diverse talent.

INTRODUCTION

The Dark Knight (2008) was the highly anticipated sequel to Christopher Nolan's *Batman Begins*, which in 2005 had pleased audiences and critics alike. A bold take on the familiar Batman character, the first film had revitalized an ailing movie franchise and moved the benchmark for Hollywood superhero movies. Making *The Dark Knight*, Nolan remained mindful of the Batman comic book source material and its devoted fan following. Nolan once again pursued his assured directorial vision, striking a judicious balance between creative integrity and mainstream appeal. He introduced two key villains from the comic books, casting Heath Ledger as the Joker and Aaron Eckhart as Harvey Dent, who later becomes Two-Face. Ledger portrayed the evil jester as a terrifying terrorist, decidedly not imitating the camp maniac Jack Nicholson had famously played in Tim Burton's *Batman* (1989).

The ensuing commercial and critical success of *The Dark Knight* (hereafter referred to as *TDK*) was also the result of a compelling script that pushed this Hollywood sci-fi action film to intellectual heights rarely reached in mainstream films. Screenwriters David S. Goyer and Jonathan Nolan (Christopher's brother) helped devise a complex story that poses difficult questions about justice versus the law, right versus wrong, good versus bad. Batman's vigilantism and moral stance are challenged with a poignancy never encountered in previous Batman films.

TDK nevertheless offered spectacular action and set pieces. Striving for realism and believability, Nolan relied on practical stunts and real sets and only occasionally drew on computer-generated imagery that so gratuitously permeates many recent superhero films. The sleek visual style of *TDK* results from highly sophisticated photography, including scenes shot in the large-frame IMAX format and subtle use of green screen to turn Chicago into Gotham City.

The soundtrack of *TDK* was equally accomplished, a highly nuanced canvas of dialogue, sound design, and music. Hans Zimmer and James Newton Howard, who had previously collaborated on *Batman Begins*, composed an extraordinary score. Building upon thematic and coloristic foundations laid in the first film, they now pushed into grittier, heavier, and darker territory. Once again, the musical language they employed was often ultra-minimalist, shunning swashbuckling themes and heroic fanfares that had typically accompanied Hollywood superheroes in the past. Howard's work on Harvey Dent's orchestral theme lent the score an air of dignified resolve that poignantly contrasted the chaos brought upon Gotham under the Joker's reign. The Joker Theme was perhaps one of the most ingenious inventions in the score, whereas the Stranger motif had a most unsettling effect (both will be discussed later). The *TDK* score departed markedly from traditional Hollywood film music and subsequently was a key driver in the stylistic evolution of contemporary film scoring towards fewer redundant musical pointers in favor of a more subliminal discourse.

It is rare for two of Hollywood's most successful composers to collaborate on a film score and James Newton Howard may not be an obvious candidate to work with Zimmer. Howard has a reputation of being quiet and very private,[1] whereas Zimmer exudes confidence and thrives in the limelight. As will be shown, Zimmer is a self-taught rebel. Howard holds a postgraduate degree in music. Zimmer is an experimenter who likes to tinker with synthesizers but does not read notation. Howard is at ease with music technology but still jots down ideas with pencil and paper. Zimmer's music has had an idiosyncratic sound in discrete time periods of his working life thus far. Howard is perhaps one of the most versatile film composers working today, with a diverse stylistic palette. And yet the two composers together crafted a score that holds together as a coherent body of work. Access to the orchestrators' scores proved invaluable in determining the composers' respective share of the workload. Ambient music designer Mel Wesson was the creative link and common denominator between Zimmer and Howard and he very generously shared his insights on the creative process.

With his contribution to *TDK*, Hans Zimmer confirmed his standing in the industry as a visionary film composer who not only delivers scores with popular appeal but also continues to push the boundaries of his craft. Although other film composers have composed more scores and won more awards, Zimmer may be the first-ever film music superstar. There is a remarkable level of public interest in his work and he has a considerable fan following.[2] Lively discussions on web forums, fan pages, and podcasts abound and Zimmer is an audience magnet wherever he makes a public appearance.[3] However, whereas Howard's music has previously been thoroughly analyzed,[4] this book offers the first treatise on one of Hans Zimmer's scores, with a comprehensive analysis and contextual discussion of the music and the creative and technical processes and practices that produced it.

This book largely follows a format that will be familiar to readers of previous entries in this series of film score guides. Chapter 1 gives a biographic overview of Zimmer and Howard and Wesson. Chapter 2 puts *TDK* in critical, textual, and historical context, tracing the origins of Batman through his many incarnations in comic books, television series, and films. It evaluates *TDK* as part of and in contrast to a growing body of commercially driven Hollywood franchises before outlining ways in which Nolan differentiated his version of Batman from previous film adaptations. Chapter 3 outlines the technical approach of Zimmer and Howard, highlighting Zimmer's groundbreaking emphasis on collaboration and how his workflow differs from Howard's. Chapter 4 comprises an analysis of the score, addressing spotting, instrumentation, and orchestration, itemizing primary and secondary musical themes and motifs and illustrating pertinent scoring techniques and devices. Since, inexplicably, the rightsholders denied permission to show detailed music examples, the score analysis here largely relies on Helmholtz pitch nomenclature and descriptions. Chapter 5 focuses on the relationship of music as part of the soundscape, exploring the collaborative creative process that brought together the music and sound design teams and emphasizing the shared sonic territory and conceptual and technical overlaps between music and sound design.

1

MUSICAL BACKGROUND OF THE COMPOSERS

Hans Florian Zimmer

Hans Zimmer was born on 12 September 1957 in Frankfurt am Main, Germany.[1] Growing up, Zimmer's parents did not own a television set because they considered television an inferior cultural medium. They did, however, have a piano in which young Hans took a keen interest. Hans's father, whom he lost at age six, was a scientist and inventor. His mother was an accomplished musician who, due to the horror and displacement of WWII, never got to pursue a professional career. Zimmer's father played jazz clarinet, which he would sometimes play for Hans in his study. By contrast, his mother preferred the "very strict and German" Bach and Mozart. When she decided to hire him a piano teacher, Hans found the lessons too structured and limiting, pressuring him to practice scales and learn to read notation. Hans quit after just two weeks. As a result of his continued refusal to receive structured tuition, Zimmer cannot read or write notation to this day.

Growing up, Zimmer was expelled from nine schools and his mother eventually sent him to Hurtwood House boarding school in Surrey, England. The artistically oriented Hurtwood offered a nourishing environment in which Zimmer fared better. Upon graduation, Zimmer pursued no higher education but instead moved to London and joined a band without a record deal, performing at working men's clubs, schools, and other small venues up and down the country. He fondly recalls the liberating and inspiring feeling of hearing and seeing the Rolling Stones and David Bowie in London, in contrast to the classical concerts his mother had made him attend in Germany. In 1977, he became a founding member of the New-Wave group The Buggles, whose 1979 hit "Video Killed the Radio Star" was famously the first video played when MTV launched in America in 1981.

In London, Zimmer also met Maggie Rodford, who at the time was running an advertising music company for producer George Martin. She noticed Hans because he was experienced in programming early synthesizers, a rare and in-demand skill at the time. Zimmer embraced emerging music technology early on and still loves experimenting with electronic instruments today, having bought up a lot of vintage analog synthesizer equipment at a time when his contemporaries were converting to digital technology. Having always preferred analog equipment, Zimmer is proud to point out that he never owned the digital Yamaha DX7 synthesizer, which in its day was very popular.

In 1980, Rodford introduced Zimmer to the Ivor Novello Award-winning British composer Stanley Myers, with whom he would found Lillie Yard Studios. Myers, who was not very technical himself, put Zimmer in charge of all electronic instruments, which were becoming part of the musical vocabulary of film and television music at the time. Myers became Zimmer's mentor, was very inclusive in his working methods, taught Zimmer about orchestration and allowed him to collaborate on projects right away rather than insisting on a more hierarchical relationship. In the ensuing formative years, Zimmer gained experience and insights into collaborative work and day-to-day creative challenges in working with directors. Even if Myers led a meeting with a director, Zimmer would still learn from observation, often working on provocative or creatively adventurous movies such as Just Jaeckin's *Lady Chatterley's Lover* (1981), Jerzy Skolimowski's *Moonlighting* (1982), and John Mackenzie's *The Honorary Consul* (alternate title *Beyond the Limit*, 1983). These were the early 1980s, the Thatcher era, when amidst socio-cultural upheaval Channel 4 was launched, a broadcaster with a bold and progressive vision to nourish new contents. Channel 4 commissioned Myers and Zimmer to score Stephen Frears's *My Beautiful Laundrette* (1985), a film about a couple in love fighting an ignorant establishment. Timely, passionate, and critically acclaimed, the film consequently got Zimmer noticed in wider circles.

In 1988, he scored his first Hollywood film, Barry Levinson's *Rain Man*. Zimmer had previously scored Chris Menges's anti-Apartheid drama *A World Apart* (1988) and Levinson's wife Diana had liked the music so much that she had bought the soundtrack CD for her husband.

When Levinson was next in London to promote his film *Good Morning, Vietnam* he visited Zimmer to ask if he would consider joining him for his next project. Following the director to Los Angeles, Zimmer ended up working on the score in Levinson's office because, as an out-of-towner, he had nowhere else to go. The experience set a precedent for Zimmer not only working close to directors, physically, but also with them, collaboratively. Working on *Rain Man*, Zimmer remembers "getting the ending right" being a major challenge, trying to ensure the film ended on a less than depressing note. Zimmer also remembers scoring *Rain Man* with a Fairlight synthesizer that offered only sixteen simultaneous notes (so-called voices), a technological constraint that must have influenced his compositional technique and style at the time.

A "Best Music, Original Score" Academy Award nomination for *Rain Man* suddenly gave Zimmer access to the Hollywood elite. Commissions to score Bruce Beresford's *Driving Miss Daisy* (1989) and Ridley Scott's *Black Rain* (1989) were a direct result of this wider exposure. Zimmer soon scored a number of big-budget features and his early scores bear a certain resemblance to one another. Over the ensuing years, Zimmer refined this style into a personal voice. In hindsight, Zimmer's near-exclusive use of synthesizers, his reliance on a pop idiom and iterative musical language may seem at odds with the respective film (e.g. the synthesized pan flute during the memorable sunset driving montage in *Rain Man* or the suitably humorous yet oddly synthetic theme in *Driving Miss Daisy*). On the other hand, this musical approach must have felt fresh and compelling at the time. The more dramatically charged synth cues in *Black Rain* hint towards an orchestral medium in terms of harmonic language and use of percussion.

Zimmer recalls that he was reluctant at first to permanently move to Hollywood because he feared he might not have a steady flow of commissions to sustain a livelihood: "I'm insecure and I always think the movie I'm working on is the last one I'm doing." These concerns soon proved unfounded and, facing an ever-increasing workload, Zimmer began assembling a team of fellow composers, technicians, and assistants. In 1989, he founded the company Media Ventures (MV) with business partner Jay Rifkin and recreated the creative and collaborative conditions he had cherished when working with Stanley Myers. Zimmer saw Hollywood as being "very closed to new composers" and feared that if no new voices were allowed in, music would eventually grow stale and clichéd. He wanted to champion new composers and counteract the loneliness that comes with working alone in a room for days and weeks on end. There "is something great about being able to walk down the hallway and get support and fresh input from a fellow musician." Over the years, MV would become the launch pad for numerous Hollywood composers including John Powell, Harry Gregson-Williams, Ramin Djawadi, Jeff Rona, Lorne Balfe, Henry Jackman, Steve Jablonsky, and many others. Following a litigious altercation between Zimmer and Rifkin in 2003, MV was succeeded by Remote Control Productions (RCP), owned by Zimmer and managed by Steve Kofsky.[2]

When he was working on *The Power of One* (1992), director John Avildsen introduced Zimmer to South African musician Lebo M, who would later sing in the opening passage of *The Lion King* (1995). Disney executives heard the score of *The Power of One* while *The Lion King* was in development and reached out to Zimmer. At first, he was not particularly interested in working on a children's musical, but Elton John, who was already writing original songs for the film, echoed Disney's interest. Agreeing to join the project, Zimmer expected a "fuzzy animal movie" that would be "fun and easy to do." Instead, he soon realized that *The Lion King* was "profoundly serious and dealt with a child's loss of his father." Given the untimely death of his own father, these were personal issues close to Zimmer's heart. This deeper emotional engagement and Disney's specific brief that this film was not a fairy tale, led to a score that is more idiomatically orchestral and musically varied than Zimmer's earlier works. It won an Academy Award (Best Original Score), Zimmer's first.

By contrast, Zimmer's score for Tony Scott's *Crimson Tide* (1995) stylistically picked up from Ron Howard's *Backdraft* (1991), blending synthesizers with live orchestral parts and low percussion. Zimmer had a prolonged disagreement with studio executives over the use of the Red Army Choir in *Crimson Tide*, which the executives felt was too daring a choice.[3] Zimmer learned that whilst composers often want to push creative boundaries, executives tend to be more conservative and prefer tried and tested solutions. Since his experience with *Crimson Tide*, Zimmer tries to be gracious and "let the slow-moving *Zeitgeist* catch up" with him and gently bring his collaborators around to his point of view. Incidentally, his score for Michael Bay's *The Rock* (1996) bears striking resemblance to *Backdraft* and *Crimson Tide*.

Both in terms of creative process and musical language, the score for Terence Malick's *A Thin Red Line* (1998) would become Zimmer's *quasi* template for many scores to follow. Malick appreciated having different musical options available and exploring different possibilities and solutions. Malick ended up refining the script for *A Thin Red Line* at the MV offices and Zimmer began writing and recording music concurrently. Over six hours of music were recorded with full orchestra, which suggests a large music budget, and the entire score was recorded before the film was shot. Only a small portion of the recordings ended up in the final film. Similarly, Malick filmed far more material than was needed (a process sometimes called over-shooting) and the film was formed and shaped during editing. Writing music prior to the shoot, away from the image, liberated Zimmer from the technical and temporal constraints of the moving image. He found this approach useful and has continued to work in this way ever since (see also chapter 2).[4] The most musically memorable cue of *A Thin Red Line* is its main theme, a series of eleven long notes that repeats identically throughout, accompanied by an ever-growing mass of orchestral and synthesizer forces. Zimmer would employ the same compositional technique in the final cue for *The Da Vinci Code* (2006, the cue "Chevalier de Sangreal") and the closing scene of Chris Nolan's *Inception* (2010, the cue "Time"), with noticeably similar results. Zimmer says he has grown weary of encountering cues from his score for *A Thin Red Line* as temp music in numerous projects since.

Ridley Scott asked Zimmer to score his film *Gladiator* (2000) for which Scott wanted to avoid overt sentimentality. Zimmer happened upon a suitable musical tone for the film when an editor lined up a Lisa Gerrard CD with the now-iconic footage of a lone hand brushing across wheat in a sun-soaked field. Gerrard's CD just happened to be to hand and the footage initially was not intended for use. However, the result struck Zimmer as so powerful that he contacted Gerrard and asked her to join the project. This eventually turned into three months of collaborative experimentation, improvising vocal lines, sometimes with Scott sitting in, listening. Executive producer Steven Spielberg was not convinced at first whether Gerrard's voice suited the film. Rather than trying to defend music itself (which is indefensible in Zimmer's view), Zimmer successfully defend ideas and concepts for the film. The score for *Gladiator* was nominated for an Academy Award and won Zimmer his second Golden Globe for Best Original Score, which he shared with Gerrard.

Working collaboratively with performers, composers, and assistants became common to Zimmer's creative approach. Composer John Powell "admires Zimmer's ability to see the big picture and delegate less-important tasks to others, especially when deadlines loom. 'Hans is the master of investing fully in the ideas of the film more than the details. By having orchestration help, arranging help, you're able to stand back a bit and have an objective view that you would otherwise never have.'"[5] It should be kept in mind that Hollywood composers have always had help. André Previn describes in humorous detail how film composers in the past had whole pools of support staff including arrangers, orchestrators, and copyists.[6] Zimmer has merely taken this to new extremes: in addition to the above, his increasingly technical process also required technicians, software specialists, and music programmers. And whereas in the past the recording sessions would have been the final stage in the composer's involvement, Zimmer's scoring process nowadays continues well past the sessions (see also chapter 2). There are also ghostwriters, of whom Zimmer is rumored to have many. One anonymous source claims that Zimmer will occasionally ask a few of his in-house composers to score the same scene in a film and then take a director or producer from one writing room to the next so they can choose their favorite.

Over the years, Zimmer's RCP has employed numerous composers who would often start out by ghostwriting or providing so-called additional music or other ancillary services before later progressing to earning their own headline composer credit. For example, Zimmer worked with director Michael Bay on *The Rock* (1996) and *Pearl Harbor* (2011) but RCP composer Steve Jablonsky has since scored Bay's *Transformers* franchise. Similarly, Zimmer worked with Tony Scott on *Days of Thunder* (1990) and *Crimson Tide* (1995) and Scott later worked with Harry Gregson-Williams on *Unstoppable* (2010). *Terminator: Genesys* (2015) was first assigned to Zimmer but then taken on by RCP composer Lorne Balfe. Given this in-house succession, it is hardly surprising when in terms of style and idiom there is a relatively high degree of similarity in the resulting musical output of RCP composers. Many critics of Zimmer have pointed out obvious similarities between not only his own scores but also between his and those of his protégés. Rarely is this more obvious than with Gregson-Williams's cue "The Stanton Curve" in *Unstoppable*, which nearly identically copies musical snippets from the cue "Bank Robbery" in *The Dark Knight* (see also chapter 4).

Admittedly, emulation and imitation in Hollywood film music is hardly a new phenomenon and musical output of a cohesive and consistent quality may have helped RCP grow and concentrate its commercial power. Hans Zimmer has built considerable clout for the RCP brand whilst at the same time divesting responsibilities and delegating much of the actual composing and producing. The financial benefits of centralizing operations and maintaining a relatively homogenous workflow and output are manifold. Studio facilities can be shared and usage optimized, project acquisition can be streamlined, and multiple projects can be run concurrently. Although the underlying process may vary in the details—and while a specific director may work with one RCP composer rather than another—production value, reliability, and quality control are assured. It is tempting to draw parallels between Zimmer's business model and a phenomenon in the food and consumables industries, whereby a progressive consolidation of brands and companies has led to a handful of large corporations controlling almost the entire market. Companies benefit from efficiency savings in the supply chain and production process and also from increased leverage in distribution and sales negotiations. Profit margins increase and customers benefit from reliable and more affordable supplies whilst a range of choice (or so-called Illusion of Choice) is maintained. The rather corporate approach and factory-like production method of RCP also has precedents in the Hollywood golden era, when films were churned out steadily and predictably.

At the same time, Zimmer has over the years changed his musical vocabulary drastically and repeatedly. He points out the need to "reinvent" his style periodically because he is being copied so readily. Sample libraries of synthesizer loops, heavy percussion, and even a *Dark Knight* pre-set for u-he's Zebra2 software instrument evidence other composers' and hobbyists' desire to imitate a certain "Zimmer" sound. Zimmer himself seems keenly aware that his cues for *Batman Begins* (strings ostinati, percussion bangs) inspired a whole new musical approach to the way film trailers are scored. Consequently, Zimmer instead favored minimalist church organ and piano to mark a clear stylistic departure with his score for Nolan's *Interstellar* (2014).[7]

The RCP model successfully interfaces with prevalent commercial filmmaking practice: Zimmer's company is exemplary in the way it integrates film music creation into Hollywood's current business model.[8] Zimmer's company may concurrently be working on several projects including feature films, television programs, and computer games.[9] It is an open secret that Hans Zimmer oversees a large number of projects while he is credited as composer on only a few. Even the scores for which he does take composer credit invariably have other composers attached. For *The Simpsons Movie* (2007), six composers supplied additional music: Ryeland Allison, Lorne Balfe, Jim Dooley, Henry Jackman, Michael A. Levine, and Atli Örvarsson. Zimmer has at least twice been disqualified in the "Best Original Score" category by the Academy of Motion Picture Arts and Sciences, for *Batman Begins* (2005) and *The Dark Knight* (2008), because too many contributors were listed on the music cue sheet (see also chapter 4).

The remarkable success of RCP is evidenced by the sizeable studio facilities the company owns in Santa Monica, California, built by studio bau:ton, a boutique architecture firm that specializes in designing and building music studios and media production facilities. A collection of custom-built structures contains writing suites, mixing facilities, recording live rooms, and a medium-sized orchestral scoring stage. In recent years, RCP has expanded further to create space for more writing rooms for computers games music and Zimmer's Bleedings Fingers production music company (a joint venture between RCP and Sony/ATV). Even if Zimmer may not always compose all of the music on every "Hans Zimmer" score, he ensures consistent quality in the output. RCP is evidently so well attuned to the industry's needs–and Zimmer so well respected within the field–that filmmakers and executives trust him and his RCP brand to deliver workable results.

Far more important than actual (or proverbial) notes Zimmer may put on score paper, he makes filmmakers feel comfortable and confident that he will take care of the music. Zimmer is the face of the RCP operation and manages creative relationships. Time and time again, sources have lauded Zimmer for his visionary outlook, his people skills and persuasiveness. Jon Burlingame quotes composer Harry Gregson-Williams: "If Hans tried to sell a minute of silence as a cue, he'd probably do pretty well."[10] Zimmer comes across as humble and personable, valuable attributes in an industry where maintaining social contacts is crucial. The author himself has encountered Zimmer at industry events where he effortlessly remembered names and pertinent details about the people he encountered. Composer Ilan Eshkeri remembers an occasion where he attended a cocktail party in Los Angeles complaining to a group of colleagues about a difficult film producer with whom he had just finished a project—only then to realize that the very producer was standing right behind him and had overheard the conversation. Zimmer was also present and, having observed Eshkeri's *faux-pas*, later teased him "this is why I am where I am and you are where you are."[11]

Zimmer has over the years developed several lasting partnerships with directors. He worked with Ron Howard on *Backdraft* (1991), *The Da Vinci Code* (2006) and *Angels & Demons* (2009) and with Gore Verbinski on *The Ring* (2002), *Pirates of the Caribbean: Dead Man's Chest* (2006), *Pirates of the Caribbean: At World's End* (2007), *Rango* (2011), and *The Lone Ranger* (2013). Zimmer's partnership with Chris Nolan began with *Batman Begins* (2005) and remains ongoing at the time of this writing. Nolan had worked with British composer David Julyan on his first three features *Following* (1998), *Memento* (2000), and *Insomnia* (2002) as well as his fifth, *The Prestige* (2006), which was interpolated with *Batman Begins* (2005) and *The Dark Knight* (2008). It is not clear why, when finally asked to direct a big-budget feature, Nolan chose to not take Julyan along, but it is possible that Warner Brothers preferred a more established composer with a proven track record.[12]

James Newton Howard

James Newton Howard was born in 1951 in Los Angeles, California.[13] He began playing the piano at the age of four and majored in classical piano at the University of Southern California School of Music and the Music Academy of the West in Santa Barbara. Howard later worked as a session musician with artists including Diana Ross, Ringo Starr, and Carly Simon. In 1975, he joined Elton John's tour band. He has worked as a songwriter, producer, conductor, keyboardist, and arranger with such artists as Cher, Earth, Wind & Fire, Rickie Lee Jones, Olivia Newton-John, Bob Seger, Rod Stewart, Barbra Streisand, and many more.

In 1982, Howard provided orchestrations for the album *Toto IV*, which won seven Grammy Awards including "Record of the Year," for "Rosanna," as well as "Album of the Year." In 1983, Howard played keyboard (a Yamaha GS-1) for veteran composer Gerry Goldsmith's score for *Twilight Zone: The Movie*. It was during this project that he first observed the film scoring process. He had not seriously considered becoming a film composer when his manager found him the comedy *Head Office* (1984), which needed an original score. Howard accepted the commission and soon found a new career in film music, turning into one of the most versatile and prolific composers in contemporary Hollywood.

Whereas Zimmer's film scores, certainly his earlier works, were clearly influenced by his background in popular music and were stylistically uniform across discrete periods, Howard has readily adapted his musical language from one project to the next. His work is equally assured in a wide range of styles and idioms and, as a body of works, defies categorization. Howard is one of the few film composers who have avoided being pigeonholed into scoring only films of a particular genre. Having composed his first fully orchestral film score in 1986 for Taylor Hackford's *Everybody's All-American* (starring Dennis Quaid and John Goodman), Howard has written large-scale orchestral scores where appropriate, for example for *The Fugitive* (1993), *Treasure Planet* (2002), and *Maleficent* (2014). Even in recent years, his more evocative scores have remained remarkably tuneful, in an age when memorable melodies have all but vanished from mainstream film music.

By contrast, his more visceral action film scores such as *I Am Legend* (2007), *Salt* (2010), and *Green Lantern* (2011) blend orchestral elements with electronic instruments and draw on rock music influences. Howard has used electric guitars in a number of scores, notably in his title theme for the early seasons of *ER* (1994–2009) but also *Collateral* (2004) and *Charlie Wilson's War* (2007). His scores for *Lady in the Water* (2006), *Snow White and the Huntsman* (2012), and the *Hunger Games* series (2012–2015) rely heavily on synthesizers. He fluently draws on non-Western styles (e.g., for *Dinosaurs* [2000], *King Kong* [2005], and *Blood Diamond* [2006]), and even composed a score with a distinct Latin flavor for Tony Gilroy's *Duplicity* (2009). Romantic scores are part of his palette (*The Tourist* [2010], *Water for Elephants* [2011]), as are more minimalist scores of a smaller scale, for example *Michael Clayton* (2007). Howard occasionally works with well-known soloists, notably saxophonist Kenny G on Joel Schumacher's *Dying Young* (1991) and violinist Joshua Bell on *Defiance* (2008).

Howard has worked repeatedly with a number of directors, including Joel Schumacher (*Flatliners* [1990], *Dying Young* [1991], *Falling Down* [1993]), David S. Ward (*Major League* [1989], *King Ralph* [1991]) and Andrew Davis (*The Fugitive* [1993], *A Perfect Murder* [1998]). He has scored five Lawrence Kasdan films (*Grand Canyon* [1991], *Wyatt Earp* [1994], *French Kiss* [1995], *Mumford* [1999], and *Dreamcatcher* [2003]). Most recently, he has been working with Francis Lawrence (*I Am Legend* [2007], *Water for Elephants* [2011]) and joined Lawrence's *The Hunger Games: Catching Fire* (2013) when Danny Elfman quit the project. Two further films have since followed (*The Hunger Games: Mockingjay—Part 1* [2014], and *Part 2* [2015]).

Starting with the groundbreaking horror-thriller hybrid *The Sixth Sense* (1999), Howard has scored all films of writer and director M. Night Shyamalan (*Unbreakable* [2000], *Signs* [2002], *The Village* [2004], *The Happening* [2008], *Lady in the Water* [2006], *The Last Airbender* [2010], and *After Earth* [2013]).

Howard also continues to work on pop songs and albums, writing, producing, and orchestrating for artists such as Cher, Randy Crawford, George Benson, the Yellowjackets, Youssou N'Dour, and Josh Groban. His experience in both the pop and film music realms has helped Howard nourish something of a renaissance of the commercially viable movie theme song: For each of the *Hunger Games* series he has written or co-written a respective theme song including "Eyes Open" (sung by

Taylor Swift) and "The Hanging Tree" (sung by actress Jennifer Lawrence). Howard has been nominated for eight Academy Awards but has yet to win.[14] In 2001, he won a Primetime Emmy Award for his main title theme for the short-lived *Gideon's Crossing*. In 1994, he also received an Emmy nomination for his *ER* title theme. Following two previous Grammy nominations, in 2009 Howard finally shared the award with Hans Zimmer for their score for *The Dark Knight*.

A substantial "James Newton Howard Collection" is held in the University of Southern California Libraries. The collection comprises orchestrations, sketches, orchestral parts, a limited amount of materials from the early part of Howard's career but extensive materials from his later works for film and television. The collection ranges from the mid-1980s to the present.

Melvyn (Mel) Thomas Wesson

Mel Wesson was born and raised in London and early on gravitated towards the synthesizer as his instrument of choice. After leaving art college, he went touring and recorded with a number of new wave bands. Wesson also began working out of Zimmer's Lillie Yard Studio where he began to explore and experiment with sound and picture as well as working with such artists as the Banshees and Brit Pop producer Mike Hedges. He worked with The Verve on their highly successful "Urban Hymns" album, featuring the hit single "Bitter Sweet Symphony." It was this album Zimmer heard in early 2000 when he spotted Wesson's credit and invited him to work on the score for John Woo's *Mission Impossible 2* (2002).

Wesson started working as Zimmer's "ambient music designer," a new role that pushed the boundaries of film music into the realm of sound design. He draws on a vast arsenal of vintage synthesizers as well as the little-known Metasynth software than allows the creative manipulation of recorded audio (see also chapter 5). Starting with Ridley Scott's *Hannibal* (2004), Wesson has worked with Zimmer on numerous films including, among many others, Chris Nolan's Batman trilogy. Wesson has also worked as ambient music designer with Howard on a number of films. Wesson has also composed music for commercials, television, and video games, as well as production music. He is a member of the recently reformed eclectic retro synth group Node.

2

CRITICAL, TEXTUAL, AND HISTORICAL CONTEXT OF *THE DARK KNIGHT*

This chapter first provides an overview of the Batman character, tracing his many incarnations through comic books, animated series, a live action television show, and feature films, in whose context Chris Nolan's approach to his three films can be seen. Capturing particular creative and commercial challenges Nolan faced in making his trilogy, this chapter sheds some light on the director's outlook on the overall aesthetic and narrative approach, including the use of music. *The Dark Knight* (in the following referred to as *TDK*) is an ambitious film that pushes the boundaries of mainstream entertainment in terms of surface aesthetic, narrative and character development, philosophical and political outlook. These are aspects and considerations that necessarily impacted upon music choices and scoring strategies.

The Dark Knight: Origins

In May 1939, Bob Kane created Batman for issue #27 of the "Detective Comics" (hence "DC Comics," the name later adopted by the publisher). Batman first appeared in his own comic book series, "Batman," in April 1940, with Robin ("The Boy Wonder") at his side. The Joker was also introduced and Catwoman first appeared soon thereafter.[1] It is worth noting that the early version of the Joker was literally an evil jester teasing with card game references: "You can't win anyway," he says to a judge in the first issue, "you see, I hold the winning card." The late American film critic Roger Ebert has pointed out that the Joker was inspired by the character Gwynplaine in Victor Hugo's 1869 novel *L'homme qui rit* and the 1928 film adaptation, Paul Leni's *The Man Who Laughs*.[2]

The Batman universe soon took shape with more villains, among others, Scarecrow, the Penguin, and the Riddler. Wayne's complicit butler Alfred was soon added and also key locales such as Wayne Manor and the Batcave with futuristic gadgetry and the Batmobile. The coin tossing Harvey Dent/Two-Face was introduced early on and in "Batman #50" the idea of a coin with identical sides first appeared (which serves as a plot device in *TDK*).

Manning describes how symptoms of the McCarthy era detrimentally affected the popularity and contents of comic books in the 1950s and summarizes this decade as somewhat disappointing in terms of Batman publications.[3] The popular character of Batwoman dates back to this era (Detective Comics #233, July 1956) as well as villain Dr. Zero (later Dr. Victor Fries/Mr. Freeze) in Batman #121 (February 1959). The "Justice League of America" series launched in November 1960 an alliance of several DC superheroes.

A highly popular *Batman* television program starring Adam West started in 1966 and ran for 120 episodes until 1968. Its camp and tongue-in-cheek tone (Robin would exclaim "holy ravioli," "holy safari," or "holy New Year's Eve"), paired with the use of comic-book-style visuals (onomatopoeic descriptions of fight sounds) became widely known.[4] There was a spin-off feature film as well (*Batman*, 1966). The television program was perhaps the first association of music with Batman. The theme, composed by Neil Hefti, was a light-hearted blues in the style of so-called surf music popular in the early 1960s. Acclaimed composer Nelson Riddle (who had scored Stanley Kubrick's *Lolita* in 1961 and would later win an Academy Award for his score for Jack Clayton's *The Great Gatsby* [1974]) composed in-episode music.

American broadcaster CBS launched the first animated series *The Batman/Superman Hour* (1968–1969), also known as *Batman with Robin the Boy Wonder*. Hanna-Barbera Productions produced their own animated series, *Super Friends* (featuring Batman, Superman, Wonder Woman, and other heroes), which enjoyed relative longevity (ABC, 1973–1986).

Whilst the light-hearted and bright live action television series had made Batman popular with mainstream audiences, it was less well received among traditional comic books fans. This prompted a new set of writers and visual artists to return the comic books to a darker tone in the 1970s. This decade saw the introduction of the League of Assassins and their leader Rā's al Ghūl (Arabic for "Head of the Demon") aka Henri Ducard (later played by Liam Neeson in Nolan's *Batman Begins* [1995]). Arkham Asylum, a mental institution that would feature in several of the later film adaptations, first appeared in Batman #258, April 1974. The 1970s took so dark a turn that Adventure Comics #263 depicted the funeral of Bruce Wayne and was titled "Death of Batman." This, however, did not deter CBS from launching a new animated series *The New Adventures of Batman* in 1977.

Nor did Wayne's death put an end to further comic books. Instead, a new series was launched with "The Untold Legend of the Batman" in July 1980. Frank Miller's "The Dark Knight Returns #1" in February 1986 and the origin story "Batman: Year One" (Batman #404–407) took yet a darker visual and narrative tone, appealing to an older age group. The latter was later cited as a source of inspiration for Nolan's *Batman Begins*. The re-launched Justice League (Justice League #1, May 1987) dropped the "American" from its name and the Joker returned in "Batman: The Killing Joke" in March 1988. With "Batman: Arkham Asylum" in October 1989, the comic books and graphic novels had finally consolidated a more mature and sombre tone, far removed from Batman's beginnings.

This coincided with the release of Tim Burton's film adaptation *Batman* in 1989. Burton ingeniously fused his signature pseudo-realistic style with hints of neo-Goth and a contemporary 1980s flair. Manning points out that the commercial success of Burton's film beneficially impacted upon the future of the comic books series, as evidenced by the launch of a new series entitled "Batman: Legends of the Dark Knight" in November 1989.[5] It is interesting to note that whilst Bob Kane is credited with the creation of the various characters in Burton's version of *Batman*, none of the DC comic book writers were part of the film's writing team. The main writer, Sam Hamm, was, however, invited by DC Comics in 1989 to contribute a three-issues story to the Detective Comics series.[6] Batman comic book sales rose in the early 1990s on the back of Burton's popular movie franchise. With films and different series of comic books being created and published concurrently, the Batman mythology effectively grew into a multiverse of several "simultaneous variants, Batmen of many worlds, coexisting across alternate earths."[7] A prolific expansion of the Batman universe contributed to the growing of the "Batman meta-text, a collected myth that constitutes the character as a whole."[8] It led to, alongside a continuation of existing series, the creation of new series including "Batman: Shadow of the Bat," a stand-alone Robin and Catwoman spin-off series, a series of hyper-real "Elseworlds" stories, and a more artistically driven series by writer Mark Waid and visual artist Alex Ross entitled "Kingdom Come" (#1 in May 1996), a speculative vision of Gotham's future. In 1992, American television network FOX launched an animated series using main title music by Danny Elfman, who had scored Burton's *Batman* and the 1992 sequel *Batman Returns*.[9] *Batman: The Animated Series* ran 1992–1995 and took a darker tone. In January 1993, the on-going "Batman" comic books presented a new villain, Bane, who was introduced with an origin story in "Batman: Vengeance of Bane." This new villain was set on breaking Batman, which he finally achieved in "Batman #497," the culmination of a series of issues under the header "Knightfall." Bane later featured as a side character in Joel Schumacher's's *Batman Forever* (1995) and was the main villain in Nolan's *The Dark Knight Rises* (2012). In the comic books, Wayne's allies Jean-Paul Valley (a darker Dark Knight who would gradually descend into murderous madness) and Dick Grayson (Nightwing) wore the cape consecutively during Bruce Wayne's recovery (in comic books, as in movies, even a broken back mends). Grayson/Nightwing received his own stand-alone series in September 1995 with "Nightwing #1." The Justice League (of America) rediscovered its patriotic roots and re-launched with "JLA #1" in January 1997. By the end of the 1990s, the Batman universe took a darker turn yet again, with the launch of "Batman: No Man's Land" (March 1999), which depicts Gotham as an isolated off-limits city with Batman temporarily missing. The premise is not dissimilar to that of Nolan's *The Dark Knight Rises*, in which Bane takes over Gotham and destroys all bridges leading to the mainland while Batman is locked away in a distant prison. The animated series *The New Batman Adventures* (The WB, 1997–1999), *The New Batman/Superman Adventure* (The WB, 1997–2000), and *Batman Beyond* (The WB, 1999–2001) overlapped at the turn of the century.

Further diversification of the Batman universe ensued in the early 2000s, with additional new comic book series started ("Batman: Gotham Knights" in March 2000, "Batgirl" in April 2000, "Robin Year One" in December 2000, a re-launched Catwoman in January 2002, "CD: The New Frontier" in March 2004, "Arkham Asylum: Living Hell" in July 2003, a re-launch of "Batman & Robin the Boy Wonder" in September 2005, and "Batman and the Monster Men" in January 2006). A number of Batman imposters appeared in the comic books in the latter half of the decade, an idea picked up in Nolan's *TDK*. A number of series and stand-alone graphic novels toy with the idea of finally killing Batman, a possibility also explored by Nolan in *The Dark Knight Rises*. The U.S. Cartoon Network ran the animated series *Justice League* (later *Justice League Unlimited*) (2001–2004). Other animated series included *The Batman* (The WB, 2004–2006/The CW, 2006–2008) and *Batman: The Brave and the Bold* (Cartoon Network, 2008–2011).

The second decade of the 21st century saw yet another complete revamp of some on-going comic book series and a cancellation of others. DC may be responding to the recent successes of the Batman feature films and the general upsurge in the popularity of superhero films. As in previous decades, the style and underlying aesthetic of emerging texts continue to adapt and cater to contemporary audience tastes.

The Hero Rises: Hollywood Superhero Franchises

Christopher Nolan's first Batman film, *Batman Begins*, was an origins story that explored how Bruce Wayne, the orphaned heir of his father's multi-billion-dollar corporate empire, became the Caped Crusader. Nolan had not initially intended for his involvement with Batman to turn into a trilogy and was contractually only committed to one film when he directed *Batman Begins*. When the box office success of *Batman Begins* exceeded the studio's expectations, the decision to produce a sequel was commercially motivated. Jeff Robinov, President of Production at Warner Bros. Pictures, first announced *The Dark Knight* as the sequel to *Batman Begins* on 31 July 2006,[10] stating that Nolan's "unique vision is what made *Batman Begins* such an outstanding film and we could not imagine anyone else at the helm of *The Dark Knight*." Nolan's bother Jonathan was announced as writer. Not only did the commercial success of *Batman Begins* spawn sequels, it also helped reinvigorate the superhero film genre that, a few years prior, Sam Raimi's Spider-Man series (2002, 2004, 2007) had returned to commercial traction.

Released in the US on 18 July 2008 (and internationally throughout July and August 2008), *The Dark Knight* had one of the biggest-ever opening weekends in terms of domestic box office gross.[11] Made for a reported budget of $185m, it eventually reached a worldwide box office gross of over $1bn.[12] Audiences loved the film. The Rotten Tomatoes audience score reached 94%.[13] The Internet Movie Database audience rating reached 9.0,[14] ranking *TDK* at number 4 on the list of the top 250 films voted by IMDb users. The film not only was a runaway commercial success, it also received mostly positive reviews. The website Metacritic shows a combined score of 82.[15] Peter Bradshaw of the Guardian called *TDK* "strange, dark, grandiose and mad."[16] Roger Ebert called it a "haunted film that leaps beyond its origins and becomes an engrossing tragedy."[17]

Hollywood has long relied on pre-existing content for its films, adapting plays and books to attract pre-invested audiences, thus maximizing the prospect of high returns. The relatively recent rise of sophisticated computer-generated imagery and digitally enabled filmmaking cater well to the heightened visual impact of spectacular comic book adaptations, which have since risen in numbers, often aiming at a younger target audience with disposable pocket money.[18] Franchises are multi-sequel film series that can comprise any number of films, resulting in sustained revenue streams for studios. Sequels and franchises are produced first and foremost to capitalize on a successful film's box office draw,[19] and the box office revenue generated from franchises that are based on comic books is staggering.[20]

As Wyatt points out, "Hollywood is only producing more of the same."[21] To try and keep a franchise fresh without disappointing devoted fans can be a daunting creative challenge. Composer John Ottman describes the pressure he experienced when working on *Superman Returns* (2006), with some fans of the older films demanding that he pick up John Williams's original theme.[22]

Tim Burton's 1989 highly acclaimed *Batman* had portrayed the conflicted hero (Michael Keaton) fighting a hilariously camp Joker (Jack Nicholson) in a dark and surreal Gotham. Danny Elfman's score underpinned the flamboyant comic book atmosphere with flair and has been analyzed by Janet Halfyard.[23] Gary Collinson traces the gestation of three sequels and refers to creative and casting decisions as being primarily driven by the commercial studio interests.[24] Whilst Burton still directed *Batman Returns* (1992), he only took a producing role on the next film. Michael Keaton also refused to return for a third installment. When Joel Schumacher took a lighter tone with *Batman Forever* (1995), its box office success assured the studios that Schumacher's approach was a "recipe for fiscal success."[25] In response to the box office success of *Batman Forever*, *Batman & Robin* (1997) was rushed into production and Schumacher's second film veered even further into the camp and kitsch realm of the 1960s TV show: garish costumes, flippant dialogue, ridiculous performances, and odd casting choices (for example, Arnold Schwarzenegger as Mr. Freeze). Even Elliot Goldenthal's admirable score could not counterbalance the fluorescent tone of the film. *Empire* magazine remarked that "the overall impact is more like the 60s TV series than anything envisaged by D.C. Comics' Bob Kane (whose consultancy credit must be largely contractual) or Tim Burton (whose gloomy architecture of the first two films is the sole remnant of his Dark Knight vision)," and called *Batman & Robin* the "camp end to dreadful era for Schumacher at the helm of the Batman franchise."[26] When box office returns slipped and profitability fell also (because budgets had been rising steadily with each film), Warner Brothers decided to put the franchise on hold. When the studio next decided it was time to attempt a re-boot, Nolan had to differentiate his film from Schumacher's.[27]

Nolan's Batman: Why So Serious?

Will Brooker stresses that a "new Batman film [had to] position itself, through connection and contrast, in relation to the vast number of existing, on-going and previous Batman texts."[28] Re-inventing and adapting Batman for the new series of films meant accessing a multiverse of characters, plot strands, and timelines that had emerged from the various comic book series and television and film adaptations. In this intertextual network, there is fluid cross-fertilization of comic books and other media, with shifting hierarchies. To appeal to the pre-invested comic book fan crowd, it was crucial to the success of the new film to remember the importance of respecting the comic book continuity, the Batman brand, and the essence of what Batman stands for. Reynolds sees the key to fan engagement and a successful film release in discourse through para-text (teasers, trailers, posters, toys, theme park rides) and a matrix that comprises the all-encompassing Batman meta-text, "a summation of all existing texts plus all the gaps that those texts have left unspecified."[29]

Previous Batman films had never adapted only one single comic book but rather drawn from a number of books. To adapt the rich source material and re-start the franchise successfully for Nolan, then, meant to retain enough of the familiar while adding enough of the new.[30] Brooker notes that the "established tradition of authorship within comic books [...] involves a complex negotiation whereby novelty is wrought from tradition; where the trick is to do something new with something old."[31]

Nolan's interpretation of Batman, starting with an origins story that had never been told in a film, took on a decidedly darker tone than previous Batman films, with emphasis on fidelity to the comic book canon but told in a markedly more realistic fashion. *Batman Begins* was an engrossing filmic narrative with broad mainstream appeal that reached beyond a comic book fan crowd. As part of an attempt to suspend his film in a timeless and geographically ambiguous setting, Nolan largely avoided connotations of contemporary pop culture, including product placements that abound in Hollywood films today.[32] He took the same approach in *TDK*, Bruce Wayne's Lamborghini being a rare exception. Nolan also shuns the use of pop songs, in stark contrast to the song compilations that accompanied Schumacher's film, including "Hold Me, Thrill Me, Kiss Me, Kill Me" by U2, and Seal's "Kiss from a Rose" for *Batman Forever* (1995) and R. Kelly's "Gotham City" for *Batman & Robin* (1997).

Commonly featured in Hollywood films to appeal to a selected target audience and to amplify a film's draw in other media, the use of contemporary pop songs also risks quickly dating a film, as may have been the case with the original Prince songs in Burton's *Batman*.[33] In the absence of pop songs, Zimmer's and Howard's scores for Nolan's trilogy are a clear contrast to Danny Elfman's flamboyant scores for Burton and Elliot Goldenthal's sophisticated scores for Schumacher.

Realism, Spectacle, Storytelling

To distance himself from Schumacher's garish excess, Nolan wanted to make as realistic a film as possible, aiming for "heightened reality."[34] Isaacs has defined "realism" in recent Hollywood films as measured by "the degree of verisimilitude of the reproductions of the real object," and posits a "broader 'realist' aesthetic" as underlying films thus inclined, which is not the same as a true realism in the vein of *cinema vérité*.[35] Nolan had previously proven his ability to successfully deliver films of a rather fantastical premise in seemingly realistic fashion (*Memento* [2000], *The Prestige* [2006]).

It is useful to consider *The Dark Knight* in the context of other, perhaps less realistic superhero films also released in 2008: John Favreau's *Iron Man*, not unlike *Batman Begins*, was also an origin story. The film derives its core appeal from high-tech gadgetry (for example, the Iron Man suit), fancy sports cars, and AC/DC songs.

Whilst *Iron Man* pitches the hero against a group of terrorists (not dissimilar to Batman's fight against the League of Shadows in *Batman Begins*), the hero's gestation is far less spiritually or philosophically charged. Louis Leterrier's *The Incredible Hulk* and Guillermo del Toro's *Hellboy II* were two other films released in 2008, the prior a reboot of an earlier failed franchise, the latter a sequel. Peter Berg's *Hancock* (2008) was not a comic book adaptation but nevertheless a superhero film, depicting a troubled and troublesome man with superhuman powers who is powerless when facing very human personal problems. *TDK* was more somber and thought-provoking and took a less gratuitously spectacular approach than its contemporaries. Nolan's Batman was dark first and foremost. Consequently, Nolan managed to make *TDK* stand apart, firstly, from the previous Batman film adaptations and, secondly, from less realistic, over-the-top films released around the same time.[36]

Aiming to craft a more realistic Batman film, Nolan restricted the use of computer-generated imagery (CGI) in his three Batman films. The Hong Kong segment in *TDK* ("LSI Extraction," see also chapters 4 and 5) is the only extended passage that draws heavily on CGI because Nolan was given insufficient access to shoot exteriors on locations. By contrast, an actual 18-wheeler truck is flipped over on a Chicago street.[37] There are subtle uses of green screen, sometimes in unexpected places such as Wayne's fund raiser for Dent.[38]

However, at times Nolan sacrifices realism in favor of spectacle. When Batman ejects out of the damaged Batmobile during the truck chase, the revelation of the Batpod is obviously created by use of CGI. Some of the gadgets Wayne uses require some suspension of disbelief. Overall, the film relies on highly constructed set pieces. These function as action-driven vignettes that sometimes feel less than prepared narratively (the bank robbery, the Hong Kong segment, the truck chase, the bomb plot that kills Rachel, the hospital bomb scare, the ferries bomb scare). These vignettes are loosely connected in an overarching narrative construct, if not always obviously so.[39] Nolan fluently subverts the narrative conventions of Hollywood film, at times obscuring cause and effect, serving so-called dialogue hooks,[40] and other standard cohesion devices.[41] *TDK* features enough spectacular action to please the mainstream, but it is more complex than the average blockbuster. It is also more nuanced than a typical so-called high-concept film, which would rely on a "simplification of character and narrative" to maximize audience appeal.[42] The plot, too, is richly layered and less than predictable. For example, it is rare in a mainstream film for two main characters to die halfway through the film (Gordon seemingly, Rachel actually).

Into Darkness: A Troubled Batman

Whereas *Batman Begins* chronicled Batman's philosophical and technological gestation, *TDK* challenges conventional notions of heroism and the repercussions of the Caped Crusader's actions. The film asks what gives any individual the moral and legal authority to uphold what they perceive as justice and whom such heroic acts should serve. Unhinging clear-cut definitions of good or evil, Batman is interchangeably referred to as a hero and a vigilante. Such multi-facetted readings of comic book Batman may not be entirely new,[43] however, it takes "a postheroic superhero movie" to challenge Batman's status as Gotham's lone savior in a Hollywood film.[44]

Batman fights a losing battle against an unpredictable terrorist. Even though he finally catches the Joker, he pays a high personal price. At the end of the film, Batman is shown limping away, running from the police, publicly accepting blame for Harvey Dent's death. Such postmodern material, "divorced from an essentialist notion of truth, right and existential purpose,"[45] perhaps resounds with audiences that increasingly experience "incredulity toward the grand narratives."[46]

A more complex filmic discourse poses intrinsic challenges for the musical score and requires different musico-narrative and aesthetic approaches. Emphasizing that Nolan's Batman is, nevertheless, still a superhero helps contextualize the style, tone, role, and function of Zimmer's and Howard's score (analyzed in chapters 4 and 5).[47]

Superheroes will often have lost their parents or have no relationship with parents or be otherwise marked out from society. Batman's parents were murdered when he was a child; Superman got sent to Earth by his parents; the X-Men are outcasts from society; Iron Man is removed from society as a technical genius and rich businessman. Superheroes will maintain an (often secret) alter ego whose ordinariness is contrasted with the extraordinariness of the superhero (for example, Erik Lehnsherr/Magneto, Clark Kent/Superman, Tony Stark/Iron Man, Bruce Banner/Hulk, Bruce Wayne/Batman). In turn, the extraordinariness of the superhero is contrasted with the ordinariness of his surroundings (for example, Wolverine stunning a police officer as he survives a bullet to the head in *X-Men 2* (2003), Batman mocking his imposter's hockey pads in *TDK*, Quicksilver outrunning and altering the course of bullets fired at him in *X-Men: Days of Future Past* (2014)). McGowan warns that the potential

> ...problem with accepting and celebrating the hero's exceptionality is [...] that this exceptionality has an inherent tendency to multiply itself exponentially. In *The Dark Knight*, this kind of proliferation occurs early in the film when copycat vigilantes place both themselves and others at risk.[48]

Many superheroes have super-natural powers (Superman, X-Men, Spider-Man) or, if they do not, they readily ally with fellow heroes who have super-natural powers (for example, Iron Man teaming with Hulk, Thor, and Captain America in the Avengers and Batman with Superman in the Justice League). Batman is one of only a few superheroes without super-human powers and thus relies on technology and his own smarts to overcome the physical limits of the human body.

Superheroes inhabit a mythical universe in which science and supernatural phenomena or magic co-exist. Gotham City is a mythical place that although is has commonly been assumed to represent New York City is never identified as such in the comic books.[49] In Burton's and Schumacher's films, Gotham is a grotesque place whose architecture and infrastructure position it outside a recognizable time period or geographic location, perhaps in a notional dystopian United States. Nolan perpetuates this ambiguity throughout his three films. Although *Batman Begins* places Gotham squarely in the early 21st century, it is not at all clear where it is. Real-world Chicago exteriors are complemented by a futuristic elevated monorail system on a stylized *Art Nouveau* steel structure. By contrast, in *TDK*, Chicago and Hong Kong are clearly recognizable to audience members familiar with these cities and no effort is made to disguise various locations.[50] At one point in the interrogation room segment, the Joker even names Chicago streets. *The Dark Knight Rises* inexplicably re-locates Batman to New York City. The very fact that Nolan is able to do so without confusing the audience underlines the fluid nature of comic book mythology and flexible narrative continuity audiences readily buy into.

The superhero will put justice before the law. Widespread property and personal damage is incurred in virtually every superhero story, seemingly justified by the wider cause. Some heroes will kill, if reluctantly, in pursuit of a justified goal (e.g., Wolverine killing soldiers invading Xavier's school in *X-Men 2*, Iron Man killing many of his captors as he escapes from the cave in John Favreau's *Iron Man* [2008]).

> The Nolans [writer Jonathan and director Chris] force an interesting dilemma on the audience: How should society combat [the Joker's] malevolence? With the shining white knight, a district attorney who plays by the rules and brings criminals to justice in a court of law? Or with the tarnished dark knight, a masked vigilante who operates outside the jurisdiction of the police.[51]

Whilst ultimately above the law (because their powers exceed those of the state: police, military, etc.), superheroes often nevertheless invest in lawfully enshrined rules and morals (restoring legal order and the balance of good over bad), patriotic allegiance (in the case of Superman and Captain America, a U.S.-American allegiance), and loyalty to public services (Batman working with Commissioner Gordon).

Many observers have picked up on underlying themes of terrorism and the post-9/11 "War on Terror" in *TDK* and some have detected in *TDK* reflections, if not an outright endorsement, of reactionary post-9/11 Republican policies. McGowan posits that

> ...the similarity between Bush and Batman consists in their joint recognition that an exceptional threat to the legal order requires an extra-legal exception in order to quell the threat. [...] The logic of the War on Terror waged by President George W. Bush and Vice President Dick Cheney derives entirely from the idea that they rule in a state of emergency where the normal rule of law will be insufficient for safeguarding the U.S. populace. One must thus carve out an exceptional position outside the law. One of the ramifications of this idea is the legitimization of torture as a normal practice during the interrogation of anyone suspected of having a link with a terrorist organization.[52]

Stevens remarks, "Nolan turns the Manichean morality of comic books—pure good vs. pure evil—into a bleak post-9/11 allegory about how terror [...] breaks down those reassuring moral categories."[53] Indeed, while *TDK* makes reference to the clear-cut dualities of good versus bad, dark versus light, perpetrator versus victim, and terrorist versus law enforcement, it also complicates matters by setting terrorist against counter-terrorist, vigilante versus law enforcement, and hero versus vigilante (the latter two embodied by one and the same character).

Batman seems to act by a vague and fluid moral compass and, as a string of unexpected challenges unfolds, he repeatedly loses control and resorts to markedly reactionary measures. Brooker identifies "War on

Terror" techniques being employed by Batman, including rendition (Lau from Hong Kong), coercive interrogation and maltreatment of prisoners (Batman beating up the Joker in the interrogation room while the police are watching, Batman throwing Sal Maroni off a window ledge to break his leg), and total surveillance (the cellphone/sonar system Batman deploys near the end of the film, which Lucius Fox dismisses as "wrong").[54] It is striking how ineffective these techniques prove, whereby Lau, having been captured, provides no useful information and is later killed. The Joker also kills Rachel Dawes, a fellow prisoner, and a number of police officers before anyone can finally stop him.[55] Batman, however, does not purposely kill people, even when he has several opportunities to kill the Joker and even though doing so would, as it turns out, save lives later. In asking why Batman does not simply kill the Joker when he has the chance, White considers the justification for the act of killing by weighing a utilitarian outlook (measure the justifications of the means by the value of the outcome) against a deontological one (whereby the ends never justify the means).[56]

Shaun Treat denies that *TDK* as a whole promotes a political agenda.[57] Manohla Dargis agrees that, "it would be reductive to read the film too directly through the prism of 9/11 and its aftermath."[58] Nolan himself claims to have aimed for a broader appeal:

> We're trying to work on a more universal scale. [In order for people] to be able to bring a wide variety of interpretations to it depending on who they are. It's allowing the characters to be a conduit to the audience. Allowing an audience to sit there and relate to Batman and his dilemma whether they are Republican or Democrat or whatever.[59]

Contrary to the 9/11 terrorists, the Joker is not the enemy of a political system or religious values. Furthermore, whilst above observers plausibly read a Republican "War on Terror"-agenda into *TDK*, any such agenda is de-coupled here from U.S. patriotism and americocentricism. This matters because previous Hollywood comic book adaptations, for example the 1978 *Superman*, overtly promoted "the American Way," and the accompanying scores dutifully served this agenda with Americana-style fanfares and swashbuckling themes. Stylistically, the score to *TDK* bears no resemblance to these more conventional superhero scores and does nothing to suggest a patriotic stance.

Focussing solely on the Joker as a terrorist also neglects the role of Harvey Dent/Two-Face. Dent aspires to become district attorney and any political agenda of his focusses squarely on Gotham City. He pursues egalitarian justice and local safety, not nationalism, social, or sectarian interests. Finally, whereas the "War on Terror" claimed to have a clearly defined goal to destroy militant extremist organizations, Batman more diffusely fights any enemy of Gotham regardless of their origin, methods, or intentions.

The Joker: Chaotic Antagonist

> Nolan leaves the character of the Joker—his origins, his motivations, his real name—a complete mystery for the spectator, but it is not a mystery that one might figure out. The mystery is its own solution. Even after the police take him into custody, they can discover no information about him. Responding to the mayor's question concerning what they know about the Joker, Gordon says, "Nothing. No DNA, no fingerprints. Clothing is custom, no tags or brand labels. Nothing in his pockets but knives and lint. No name, no other alias." This complete absence of identifying information is not an indication that the Joker has successfully hidden who he really is but that he has no identity to hide.[60]

It is fascinating that Zimmer's Joker Theme (discussed in chapter 4) fulfills two purposes with utmost economy: the nervous buzz tone on the one hand delivers a sound "people can really hate,"[61] underlining the villainous quality of the character. On the other hand, the low-profile non-melodic theme is devoid of any cultural connotation or other extra-musical signifiers that might infer too much about the character. The Joker is to remain a mystery and his theme must not give too much away. A quote from the late David Raksin comes to mind, remembering that, "Oscar Wilde once said, to be understood is to be found out. And the biggest way to risk that is to write a melody."[62] In its opaque and understated nature, the Joker Theme is ugly and terrifying but at the same time supple, fleeting, and shifty, just like the villain it accompanies.

The Joker is not a larger-than-life villain as they feature in so many other superhero movies (such as Magneto, Ultron, Apocalypse, Mandarin, Sandman, Thanos and the Sentinels). A mortal human can perform his acts of terrorism. "We wanted the Joker to represent pure, unadulterated evil, in the sense that he has no logical motivation for his actions. That is what we wanted to unleash on the city of Gotham. He is an absolute," Nolan says. "The Joker is terrifying because there appears no rhyme or reason for what he does. He's just a force of nature tearing through."[63]

The Joker is a volatile character who lacks any sense of direction and allegiance to anything other than chaos. His effeminate stagger, his affected voice and disfigured face amount to a terrifying presence. Ledger is said to have based his version of the Joker on Sid Vicious (bassist of the Sex Pistols) and Malcolm McDowell's Alex DeLarge in *A Clockwork Orange* (1971).[64] It is quite possible that Ledger, a native Australian, also found inspiration in a Tom Waits interview with Australian TV host Don Kane in 1979.[65] Stevens notes that the Joker, not unlike Waits, is "also very funny—a funniness that has more to do with timing than with the usual villainous catchphrases."[66] For example, one of the funniest moments occurs when the Joker appears as a female nurse in Dent's hospital room and coyly but simply says, "hi."

Brooker flags that there is a lingering ambiguity over the Joker's sexual orientation, which adds to the overall mystique of the character.[67] He is strikingly flamboyant, wears thick colorful make-up, and elegant, if garish attire. Admittedly, heterosexual men commonly wear make-up nowadays and so too does Batman, whose black eye shadow helps blend his face with his masks. But when challenged by Rachel, the Joker says, "you got a little fight in you. I like that." He, notably, does not say "I like that in a woman." Elsewhere he refers to a wife in an anecdote about a failed marriage. There is at least a hint of suggestiveness when he swoons "you complete me" to Batman. When, shortly afterwards, Batman beats him up in the interrogation room, his response is poignantly masochistic: "Ooh, look at you go!" He remains passive and timid towards Batman throughout. Only after the truck chase, when Batman lies unconscious on the ground, does the Joker dare to approach him, gun in hand.

By contrast, there is something deeply heterosexual about Batman, despite his black skin-tight outfit. Bruce Wayne does show a softer side, for example when after Rachel's death Alfred serves him breakfast and he whispers, "She was going to wait for me, Alfred." But his caped alter ego is an alpha male who trumps the Joker in vigor and physical strength, if not in intellect and cunning. It is compelling to think what turn the story would take were the Joker to find out Batman's true, softer identity. The bipolar opposition between Nolan's Batman and Joker is striking:

Table 2.1. Comparison of Batman and the Joker

Batman	Joker
Costume: black Kevlar full body armor, black memory-cloth cape, mask and helmet with stylized ears	Costume: purple trousers, purple long coat, grey suit jacket, poison green waistcoat, grey shirt with honeycomb weave, grey tie, grey shoes, purple leather gloves
Subtle make-up: black eye shadow (to blend with black mask)	Garish make-up: black eye shadow (to contrast white face) white face paint / concealer, scars across the mouth accentuated with red face paint / lipstick, green hair streaks
Voice: small pitch range, low	Voice: wide pitch range, low when calm / manipulative, high when teasing / mocking
"I don't wear hockey pads" = "I am not ridiculous"	"I'm like a dog chasing cars" = self-deprecating / "I am ridiculous"—but also: "I am not crazy. I'm not." (See below.)
Clear sense of agency but not clear in whose name	Claims to have no sense of agency
Hides identity, but back story known to audience	No known identity, no known back story
Attitude: serious, measured, aggressive	Attitude: flippant, impulsive, cruel
Excessive force	Excessive wit
Problem solver	Problem creator
Removing obstacles	Creating obstacles
Solution	Puzzle
Justice	Injustice
Order	Anarchy

At one point the Joker emphatically snaps at Mafioso Gamble, "I am not crazy!" Reynolds suggests that comic book villains, "all are corrupted by power and power in the particular form of knowledge."[68] In the case of the Joker, he knows, first and foremost, what his next move will be, whereas no-one else does. Incidentally, the Joker and Batman spend the first half of the film not knowing of each other's whereabouts and looking for each other. Trying to convince Dent, whose fiancée Rachel he has just murdered, to join him, the Joker lies,

> I don't have a plan. The mob has plans, the cops have plans. You know what I am, Harvey? I'm a dog chasing cars. I wouldn't know what to do if I caught one. I just do things. I'm a wrench in the gears. I hate plans. Yours, theirs, everyone's. Maroni has plans. Gordon has plans. Schemers trying to control their worlds. I am not a schemer. I show schemers how pathetic their attempts to control things really are. So when I say that what happened to you and your girlfriend wasn't personal, you know I'm telling the truth.
>
> (The Joker to Harvey Dent/Two-Face)

The Joker does show a certain level of short-sightedness when he burns his share of the mob money, considering the presumed cost of maintaining his loyal gang of thugs. And yet, claim though he may that he is not a schemer, his schemes are actually most elaborate (stealing mob money, bribing officer Ramirez, scouting out high-profile locations, running a well-equipped terrorist organization, planting bombs, wiring a hospital for demolition). It may be true that he has no clearly defined goals other than creating chaos and terror, but to dismiss the Joker as a mere lunatic would fail to acknowledge just how twisted and brilliant his schemes are. Throughout the film, he also remains largely in control. Even when he is arrested by Gordon (whom he thought dead), this is only a temporary glitch whilst the next scheme is already underway.

The making of *TDK* was overshadowed by a number of accidents,[69] notably the death of Heath Ledger (the Joker) of an accidental drug overdose in January 2008.[70] The media was quick to speculate whether his use of prescription drugs was linked to the traumatizing experience of playing the Joker.[71] Ledger's untimely death did not stop Warner Brothers from using him and the Joker prominently in promotional material. Heath Ledger's performance as the Joker was hailed widely. Empire online called Legder's Joker "a towering performance."[72] *New York Times* critic Manohla Dargis saw him as "some kind of masterpiece."[73] Ebert correctly predicted that Ledger might be the first posthumous Oscar winner since Peter Finch (he won for his role in Sidney Lumet's *Network* in 1977).[74] Ledger won the Academy Award for Best Supporting Actor in 2009.

3

THE TECHNICAL APPROACH OF THE COMPOSERS

Zimmer's Technical Setup

Since gaining widespread attention with his score for *Rain Man* in 1989, Zimmer has been leading the way in popularizing the use of emerging music technology in Hollywood film music. Through his visionary and often technically pioneering work he has influenced contemporary film scoring practice in every aspect of the creative and technical process as well as aesthetic and idiomatic trends. Zimmer's musical background, professional experience, and inclination towards evolving technology have continued to steer his scores into new directions technically, stylistically, and sonically.

Zimmer's approach to composing is facilitated, and perhaps in turn guided, by the technology he uses. Even though in many interviews he has referred to his compositional process as "writing," he does not actually use pen and paper to write notes. His creative process relies on assembling ideas by use of music technology and hearing them played back by machines. Real orchestral parts may complement or be substituted for synthetic elements but they are added only later, at a stage when Zimmer's score is already conceptually advanced.

Music technology does not make Zimmer's creative process easier or quicker.[1] Finding suitable sounds, programming performance parameters (whereby composer-programmer effectively takes on the role of the performer), recording, editing, processing, and mixing takes a considerable amount of time.² Zimmer himself points out that every note in every score of his has at some point been conceived, performed, and manipulated by him. It is also important to remember that the decision to rely on cutting-edge music technology in the late 1980s was certainly not a cheap option: many of the tools Zimmer used such as, for example, the Fairlight synthesizer and rack-mounted Akai S900 samplers were extremely expensive at the time, costing $6,345 (in 2015 money) when they were first released in 1986. To assemble a virtual orchestra by use of Akai samplers, composers had to use multiple machines because each sampler could only provide one instrumental patch at a time.

Given his background as a keyboarder, it is understandable that with his early film scores Zimmer relied on a synthesizer medium (the Fairlight synthesizers has a standard keyboard interface). He then gradually expanded his instrumental range to encompass a wider palette including extended orchestral elements. It is unlikely that Zimmer ever saw the use of synthesizers and symphonic orchestra as a bipolar dichotomy whereby synthesizers replaced the orchestra. Instead, the autodidact would break with conventions, explore, and experiment, layering musical elements to suit his creative intuition.

By 1996, Zimmer had grown dissatisfied with commercially available sample libraries. His then recent successes allowed him to record his own samples at Air Lyndhurst Studios in London. At this point, his studio setup comprised eight Roland S760 samplers.³

> I sit in front of a pair of speakers all day long and that's how I spend my life, so I thought I might as well sit in front of a pair of speakers and listen to sounds that I actually think are good. [...] I always work with pretty much the same orchestra in London, so I did a deal with them, which was basically "Let me go and sample you guys at Air Lyndhurst sitting in the chairs you sit in whenever we do an orchestra recording, so the perspective is right." And the other part of the deal I made with them was that I wouldn't use the samples without using any real musicians—it wasn't to replace real musicians. In fact, I think 90 percent of the movies I've done ever since I've recorded in London and kept those musicians busy.⁴

Zimmer's commitment to keeping orchestral players employed is a laudable *Arbeitsbeschaffungsmaßnahme*.⁵ Zimmer retains a strong ethical sense to secure fellow musicians' livelihood and he will painstakingly supplant samples with real instruments where appropriate. For example, for Nolan's *Interstellar* (2014), he recorded organist Roger Sayer on the organ at Temple Church, London, even though he had already used samples of that same organ (which in fact he had sampled himself) for the demos.[6] It is ironic, however, that Zimmer's use of increasingly sophisticated samples pushed his peers and contemporaries to pursue similar working methods, creating a growing demand for sample libraries that has resulted in the proliferation of ever-cheaper commercially available products. One of the lamentable side effects has been an industry-wide downward spiral in music budgets, particularly in television and advertising where convincing samples have rendered live musicians redundant.

Into the new millennium, Zimmer's studio setup continued to expand in line with improving computer processing speeds and decreasing cost of memory required for loading samples. By 2002, his hardware samplers had been replaced by ten rack-mounted PCs that hosted the multi-timbral software sampler *GigaStudio*, offering a combined 1,600-voice polyphony. This setup for orchestral samples complemented a vast array of hardware synthesizers such as Minimoogs, a Waldorf Microwave XT, Roland MKS80 analog modules, a Jomox SunSyn, Access Virus B, a Clavia Nord Rack modeling synths, a Studio Electronics Omega 8 analog synthesizer, a Novation Supernova, and an Access Virus Indigo, among others.[7]

By 2013, computer-processing power had improved even further, allowing for a streamlined setup. Zimmer had replaced *GigaStudio* with his own custom-built software sampler SAM to host his latest 5.1 surround sample library. Zimmer's London studio now relied exclusively on software synthesizers whereas the hardware synths were mostly stored in his Santa Monica headquarters.[8] A guest bedroom housed three large flight cases, with thick strands of cables running into the main reception area where Zimmer worked. The flights cases contained:

- One MacPro for the Cubase sequencing software which hosts a template of 350-tracks,
- one MacPro for video playback, synced to Cubase via a MIDI timepiece,
- one computer to run Pro Tools to record audio stems and mix-downs,
- one PC to run an A3-sized touch-screen interface to control continuous MIDI controller data in Cubase,
- two Digidesign 96 I/O digital audio interfaces,
- four PCs to host SAM software samplers,

- one PC to host Vienna Ensemble Pro software and samples,
- several backup battery systems to boost the power supply in case of an outage.

In the lounge, a very large LED plasma screen displayed Cubase. A small mixing desk served to control playback volume only. Various MIDI keyboard interfaces were connected to the sequencer. Mid-field monitor speakers and a subwoofer were used for 5.1 surround playback. At the time of this writing, Zimmer has more than 30 similar setups in the RCP compounds in Santa Monica.

Whereas composers in the past would have distinguished between, firstly, writing music, secondly the interpretative layer of musical performance and, thirdly, the final recording, Zimmer's approach conflates the three stages into one holistic process. Using a custom-built software sampler is typical for Zimmer, who has continued to push beyond the capabilities of existing, commercially available music technology. In pursuit of his vision, he can be quite demanding. For example, he has been known to phone up his contact at Cubase manufacturer Steinberg in the middle of the night if he needs a software glitch fixed.

His inquisitive approach to learning has led to some fascinating innovations, including a 22-inch multi-touch pad he uses to program continuous controllers, which trigger MIDI performance parameters such as dynamic or timbral changes.[9] This interface allows the composer to intuitively input performance parameters through touch and movement, resulting more readily in musically rewarding results. Zimmer has also championed the ROLI "Seaboard," a keyboard interface with soft silicon keys and revolutionary after-touch capabilities that promise compelling new ways of capturing live performance parameters.[10]

Pre-Production: Inventing the Language

For Zimmer, every score starts with finding suitable colors and assembling a virtual ensemble. Revealing trepidation of the unknown, he confesses, "the first few weeks on a film are so painful, because I am trying to invent the language."[11] What Zimmer calls "language" need not yet involve specific musical ideas but rather a sound palette: for *The Power of One* (1992) this was the use of choir, percussion, and piano. For *Man of Steel* (2013) it was guitars, and a large number of drum kits. Zimmer's generic Cubase template contains 350 tracks with a wide range of sounds already loaded, which he customizes for each project. He loathes pre-sets and out-of-the-box solutions and consequently may spend whole days trying to create a particular sound patch on a synthesizer. This way he devises sounds that are uniquely his and not used by other composers. At the same time, he acknowledges that one of his biggest struggles is to keep his music sounding fresh and innovative, staying ahead of imitators. Zimmer's music has widespread reach and exposure and he is keenly aware of "innovation getting used up" and the need to re-invent frequently.

When pressed on the matter, Zimmer is happy to acknowledge that he often uses a simple harmonic and melodic vocabulary. For example, his theme "Time" for *Inception* (2010) repeats the same four chords throughout. The melodies in many of his most cherished themes comprise only a few repeating notes, including the theme for *The Thin Red Line*, "Chevaliers de Sangreal" for *The Da Vinci Code*, the final cue of *The Dark Knight Rises*, and many others. In a creative period that perhaps ended with his work on the *Pirates of the Caribbean* franchise (2003–2011), many of Zimmer's scores would rely on rhythmic figures comprising sprightful *marcato* strings, heavy, driving percussion, and brass fanfares (for example *Crimson Tide*, *The Rock*, and *Backdraft*). Although these scores also feature some melodic themes, they heavily rely on rhythmic accompaniments that resemble rock guitar riffs.

During his early Hollywood years, Zimmer's compositional process was somewhat more traditional, whereby he would wait for edits-in-progress or even so-called locked picture before composing. These days, Zimmer likes to get involved in projects as early as possible, inviting directors to participate in finding the musical palette for their film early on. Zimmer spends a lot of time with directors during pre-production, sometimes even on location. Zimmer might ask, "What are we trying to achieve? What is the tone of this scene?" For *Frost/Nixon* (2008) Zimmer spent weeks with director Ron Howard discussing songs of the time period in question, only to eventually dismiss the use of songs altogether. He would also discuss the films in terms of musical rhythm and dramatic flow, offering the director a different point of view. With Ridley Scott, Zimmer would meet to talk about a film over dinner. When working with Chris Nolan, Zimmer is one of the very few people who get to read the script in advance. This allows him to start experimenting long before the film is shot.

Zimmer wants directors to "be part of the band," and, crucially, Zimmer never relies on specialist music terminology when talking about his scores. This is where his own lack of traditional musical training decidedly plays in his favor: he conceives of his scores in terms of choice of instruments, colors, timbre, rhythm, tempo, dynamics, which are aspects even non-musicians can relate to. Given his childhood aversion to music theory, it is understandable that Zimmer does not intellectually ponder musical elements of harmony, melody, counterpoint, or motivic development. Instead, these emerge through free improvisation, trial and error, in a collaborative creative process.

Demos and Suites

Zimmer relies on his intuitive approach to scoring at the keyboard and the computer as guiding principles to his musical creativity:

> For me to orchestrate things—and I like doing all the stuff myself—I needed to be able to hear it. And the other thing is, it's very hard to tell a director when you're plonking [sic] around on the piano how it's all going to sound with eight horns and 32 violins, because the emotional gulf between tinkling on the piano and having the chaps sit there and giving it some is enormous.[12]

Working on musical ideas for *TDK* and specifically the Joker, Zimmer handed Nolan an iPod that contained 3,000 bars of continuous music, numerous variations on what would end up being the Joker Theme: a long distorted drone comprising synthesized element, electric guitars, and electric cello (see chapter 4). Nolan recalls that he "dutifully listened" to the whole recording, which he remembers as an "unpleasant experience."[13] Nolan's feedback to Zimmer was that he was not sure where exactly the Joker Theme was in those 3,000 bars but that it was certainly "in there." He then left it to Zimmer to devise something workable for the final score.

On the one hand this anecdote seems to illustrate a wasteful and less than focused approach to collaborative creativity, because so much excess material was produced only to be discarded. On the other hand, those 3,000 bars contained pre-selected ideas in terms of the general direction Zimmer wanted to take with the Joker Theme. The demo recording served illustrative purposes and facilitated a dialogue with the director. Zimmer knows that whilst he can reason with a director over a given cue's supposed meaning, he cannot defend his ideas, only what effect he thinks his ideas might have in the context of a film. Zimmer describes a dialectical process that he likes to maintain throughout a project: "I create problems for directors on a daily basis. I provoke. I ask 'what if we did something entirely different here?'" Nolan has said of Zimmer, "I have never worked with someone so dedicated to the idea that the real risk is in playing it safe."[14]

Zimmer's technical setup serves to create scoring demos that closely resemble the final score. Producers and directors welcome these demos because few of them can imagine what music they want (or whether the composer will give them what they think it is they have requested) until they hear a demo. Those funding the film often will not approve financing for the recording sessions until they have heard demos and believe the final score will successfully serve the film. In relying on samples and other electronic sources for demos, the risk and temptation may be to compose and demo only what sequences and samples well. Sequenced performances often lack some of the inflections and expressive nuance human players will bring to a performance. Zimmer, who pays close attention to sonic qualities in his work, frequently works with soloists at an early stage. He actively invites these musician's input and creative contribution, including Lebo M for *The Lion King*, singer Lisa Gerrard for *Gladiator*, and guitarist Johnny Marr for *Inception*.[15] For *TDK*, Zimmer worked with cellist Martin Tillman, who provided some of the many sonic layers of the Joker Theme.[16]

Zimmer will often double orchestral samples with synthesizer sounds and these doublings will usually remain in the final score. The technique can lead to somewhat odd recording practices. A violist of the London Symphony Orchestra, who has asked to remain anonymous, shared an anecdote about a Zimmer scoring session: the printed strings parts had numerous dynamic markings across gradual *crescendos*, in order for the players to match as closely as possible the dynamics of the sample-based demo.[17] Such carefully controlled instructions potentially restrict the contribution and musical interpretation of the live ensemble. Wesson recalls a scenario during the scoring sessions for *Batman Begins*:

> I do remember the first time we ever did the ostinatos on the Batman trilogy, on *Batman Begins*: It was pure hell. We had all these poor guys sitting in there. I don't know how many strings we had in there—80 players or whatever and they tried all day long to get it as tight as the samples and it was difficult, but they got there. They worked hard. They pushed hard. And then everybody was waiting for cabs and everybody's going home. [Engineer] Geoff [Foster] looked around and there was no Hans and he [says to me,] "Come here." Plays these guys, the guys that were in the hall. And by this time they'd gone into Pro Tools and they'd been quantized. With digital recordings you can edit anything you want. There were thousands of

edits. There was some poor music editor, as this stuff was being recorded, chopping it. [...] At the end of the day we sat there and we played back: we have the live orchestra at great expense with the same microphones in the same positions [as were used for Zimmer's samples], the same instruments, recorded, put through Pro Tools, quantized there. Or we've got the samples, which are the same players in the same room—and they're almost indistinguishable![18]

Whilst cue-by-cue demos have become an industry standard, Zimmer likes to create longer form pieces he calls suites that are musical exposés of sometimes up to 25 minutes in length. These pieces are often fully sequenced, but they may contain live recordings of soloists. Because Zimmer's sample libraries sound close to the studio session recordings that will eventually be added in, directors and producers get a very good impression early on what their score will sound like. The material contained in the suites will later be tailored to fit the film. Producer Jerry Bruckheimer likes Zimmer's suites because they provide "the launching point for more scene-specific music later on."[19] With his musical sketches done, Zimmer may not himself need to be involved in every (technical and time consuming) step along the way to the final score.

Music Production: Crafting the Score

Zimmer warns that the "mechanics of making a movie can really get in the way of creativity," which is why he prefers to compose music before a film is shot.[20] He acknowledges that there is no such thing as locked pictures anymore whereby composers might write music to a film edit that will not be altered. Zimmer welcomes this development because he wants the director to have the ability to revise ideas and keep trying different solutions. Zimmer says that Chris Nolan protects him from being caged in by the mechanics of the process: "We work together trying to make the best movie we possibly can." Ultimately however, Zimmer concedes, "picture is king" and music will submit (or be submitted) to the requirements of the film.

To cope with inevitable demands for change, Zimmer has adapted his working method to be compatible with prevalent working conditions in mainstream commercial (Hollywood) film production.[21] Traditionally, orchestral film scoring sessions served the purpose of recording complete musical cues and constituted the definitive conclusion to the scoring process. For Zimmer, this linear approach to film scoring is now virtually obsolete. Orchestral elements recorded in the scoring session may replace or complement elements of the demo. Acoustic parts may be doubled with synthetic elements. As will be shown in chapter 4, some cues of *TDK* contain only few live elements, or none at all. Other cues may feature strings and brass recorded live alongside layers of synth drones and heavy percussion (not recorded in the same session), as well as Mel Wesson's so-called ambient music. Zimmer also tends to use numerous pick-ups and overdubs, such as instrumental effects that he may add to cues where needed. Because some recorded material may already exist prior to the scoring session (e.g., suites, demos, soloists) and because additional material may later be sourced from elsewhere, the orchestrated session score of a Zimmer cue sometimes looks rather bare on the page. The sound of recorded live elements will, furthermore, be edited and mixed, sometimes with striking effect. Zimmer fully exploits cutting-edge recording techniques (including the inventive use of different microphone positions) and music production tools (including analog and digital effects), to produce a more cohesively affective and impactful sound.

In order to be able to adjust his music at every stage along the way, Zimmer uses numerous separate tracks in large Cubase or Pro Tools sessions. As a result, elements can easily be added or withdrawn, instrumental choices revised, balances redressed. Taking a flexible approach to the final product, Zimmer can act as an integral part of the filmmaking team rather than a contributor whose work will be left at the mercy of others, as has traditionally been the case with film music.

Zimmer's Collaborators

Over the years, Zimmer has assembled a team of trusted collaborators. Bruce Fowler has been orchestrating Zimmer's scores since *Bird on a Wire* (1990). Fowler's younger brother Walter has also been orchestrating for Zimmer sporadically since *The Rock* (1996), including on *TDK*. Bob Badami, who first started out as music editor in 1970 and worked as music supervisor and music consultant in the 1990s and early 2000s, has been credited interchangeably as Zimmer's "score wrangler" or "music wrangler" since 2010 (though, notably, he was not involved in the Batman trilogy). Alex Gibson is Zimmer's supervising music editor. Scoring mixer and music producer Steve Lipson and mixing engineer Alan Myerson have worked for Zimmer on many scores. Mark Wherry is Zimmer's director of music technology and responsible for a number of custom-built software and hardware solutions at RCP, including the SAM software sampler.[22] There are many other people involved in every Zimmer score, including additional composers, technical assistants, programmers, and runners. The sheer size of Zimmer's team invites speculation as to how much of the composing he undertakes himself. Zimmer is certainly not the only composer in Hollywood who has been accused of employing ghostwriters. Wesson explains:

> I'd go so far to say that most Hollywood composers use assistants and ghostwriters that most do not credit. [Challenged as to what all those people are doing for him, Hans says:] "It's like a bank job. I've got this guy here: he's the safecracker and you're the getaway driver and you're the jelly man and these guys, they're all lookouts." And he's absolutely right. It's a team of specialists and everybody has their place and everybody has their job.

Ambient music designer Mel Wesson has been working regularly with Zimmer since *Mission Impossible 2* (2000). His role and contribution will be addressed in more detail in chapter 5.

The Changed Purpose of the Scoring Session

Just as the notion of locked picture is now obsolete, so is the concept of "writing" a score, according to orchestrator Patrick Russ.[23] Traditional, linear film scoring workflows (spotting, writing, recording, dubbing) are incompatible with prevalent modes of digitally enabled film postproduction: filming on digital media, digital sound recording, virtual editing, reliance on computer-generated imagery (CGI), digital sound editing, and mixing and digitally enhanced sound design. The widespread use of stereo or surround sound has led to an increase in sonic competition between the component parts of the film soundtrack (dialogue, music, sound design). The transition to digital production and post-production means that picture and sound can now change up until very close to the final delivery deadline. Changes to the score are demanded later and later in the post-production process and decisions about the final place and placement of music are commonly deferred until the dub. Contemporary Hollywood composers know to expect frequent picture changes and also often have to accommodate changing demands on their music in terms of tone, style, and function within a film. As a result, the film scoring session is no longer the conclusion to the film composer's creative involvement. It is now a stepping-stone in the scoring process that provides essential building blocks for the final score, but not the final score in itself. Rather than recording the orchestra *tutti*, composers often record so-called stems (or stripes) to maximize potential for flexible music editing later on: being able to single out, for example, percussion only or to drop all brass at given moments provides more options later on.

Navigating emerging obstacles, Zimmer has adapted his working methods to interface flexibly with the post-production processes. As a composer with a less than traditional background and an unconventional approach to learning and creativity, Zimmer thrives in a technically progressive environment that works with a mixture of proven and speculative methods. He appreciates the benefits of joining a project as early as possible, not only to bring the director on his side, but also so he can liaise with the sound design team, the film editor, and other members of the post-production team.

Former RCP composer Klaus Badelt reflects on this strategy, which he himself has adopted for his own scores:

> I build my method of writing in such a way that there are no one-way streets and no milestones where I cannot return. There are no transitions into other phases of production: the first moment I sit down and tinker on a piano sound [...] it's the same production environment I use at the very end to mix the finished score. That has the benefit that I can always go several steps backwards and make changes [...] You're constantly re-addressing ... You go to the final dub stage and suddenly think "no, I get it, now I understand." Even in the finished, mixed cue I can make changes to a synthesizer sound or a melody. [...] I don't have to rely on others to cut my music around and I have a lot more creative freedom that way.[24]

Organically incorporating session takes into the evolving score-in-progress, Zimmer keeps his scores malleable in adjustable musical layers. Figure 3.1 illustrates the different key stages at which certain team members were involved in *The Dark Knight*. Zimmer's creative strategy was to get involved early and then to stay involved until the dub, where he helped shape the use of his music in the final mix. By contrast, James Newton Howard chose to end his involvement before the dub (see also below).

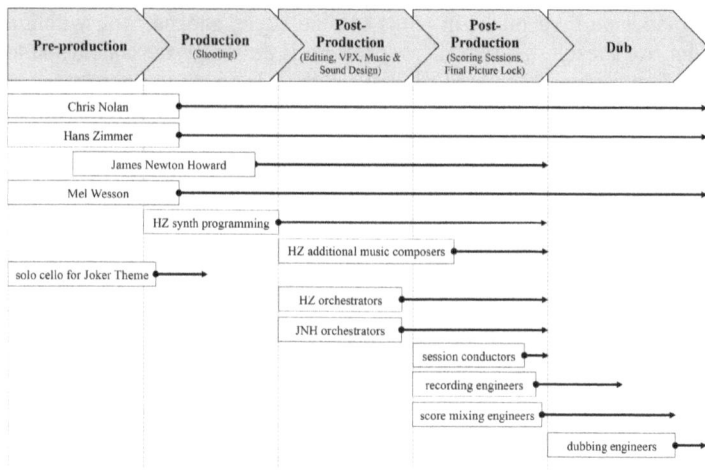

Figure 3.1. Collaborators getting and staying involved in *TDK*

Zimmer at the Dub

Many film composers tend not to attend the final dub, primarily because they resent the potential frustration that can arise from being there. Music often needs to give way to sound effects and dialogue by means of lowered volume or re-adjusted balances between individual music stems. This can significantly alter how the composer's intentions translate to the final soundtrack. Filmmakers who are suddenly unsure of their film or otherwise reconsidering their approach may request changes to the music. Studio executives may also weigh in with their opinion. The dubbing engineer and his team may spend only a few days with each film whereas the composer and others have spent many weeks or months. Whilst creative control ultimately remains with the filmmakers, dubbing engineers have a great deal of influence on balancing the film soundtrack. It is not uncommon for musical cues to be omitted, repeatedly re-mixed (within music stems or relative to sound effects), or even moved to a different point in the film at this final stage of audio post-production.

James Newton Howard tends not to involve himself in the dubbing process: "I try to stay fairly calm about cues disappearing under cars. What are you going to do?"[25] Wesson explains that the process of revising and adapting the score

> ...goes on and on until we've finished. Which, in a James movie, is when James has decided the score is approved and James is perfectly happy and we all breathe a sigh of relief. [...] James Newton Howard is much more of a gentleman. He likes things to be approved and move on.[26]

Zimmer sees the dub as a final opportunity to improve his scores. According to Wesson, even after the filmmakers have approved the score,

> ...Hans is still at the dub stage saying, "I can write a better one—oh, you're not using that—oh, don't do that." [...] I do remember the first film I worked on with Hans, which was *Mission Impossible 2* in 2000. And the night before print mastering, the movie got later and later and later and there were posters up in Remote Control and it would say *MI2* with a big picture of Tom Cruise pulling a helicopter or whatever and it said "May 2000" and we had gone so close to any possible deadline that somebody had actually written "MayBE 2000." [...] Hans will play it right to the last minute.

Being involved at this final stage allows the composer to fully explore the affective possibilities of his score, drawing on a wider sound palette that is better integrated in the overall soundtrack and, ultimately, may serve the film more effectively. As will be shown in chapter 4, this relatively new approach to film scoring can result in music that is structurally better suited to the narrative requirements of a contemporary film. Wesson also describes how, in the case of the *Dark Knight* trilogy, loosened financial restraints allowed room for experimentation at the dubbing stage:

> When you're on the dub stage [...] it's your last chance [...] to really change what you've done or to make absolutely sure that your idea is what you really intended [...] I can't understand why a composer wouldn't go. [...] Things get changed constantly there. I think it's important to consider the dub part of the creative process, not just the mix. It's more than that. It's the opportunity to experiment, if you've got time. [...] And when we were mixing [with Chris Nolan], we were mixing on the dub stage and we had seven days a week for six weeks. [...] It was an open-ended day, so if Chris wants to keep people there 14 hours on a Sunday and he's paying them triple rate, he doesn't care. And it's just Warner's problem. [...] In an environment like this, it's all about experiment. Try things out. But it's a very expensive way [in] a very expensive place.[27]

Openness to experimentation at the dub comes at a cost that, as yet, prohibits a more widespread use of this creative approach in the industry. Other threats include potentially inefficient and redundant workflows, an excess of expressive options and deferred authorial control over the score, in which cynics might see a lack of the composer's core competence to direct the scoring process. In traditional, pure musical terms, technically enabled flexible scoring methods are at odds with well-developed film music (tonal language, structure, themes, etc.). On the other hand, Zimmer's method of working has placed him at the top of his field in terms of commercial success and influence on common practice. He has continued to accept changes to prevalent working conditions in filmmaking and post-production practice, adapted his workflows and working methods, pursued emerging music and sound technology, and adopted new techniques and communication strategies. He embraces co-operation and active dialogue across all film departments, with the ultimate aim to serve the film at hand.

On a side-note, it is perhaps ironic that as a side-effect of Zimmer's workflow, the soundtrack recordings cherished by film music fans are now rarely the mixes heard on the film's soundtrack. These days, his score albums are usually mixed especially for the album release and can sound quite different from the dubbed cinema mix. The soundtrack album for *TDK* shares very little actual material with the score that is heard in the film.

Zimmer/Howard Collaboration

It is rare for two composers of Zimmer's and Howard's stature to collaborate on a score. Usually, a shared credit suggests that one composer has replaced another. For example, Randy Edelman replaced Trevor Jones on *The Last of the Mohicans* (1992) because the project ran over schedule and Jones had already committed to *Cliffhanger* (1993). Marc Streitenfeld took over from Harry Gregson-Williams on *Prometheus* (2012) and the latter received credit for his themes. John Williams's various themes in the *Harry Potter* and *Jurassic Park* films were adapted by other composers for the respective sequels. A composer partnership of equals can sometimes be found with more progressive film scores such as the score for *TRON: Legacy* (2008) by pop duo Daft Punk, Trent Reznor's and Atticus Ross's score for *The Social*

Network (2010), or Klimek's, Heil's, and Tykwer's score for Tykwer's own *Cloud Atlas* (2012).

Zimmer's and Howard's respective styles, personally and creatively, might not seem immediately compatible. Zimmer keeps a haphazard schedule, rises late, and works well into the early morning. He expects his team to work whenever he is working, invites a team effort, but remains fully in charge. Howard keeps a more reasonable schedule. According to Wesson, Howard will have pencils and stacks of paper neatly lined up on his desk. Zimmer is the chaotic opposite. Aside from the fact that he does not use pencil and paper, his own writing spaces in Santa Monica and London feel equally "lived in," even if the facilities surrounding him are modern and sleek. The self-deprecating and lax attitude Zimmer displays when speaking publicly masks the controlled and calculating manner he reveals in private meetings. Inasmuch as Zimmer can seem outgoing and forward, Howard comes across as soft-spoken and introverted. Howard has been known to be very private and guarded about his work. He prefers to work on his own and will consistently turn down interviews.[28] On one occasion, the author has witnessed Howard avoiding the hustle and bustle of a scoring session at Abbey Road by hiding away in a back room to make phone calls to friends.

The two composers also have a contrasting aesthetic and musico-narrative outlook. Although they both have a background in popular music and whilst they are both accomplished keyboarders and (pop) music producers, their film music nevertheless differs considerably. Zimmer's composing by additive layering contrasts Howard's more florid and developmental style. Zimmer's aforementioned focus on serving the film (which one might summarize as "picture is king") diametrically opposes Howard's view that in his scores the "theme is king."[29] For *TDK*, Mel Wesson was a common denominator between the two composers, as he had worked with both previously.

The following quote from Zimmer sheds some light on the partnership, explaining how the collaboration with Howard on *Batman Begins* came about in 2005 and then on *TDK*. It is interesting to note how the two composers interfaced with each other and with Chris Nolan:

> I really wanted to work with Chris Nolan, but I wasn't sure I wanted to be part of reinventing Batman. It came with a lot of baggage. I thought Danny Elfman had done a fantastic score for Tim Burton and I couldn't think how to do something different. The other problem was that I kept thinking about the duality of Bruce Wayne and the Dark Knight. I wasn't sure how one person could handle both [...] I

was quite ready to go and be the Dark Knight, but I didn't know how to do the love story. I kept hedging and being coy until Chris asked what the problem was and I said I didn't want to do the lovey-dovey stuff! So he suggested I work in collaboration with someone else. James Newton Howard and I had been saying for years that it would be fun to do a score more collegially, more like a band [...] When you work alone you talk yourself out of your crazy ideas, but a partner gives you the encouragement to go forward with them. It was a really interesting process between myself and James and Mel Wesson and whomever else we pulled into the band. It was never this uncreative sort of process of the director coming to listen to what the composer has prepared a little earlier, that dry conversation. [...] Chris kept phoning and describing films to me that he was shooting. I didn't have any footage, he was just telling me what he was doing on the phone and saying, "I can't make this scene work and I don't know what music to put in and I don't want to use other people's. Can you just dash something off?" So even though I was working on something else, somehow or other James or I would dash something off and send it over. A lot of the stuff developed that way, sort of in the periphery of my vision, in a way. It was actually quite nice. By the time we came to London to see Chris' first cut, the movie was populated with all these little ideas and vignettes that we had written [...][30]

Zimmer recalls that he was hired to score *Batman Begins* first and then invited Howard along. Howard corroborates this recollection:

I think first of all this was Hans's gig so [...] he asked me to join in on *Batman Begins* because we had wanted to work together for a long time and we were already good friends. It's a tribute to the collaboration that we're better friends now. Somebody had to be designated leader and that's Hans and I love that because it's the only time in my musical life where I've had somebody essentially producing my music, so to say, in such a wonderfully intelligent and insightful way. For a modern composer, that just doesn't happen.[31]

Whereas at first Zimmer and Howard felt it was a good idea to work together, their relationship seems to have deteriorated over time. In a short interview after the 2009 Saturn Awards (where Zimmer and Howard were honored for their *TDK* score), Howard seems impatient and clearly wants to leave as soon as questions are asked about the film and their collaboration.[32] Subsequently, Howard did not work on *The Dark Knight Rises* (2012). Although it cannot be ascertained what exactly led Howard not to work on the third installment of the trilogy, sources suggest that hurt feelings and creative frustration may have been a factor: "James [...] mentioned that it was his decision to bow out of the next film. He stated that Nolan and Zimmer had established such good chemistry working on *Inception* and he didn't want to be a third wheel."[33]

On *TDK*, the division of labor between Zimmer and Howard is not always entirely clear in terms of the themes the two composers wrote respectively, as will be shown in chapter 4. Incidentally, Zimmer's work on Nolan's Batman films has effectively made Zimmer the go-to composer for superhero movies [*Man of Steel* (2013), *The Amazing Spider-Man 2* (2014), *Batman v Superman: Dawn of Justice* (2016)] whereas Howard has since scored a more eclectic range of films.

Howard's Technical Setup

Although his training as a classical pianist might have steered him in a more traditional direction, Howard embraced music technology early on: "I'm quite comfortable working with electronics [...] I try and blend electronics as part of the orchestra. I spend a huge amount of time producing."[34] Whereas Zimmer tried to avoid out-of-the-box solutions, Howard gladly relies on commercially available products. For example, in a short promotional video he has endorsed Yamaha and its iconic Yamaha DX7, the very instrument Zimmer is proud never to have owned. Howard remembers the synthesizer fondly from the early 1980s for its "musician-friendly quality."[35] He has also supported software developer Spectrasonic, lauding their Omnisphere synthesizer for its ease of use.[36] Wesson, who has worked with Howard on a number of scores, points out:

> People listen to James' scores and think of him as being very traditional. He's unbelievably adept at dealing with electronics. He has one screen on the left-hand side of his writing rig which [runs] Ableton Live, so anything I send him, like this, he can do whatever he wants. He can shift tempos, he can edit, shift pitches. Whatever he wants. And he does and he's very, very adept at it.

In 1997 architectural firm studio bau:ton completed the design and construction of a 4,500 square foot recording studio facility for Howard in Santa Monica, California.[37] This was significantly expanded in 2007 to include a second live room and common areas. The overall setup is perhaps more traditional than RCP's in terms of equipment, certainly more modest in scale. Nevertheless, Howard uses a state-of-the-art Euphonix System 5 mixing console and a Euphonix MC Mix Controller for Pro Tools, housed in custom-built studio furniture. Besides a large array of outboard effects processors (compressors, preamps, etc.), Howard also uses multiple MacPros running Cubase and Pro Tools, the same sequencing and recording software used at RCP. The studios house a Yamaha C6 grand piano as well as a Steinway & Sons grand. Commercially available software instruments such as Project SAM True Strike (not to be confused with Zimmer's SAM software sampler), Native Instruments Komplete, Trilogy, Zebra, and the EastWest PLAY sampler run from *GigaStudio* computers. Howard has also adopted several of Zimmer's custom-built 22-inch control surfaces.

The Yamaha promo mentioned above shows Howard writing on manuscript paper with pencil and ruler in hand, perhaps to emphasize that he is a contemporary film composer equally comfortable with traditional and modern ways of composing. In fact, his studio facilities are ideally suited to accommodate the eclectic and versatile nature of Howard's music, which has comprised a wide range of symphonic, electronic, ethnic, and popular idioms.

Howard's Suites and Collaboration

Starting out on a new project, Howard prefers to be involved early (see also Figure 3.1 above), based on his positive experience with M. Night Shyamalan. Like Zimmer, since the early 2000s, Howard has been writing long-form suites for each project, which he demos before shooting commences, drawing inspiration from the script and storyboards. For every Shyamalan project since *Signs*, he has composed these suites that may last between 10–20 minutes. He has done the same with *Water for Elephants* (2011) and the *The Hunger Games* series (2012–2015). These pre-shoot suites allow Howard to find a suitable palette and musical language for a film and engage directors in a creative dialogue over the music, before they become preoccupied with the production process. He points out that with the director "having heard all the demos there are usually very few surprises come recording day."[38] The use of suites must offer reassurance for the composer, knowing that, once approved, the musical landscape for a film is broadly established.

Howard likes to work closely with directors but knows from experience that some directors are reluctant to be involved in the scoring process.[39] He is confident that his music can have a profound affective impact on a film and, in turn, the audience, pointing out that "oftentimes we (composers) take a scene that is okay and make it much, much better."[40] For *The Sixth Sense*, Shyamalan initially felt that no music was needed ("I don't need any help here"), until the film was received poorly in test-screenings and convinced him otherwise.[41] Howard is confident about his contribution to *Signs*: "[The film] wasn't scary without music, I guarantee you."[42]

Howard's music is often motivic, even melodic, and he is one of the few contemporary Hollywood composers who continue to write tuneful scores where appropriate (for example, *Maleficent* [2014]). As mentioned above, he champions strong musical themes, which need not consist of extended melodies. He likes to exercise "calculated restraint" but feels that "the hallmark of what I do […] is a very melodic kind of take on a piece, even in tiny little bits and pieces, little motifs […]."[43] Howard's theme for Harvey Dent in *TDK* is a short regal two-phrased melody that keeps a relatively low profile (see also chapter 4).

Howard notes that today the scoring process is "demo-dependent, which most people are now."[44] He relies on a demo process enabled by technology:

> I always mock up and orchestrate as I write and that includes electronic as well as orchestral elements. To me they're inextricable—they always have to work in concert. Mocking the cues up and essentially mixing as I go is the only way to know for sure that they're going to work in the final film. I like to get my music in the movie as early as possible, to replace the temp score and really help the film find its voice. Often, my synth demos are used in the preview screenings since they're so close to what the final will be.[45]

It is interesting to note that Howard distinguishes between programming ("mock up and orchestrate") and composing ("writing"), even if he experiences them as processes occurring in parallel. This sets him apart from Zimmer, who practically does not make this distinction. Once there is an edit-in-progress of the film at hand, Howard can edit elements from his suite to the film on a cue-by-cue basis. It is fascinating that on projects where Mel Wesson is involved, he might act as a mediator, placing ambient music stems in an edit-in-progress and send Howard these versions, which help Howard find access points for his music:

> James Newton Howard is a big fan of this: I'll go way ahead of him and I'll feed stuff back so when he gets to a given cue, it's not a completely blank canvas. There is something there. There's maybe

some sort of a structure. Even if it's a very rudimentary sketch, there's dark rumbling stuff because something terrible is going to happen, or there's high-end tension stuff because somebody's around that corner.

Howard's diverse musical output over the years defies categorization. Although some of Howard's scores in the past have been purely orchestral, these days he combines electronics and synthesized elements with orchestral parts. The resulting sound, as he himself acknowledges, transcends the sound of a real orchestra towards something more stylized and blended aesthetically.

> It's very produced, high production value, we're very careful about all the synthesizers, all the electronic sounds, we record all the percussion separately, we get it all sounding amazing, then we layer it with the orchestra, get that sound amazing. So in the end you're bringing to the mix five Pro Tools rigs with a thousand tracks of information. Just massive amounts of stuff, that then has to be mixed. It's not like recording an orchestra live. There's a huge amount of layering, pre-recording, over-dubbing that goes on for months.[46]

> I produce my scores like a record, which is why Hans Zimmer and I got along so well [working on *TDK*]. We take great care with the rhythm section. We take great care with the programming. It's recorded in a very pristine fashion and the whole thing is cumulative in its impact. As opposed to synthesizers and electronics just being an afterthought. They are really carefully conceived from the beginning.[47]

Howard usually works with the same orchestrators, mostly Brad Dechter, Pete Anthony (who has also conducted many of Howard's scores), and Jeff Atmajian. As is standard practice across the industry, the orchestrators will take MIDI files of Howard's approved cue demos and translate them into notation, making necessary adjustments to ensure parts are idiomatic and effective on the scoring stage.

Whilst Howard readily uses music technology when conceiving of his score and whilst he is fluent in a range of styles that often incorporate an electronic and synthesizer medium, he is nevertheless aware of certain threats technology poses. He is also critical of some of his contemporaries:

> This whole technology issue is obviously a mixed bag. For the first time in history it's allowed non-musicians to write music, which is kind of regrettable in many cases. [...] I think complexity is part of

what's been set aside as well, that with the technology, somehow intricate writing and moment-to-moment architecture of the scoring has become much less fashionable.[48]

This statement might very well describe the kind of technologically driven scores Zimmer is known for, comprising musical material that may seem less than elaborate at surface level. Then again, the next two chapters will show that the score for *TDK* is actually most intricately tailored to the film it accompanies. The next two chapters also explore Zimmer's and Howard's collaboration in more detail as part of a wider score analysis (chapter 4) and music in relation to sound design (chapter 5).

4

ANALYSIS OF THE SCORE AS MUSICAL TEXT

This chapter first gives an overview of the spotting of *The Dark Knight* (hereafter *TDK*), detailing the use and placement of different types of newly composed and sourced music in the film. An outline of the instrumentation and orchestration follows, including considerations of recording techniques used to capture the orchestral elements of the score. The next section provides detailed illustrations and analysis of primary and secondary recurring themes and motifs. A discussion of scoring techniques and devices, notably the use of ostinato, building tension by additive layering of musical strata and the use of thuds, bangs, and swells, is prefaced with a look at the differences and similarities between Howard's and Zimmer's cues.

Since the rightsholders refused to grant permission to show many of the author's more detailed music examples, reference will be made to rhythms and pitches descriptively, using Helmholtz nomenclature (Figure 4.1) for labelling of respective octaves.

Figure 4.1. Helmholtz nomenclature

Spotting

There is a remarkable amount of music in *TDK*. The film lasts 153 minutes and, according to the PRS cue sheet,[1] features 135 minutes and 40 seconds of music. In other words, nearly 90 per cent of the film is accompanied by music. The majority of this music is newly composed underscore. The remainder comprises previously released tracks licensed for synchronization.

Original Music

The PRS cue sheet lists all newly composed music under the title "Dark Knight," with the work number 062635HN T-903.042.602-9. This one entry comprises the musical contributions of six composers with a combined duration of two hours, seven minutes, and 37 seconds. This includes all music cues originally composed for the film as well as Wesson's ambient music design. The distribution of performance royalty share for "Dark Knight" (and, by inference, the amount of work each composer has contributed), breaks down as 17.25% for Zimmer, 12.5% for Howard, 9% for Wesson, 7.5% for Lorne Balfe (a Remote Control Productions composer), 2.5% for Henry Jackman (also RCP), and even 1.25% for supervising music editor Alex Gibson (RCP). Universal/MCA Music Publishing claims the other 50%, a common arrangement in film music publishing. It is noteworthy that Wesson's contribution was deemed so important that he was given a substantial share of performance royalties. Similarly, Balfe and Jackman both receive a considerable share of performance royalties even though they do not receive prominent billing in the film's credits. For supervising music editor Alex Gibson to receive even a small share of royalties suggests that his contribution to the final score was deemed sufficiently important. Taking into account his job title, it is likely that Gibson played an important role in the placement of cues within the film and helped with creative editing decisions.

    A second entry in the cue sheet, also titled "Dark Knight," has a different tune code (062635GW T-903.041.755-1) and is used for four minutes and five seconds. Zimmer receives the full 50% of the writer's share. This track was used in the closing credits of *TDK*.

    The table in Appendix I lists all music cues in the order they appear in the film. The table shows that there are few gaps of silence be-

Analysis of the Score as Musical Text 55

tween music cues. Relatively longer passages without music include the fight scene in the parking garage early on, two minutes after the Joker has visited the mob bosses and just under two minutes in the segment following the Hong Kong sequence. There is an almost 7-minute stretch without music during the truck chase, interrupted only by a brief music cue when the Batpod is revealed. Elsewhere, cues follow in close succession. It is important to remember that the table in Appendix I does not indicate the nature of the music in each cue, nor the instrumentation, orchestration, dynamics, and relative volume against other soundtrack elements. Some cues comprise extremely quiet ambient murmurings, soft tones, subtle pulses, that can barely be heard.

Whilst Zimmer's scoring method and music production technique allows for music to be flexibly adjusted during post-production, it is interesting that the spotting of the film actually remained fixed in terms of number of cues and cue order. Table 4.1 displays cue numbers as shown in the orchestrator's scores that can be matched and compared with the order of cues as they occur in the film, listed in Appendix I.[2] Copies of the orchestrations, session, and conductor's scores are held in the James Newton Howard Collection, part of the University of Southern California Libraries Special Collection in Los Angeles and can be viewed by appointment. As per convention, the cues in *TDK* have been numbered consecutively, based on the initial spotting. "1M1" refers to reel 1, music entry 1. A start point for 1M1 would also have been agreed to, usually down to the exact frame in terms of SMPTE time code (reel:minutes:seconds:frames).

For the purpose of spotting, films are still commonly broken down into reels, even if the physical medium quickly is growing obsolete. In the days of analog film, physical reels were ten minutes long and would be delivered to cinemas as 20-minute double reels for assembly by the projectionist. A 120-minute film thus comprised twelve reels or six double reels. Somewhat oddly, the reel IDs in the *TDK* cue numbers refer to double reels: 1M1 points at double reel 1 and the first music entry ("M1"). Accordingly, "2M9" is the ninth music entry overall and occurs at the very beginning of the second double reel, almost exactly 20 minutes into the film (see also Appendix I).

Table 4.1. Cue numbering in the orchestrators' scores

Cue #	Cue Title
1M1	Bank Robbery
1M2	Find the Batman
1M3	Buyer Beware
1M4	Dirty Cash
1M5	The New DA
1M6	Hostile Witness
1M7	Bank Warrants
1M9	Who Appointed Batman?
2M9 [sic]	Who Appointed Batman? [sic]
2M10	Move the Money
2M12	Halfway to Hong Kong
2M13	Trip to Hong Kong
2M14–15	Put A Smile on That Face
2M16	LSI Extraction
2M17	Mobsters Taken to Justice
2M18	Are You Up to It?
3M20–21	Hero Without a Face
3M22	Joker Crashes Party
3M23	Panic Room
3M24–25	Then You're Gonna Love Me
3M26–27	Lau, Watch the World Burn
3M28	Loud Enough?
3M30	Speech Ambush
3M32B	Gordon Is Dead
3M32J	Dent to Van
4M34–35	?
4M37–38	I Don't Know Anything
4M38ALT	Overlay
4M39	Blood On My Hands
4M39B	LB's High Strings
4M40	I Am the Batman
4M42	Pod Deploys
4M42b	Batman Down

Cue #	Cue Title
4M43	Gotcha
4M44	Gordon Returns Home
5M42 [sic]	BB 5M42 Backup RFK v1.0 LB
5M46–47	Wired
5M48–49	Harvey Two-Face
5M50	This Is My City
5M51–52	Hospital Bomb Scare (posted as "Gotham Towers" on Lorne Balfe's website)[3]
6M52b	Hospital Bomb Scare [sic]
6M55	The Boats
6M56–57a	Always a Catch
6M57	Storming Pruitt Building
7M58	Give It to Me
7M59	A Little Push
7M60	An Eye for an Eye
7M61	I'm Not a Hero
7M62	A Dark Knight

Where cues are omitted in Table 4.1 (see non-consecutive cue numbers, for example missing 1M8), those music entries are either diegetic (see above) or have been scored without live orchestral elements. Cue 1M4 "Dirty Cash" was not used in the final film. It was probably intended to accompany the conversation between Batman and Gordon in the vault of the bank the Joker has robbed. The absence of underscore in this scene results in a relative silence that adds to the clinical and claustrophobic feel of the harshly lit bank vault. The consecutive cue numbering skips number 1M8, which allows for the source cue of the string quartet playing in Wayne's restaurant. The fact that the number was skipped in the orchestrations indicates that the placement of this source cue in the running order of composed cues was known quite early on, perhaps at spotting, but certainly when the cues were being orchestrated and labeled with their respective numbers.

The duplicate entry for "Who Appointed Batman?" (1M9 and 2M9) results from two different versions of the same cue being orchestrated and, presumably recorded. 1M9 was composed by Howard and orchestrated by Brad Dechter (see also below). The cue is 22 bars long and starts at 49bpm, with a slight *ritardando* in the last three bars (down to 45bpm). Scored for harp and high strings, this sparse and gentle cue states the Harvey Dent Theme (see also below). Dechter also orchestrated 2M9 by the same composer. He adds a disclaimer on the first page of this version, presumably addressing Howard: "This is very much like 1M9v2 which was orchestrated first. This version (2M9) include[s] the addition of celli harmonics doubling the string pads. You may want to consider doing the same for 1M9, which I added in a 1M9Alt version)." 2M9 is not only orchestrated in a slightly different way: at 15 bars, it is also shorter. It starts at the slower tempo of 48.50bpm, a slight difference that nevertheless results in quite different image synchronization over the course of 15 bars. Rather than changing tempo gradually, this version of the cue changes immediately to 50bpm on the downbeat of bar 10. Both versions of this cue were likely being tried against different picture edits. If so, then this shows that Howard copes with changing picture requirements rather differently than Zimmer: whilst the latter will keep his music changeable by use of adaptable compositional, recording, and production techniques, Howard takes a more traditional approach by simply recording two alternative versions of the same cue.

2M11 "Kill the Batman" is skipped in the list of orchestrations. This cue, heard when the Joker joins the meeting of mob bosses and proposes to kill Batman, does not use orchestral parts. The cue 2M12 "Halfway to Hong Kong" was spotted, orchestrated, and recorded but later omitted from the film. It is, however, featured on the soundtrack album. The missing cue 2M19 in the list accounts for the diegetic string quartet playing at Wayne's fund raiser. Once again, the orchestrators must have been aware of this source cue early on to allow for consecutive numbering to account for this cue.

The "Speech Ambush" segment is the only section in the film where the cues do not appear in the order they have been spotted and numbered. 3M28 "Loud Enough" is heard when Wayne fires bullets into blocks of concrete to reconstruct fingerprints from the shrapnel (comic book forensics!). As it appears in the final film, this cue is intercut with an aerial shot of the marching band playing Balmoral. After Wayne has left the lab on his Ducati, we cut back to the parade with Balmoral playing again. These two entries of source music, listed in the PRS cue sheet, have not been accounted for in the consecutive cue numbering. 3M29 is "Kitchen Timer," a slow gnawing ascend of a terse tone (the Joker Theme, see also below) as an assassination attempt on the mayor unfolds. 3M30 "Speech Ambush" is a short mournful moment in the upper strings that laments the death of Gordon, who has taken a bullet to save the mayor. 3M31 is skipped in the numbering but there is no cue in between "Speech Ambush" and 3M32J "Dent to Van," which segues out of the prior. Confusingly, 3M32B is actually "Gordon Is Dead," an extended version of "Speech Ambush" that is heard *after* 3M32J, when the police inform Gordon's wife that her husband has been shot. The very same music is reprised, and expanded upon, when Wayne later mourns Rachel's death (5M46–47).

3M33 is skipped altogether, which possibly accounts for the diegetic dance music in the club where Batman seeks out Maroni (Eric Roberts). Accordingly, 3M36 would account for the second use of dance music, heard quietly from outside the club where Batman interrogates Maroni. 3M34–35 is an unused cue by Howard for meandering brass and low strings, presumably scored for the Maroni interrogation.

4M41 introduces the truck chase segment and features the Joker Theme. It does not contain orchestral parts. 5M42 is labeled "BB 5M42 Backup RFK v1.0 LB." "RFK" stands for "Rory's First Kiss," the working title of *TDK*. "LB" stands for Lorne Balfe, who will have worked on this cue. Balfe's initials appear on several of the orchestrations. "Backup" suggests that this cue was supposed to supplement or serve as a stand-in for another cue, presumably 4M42 "Batpod Deploys." In which case "BB" perhaps stands for "BatBike?" Musically, Balfe's backup is very similar, featuring the Batman ostinato (see below) and hits in low percussion. It is more elaborate and rhythmically busier than 4M42. However, 5M42 was not used in the final film.

5M51–52 is titled "Hospital Bomb Scare" in the orchestrations and the exact number on the score is "5m51-52 v9.01_o p7r." Remarkably, Lorne Balfe has posted this exact version of the cue on his website, under the title "Gotham Towers" (see table above). This seems to suggest that he composed it and not Zimmer, who is stated as the composer on the score.

Cue numbers 6M53 and 6M54 actually cover three music entries: "Dent Kills Wertz,"[4] [*sic*] "Sonar System," and "Unlucky Driver," neither of which featured live orchestration.

Licensed Music

When Lucius Fox meets Bruce Wayne in a public pedestrian passageway in Hong Kong, there is music playing through a PA system. The innocuous piece is the kind of generic easy-listening music one would expect from a shopping mall or tourist attraction. Incidentally, Wayne is posing as a tourist, wielding a large camera. The track is "Bamboo

Rafting" by Miklosh, published by JW Media Music, a London-based production music company.[5] The PRS cue sheet for *TDK* indicates that the piece plays in the background for 32 seconds. It is interesting to note that production music was used here, which is far cheaper in terms of production and licensing cost than bespoke music or music released commercially by a major label. The relative obscurity of this particular track also ensures that very few audience members will recognize it or have extra-filmic associations (at worst, mundane or dated) that might distract from the film and disturb its make-belief integrity.

In the restaurant where Bruce Wayne and his Russian ballerina girlfriend intrude on Harvey Dent's and Rachel Dawes's dinner, a string quartet performs Schubert's String Quartet No. 13 in A minor, D. 804. Since the piece is in the public domain, the PRS cue sheet states no publishing interest. No further information is available as to the origins of the recording and the ensemble that can be seen briefly on screen is not credited. The piece is not featured on the *TDK* soundtrack album.

When Wayne later hosts a fund raiser in his penthouse in support of Dent's political ambitions, the diegetic background music is the "Whitol-Minuet" from "Les Vendredi," a collection of Russian folk music. The track was taken from the production music album "Classical String Quartets" released by Chappell Recorded Music Library Ltd.[6] No information on the performers was available at the time of this writing. The piece is not featured on the *TDK* soundtrack album.

The PRS cue sheet lists two entries for "Balmoral," once for 12 seconds as "background" and then 31 seconds as "featured." The traditional bagpipe tune was performed on location by the Pipes and Drums of the Chicago Police Department. The "background" use is heard during a brief aerial long shot of the streets of Gotham (Chicago) before these are followed by closer shots, with the music and marching band much closer.[7]

Two tracks by Tokyo electronic-pop duo Boom Boom Satellites (singer/guitarist Michiyuki Kawashima and bassist/DJ Masayuki Nakano) can be heard inside and outside the nightclub where Batman seeks out mobster boss Sal Maroni. When Batman fights his way through Maroni's goons inside the club, the track "Scatterin Monkey" amplifies the action with its aggressive beats and jarring textures, in tandem with the stroboscopic club lighting. When, shortly after, Batman has taken Maroni outside and threatens to throw him off a fire escape, the track "A Moment of Silence" can be heard thumping from inside the club. Both tracks are taken from Boom Boom Satellites' 1999 album *Out Loud*.

Instrumentation and Orchestration

Most cues in *TDK* contain orchestral parts but few cues, if any, use orchestral parts exclusively. In most cues, acoustic elements recorded at the scoring sessions are blended with pre-recorded sampled and synthetic elements, as well as Mel Wesson's ambient music (see below). The written orchestrations rarely contain all the instruments heard in the final score. The final mix of the music, as it appears in the film, does not maintain a natural balance between the instruments. Zimmer tends to double acoustic instruments with synthesized sounds. Whilst this considerably expands the sonic palette of the score, the resulting sound is a clear departure from realism. It is ironic that although Zimmer has repeatedly said he likes to draw on orchestral sounds, the overall aesthetic of his music veers towards the synthetic and electronic, readily supplanting acoustic sounds.

The table in Appendix 2 lists all cues that were orchestrated for *TDK* to record orchestral parts. Zimmer and Howard worked with completely separate teams of orchestrators. Of the numbered cues (spotted for specific moments in the film), Zimmer composed 29 cues and Howard composed 20. Brad Dechter orchestrated ten cues for Howard, Jeff Atmajian orchestrated seven cues, and Randy Kerber three cues. Bruce Fowler orchestrated nine cues for Zimmer, Walter Fowler orchestrated eight cues, Suzette Moriarty seven cues, Kevin Kaska three, and Elizabeth Finch two.

A look at the instrumentation of the orchestration for *TDK* should be prefaced with the observation that the budget for the film was very large even if, at an estimated $185m, it was relatively modest compared to Hollywood's escalating budgets around the same time.[8] It is worth remembering that commercial mainstream cinema will quite readily expend vast amounts of money, for example on labor-intensive visual effects, if this promises to increase box office takings. To Hollywood cinema, profitability matters more than up-front expenditure. Since *TDK* did not rely on many CGI shots, relatively more money could be spent in other areas. The dubbing sessions for *TDK* took place with a focus on experimentation and collaborative creativity, relatively free from budgetary concerns (see also chapter 3). It is highly likely that the scoring sessions enjoyed a similar degree of fiscal freedom, allowing for instrumental forces in numbers not commonly encountered in contemporary classical music, opera, or even film music. Although the composers worked with discrete teams of orchestrators, there appears to have been consensus as to the overall orchestral forces that would be used for the scoring sessions: the numbers of brass and strings match up fairly consistently. Agreeing on live ensemble size and instrumentation up front allowed Zimmer and Howard to record with the same ensemble in the same studio.

The orchestrations of Zimmer's cues generally do not use woodwinds, except 3M22 "Joker Crashes Party," where an oboe plays a short line for six bars (it is hardly audible in the surrounding texture of the final mix) and 6M55 "The Boats," where orchestrator Moriarty asks for two contrabassoons. These add color to chords of long held notes in synthesized parts, brass, and strings. It is possible that woodwinds were felt to be too weak and completely get lost in the texture and visceral force of many of Zimmer's cues. Not counting the un-numbered effects cues, 25 of Zimmer's cues employ brass and often call for nine horns, up to three trumpets (e.g., 4M42 "Pod Deploys"), up to six trombones (in 6M56–57 "Always a Catch"), up to three bass trombones, and even an additional three bass trombones in overdub for 6M57 "Storming Pruitt Building." Where he calls for tubas, he consistently asks for two (e.g., 1M5 "The New DA"). In 2M16 "LSI Extraction" and 2M18 "Are You Up To It" two cimbassi reinforce the brass.

Eighteen of Zimmer's cues require up to five percussionists (largest number in 6M57 "Storming Pruitt Building") playing a varied array of toms, taiko, gong, surdo, gran cassa, Verdi bass drum, "big drums" (in 4M42 "Pod Deploys"), timpani, and a "big low drum" (4M42 "Batman Down"), as well as "KA rims" [sic] (NB: these are rim strikes on a taiko drum), "huge taiko" [sic] and "doepher" [sic] in the unused 5M42. Ten cues use piano and 3M22 "Joker Crashes the Party" uses two pianos. Twelve cues use harp.

The strings section for Zimmer's cues was very large. Although not every cue specifies the exact number of strings needed, it is likely that multiple cues shared the same group of players. 2M14–15 indicates 12 violins I, 12 violins II, 14 violas, 14 violoncellos, and eight double basses. The somewhat unusual balance within the section favors the lower end of the register (a setup of 12/10/8/6/4 would be more conventional). Some cues call for 28 cellos, for example 2M18 and 6M56–57, which were recorded at a separate overdub session. For 3M26–27 parts for a 28-cello overdub were prepared also but it is not known whether they were eventually recorded and used. A number of cues use strings 12/12/14/14 but omit double basses, for example 1M9 and several of the special effects cues. The score for "New Batman Theme vSAD48 Str" indicates that Zimmer used 24 violins, 14 violas, 42 violoncellos (!), and 8 double basses.

The orchestrations of Howard's cues do call for woodwinds, albeit sparingly. Cue 1M5 "The New DA" requires bassoon and contrabassoon, but in the orchestration they are shown as "cue only," meaning they were an option to fall back on at the scoring session. There is a short succession of held chords in 1M7 "Bank Warrants" for English horn, bassoon, and contrabassoon. Two bassoons are required for 2M12 and 2M13 and an English horn in 2M17. Where Howard's cues call for brass, the forces are similar to those of Zimmer's cues: twelve cues use nine horns. The only other cue using horns uses five (4M38ALT "Overlay" for "I Don't Know Anything"). Three trumpets are used in four cues (1M4, 2M17, 4M37–38 and 5M48–49) and 3M20–21 uses solo trumpet. Twelve of Howard's cues use various combinations of three to six trombones and up to three bass trombones but never more than six trombones in total. Eleven cues require two tubas and two cues use two cimbassi instead.

As for percussion, Howard's cues use a range of combinations of gran casa, Verdi bass drum, taiko, slapstick, tubular bells, odaiko, roto toms, gong drum, and timpani. Five of his cues use harp and seven piano. Eighteen of his cues use similar strings forces as Zimmer, with some peculiarities: 1M9 "Who Appointed Batman?" and 3M20–21 "Hero Without a Face" are without double basses and 4M43 "Gotcha" is without violins. The biggest strings section used by any of Howard's cues is 2M18 "Are You Up to It?" with 16 violins I, 14 violins II, 12 violas, 28 cellos, and 8 double basses. 3M32J "Dent to Van" uses the same setup but omits violas. 4M34-35 and 4M38ALT use only overdub strings (28 cellos and 8 double basses).

Recording the Score

Film music exists first and foremost in recorded form. Film composers have always explored emerging recording technology and the new creative possibilities it unlocked, notably enhancing and manipulating the orchestral sound palette beyond what is physically available from the medium itself. As early as 1937, Aaron Copland used over-dubbing on the score for *Of Mice and Men*.[9] Zimmer and Howard recorded over-dubs for *TDK*, which is not common practice at film scoring sessions in the UK, for reasons of added cost. The two composers used two types of overdubs and there is a qualitative and budgetary difference between them. The first type calls for 28 cellos to be recorded on top of strings already recorded. Because these 28 cellos were hired on top of the strings consort, the cost increase would have been linear. The second type of overdub, however, calls for the small group of players to record takes on top of identical parts already recorded, for example, to make it sound as though a larger group of players had been hired to begin with. Prevalent musician's union rules dictate that players must be compensated additionally for the latter type of overdubs and rates are punitively high to prevent composers from employing this method to try to cut down the number of players used. For Howard's 7M60 "An Eye For An Eye," orchestrator Jeff Atmajian recommends "Ideally this should be done in 3 sessions: twice with full strings and once with the 28 vc/8 cb. It must at least be done once with each of the two types of sessions!!" Not only does this comment stress the orchestrator's demand for a very large group of string players. The reference to *"the* 28 vc/8 cb" also shows that the orchestrator already knew an overdub session with this large group of low strings was planned. Therefore, the need for such a session did not emerge in the process of orchestration but was pre-determined.

An orchestral album recording or radio broadcast of an orchestral concert will usually strive to capture and transmit the live performance as truthfully as possible. Emerging modern recording techniques (i.e., how sound is picked up at the source, including types of microphones used) and continually improving recording technology (recording, storage, and editing media, including digital hardware and software) have made it possible to render and reproduce live sound accurately with stunning results. The recording or live broadcast can be judged by the level of fidelity to the original: how closely does the recording resemble the experience of being in the same room as the ensemble? The aim is to render inaudible or mask any manipulative effect of the recording, editing, and mixing process.

Film music recording poses unique challenges that differentiate it from other (orchestral) recordings. Traditionally, synchronization to picture was perhaps the most obvious requirement, met by use of visual conducting aids projected during recording, use of click tracks, or stopwatch. Ensembles performing film music, and in turn the performance of film music, have, therefore, always been confined to certain technical strictures, most notably timing. As multi-track recording became readily available (allowing for many microphones to simultaneously record sections of the orchestra from close proximity), film composers pounced on the opportunity to refine the sound of the orchestra in ways they deemed palatable and effective. Film composers can choose to alter the sound of selected elements within the orchestra through creative editing, use of effects such as dynamic processors and equalizers, and mixing. Digital technology has made this process ever easier and cheaper. A changed aesthetic outlook on sound qualities has eroded in film music any sense of the sound of a "real" orchestra: during film music production, it is not the balanced sound of the actual ensemble that matters but the blended, stylized, and polished sound of the manipulated whole.

Placing microphones close to the instruments, as opposed to recording the overall ensemble with stage microphones and outriggers in stereo pairs, gives the engineer and the composer much more control over each sound. For the purpose of separation and isolation, close-mic positions are a valuable tool that can be used to great effect. In 2M16 "LSI Extraction" (discussed in more detail later) the orchestration spells out a rhythmically complex web of strings cumulatively playing a D-minor (add2, add9) chord (the pitches D, E, F, G, A in different figurations and octaves), at a generally quiet dynamic (pp-mf). The arrangement gradually adds layers until the full texture is reached in bar 18 of the orchestration. Listening to this cue in the film reveals how little of this intricate texture is actually audible. Instead, the mix favors individual lines at one point or another, flexibly changing the balance of the strings between each other and also against other elements in the mix (synthesizer pads, the Batflaps sound effect [see below], percussion, etc.). Such manipulation of the recorded sound is facilitated by close-mic positioning, with decisions about instrumental balance deferred until mixing.

The recording of separate stems (or so-called stripes) gives greater flexibility to the composer during editing and mixing. When the orchestra is recorded *tutti*, instrumental parts tend to spill into respective microphones that are meant to pick up other sections. A loud brass chord, for example, will be audible in all microphones, making it impossible to omit later, should this become desirable. If sections are recorded separately, this renders a natural balance within the orchestra impossible, whereby players would listen to one another and blend as they have learned through years of training and experience. Instead, these decisions are placed with the composer and the engineer. Although in *TDK* it is not always clear from listening to the final recording whether and where stems and overdubs were used, there is clear evidence that they were used in some places. For example, in 2M16, heavy driving percussion helps build the tension as Batman abducts Lau from his office.

However, the orchestration for 2M16 contains no percussion at all, indicating this was either pre-recorded (and probably sequenced) or recorded separately on a different occasion.

Zimmer's and Howard's scores, consequently, are the product of a highly technical process, not only at the early conceptual stage (finding the language and writing demos) but also during recording, editing, and mixing of the music. It is hardly surprising, then, that the final score fluidly blends acoustic and artificial elements, explores an extremely wide frequency and dynamic range, and is subtle where required, visceral where appropriate, and overall highly nuanced. By its very nature, the sound of a real orchestra cannot match this sound and it is compelling to note that the polished and glossy sound of Zimmer's and Howard's scores effectively agrees with the heightened realism Nolan aspired to devise when he created *TDK*.[10]

Pertinent questions arise as to the function and purpose of the elements recorded during the scoring sessions in the context of a score that relies so much on production, pre-recorded samples, and non-orchestral elements. Perhaps Zimmer and Howard opted for live recording sessions out of convention, i.e., scoring sessions were expected of them. Perhaps scoring sessions were held out of a sense of creative integrity, respect, and nostalgia for the craft of film scoring. Then again, one can hardly imagine reasonable artistic grounds for the use of 28 violoncellos.[11] Zimmer has previously expressed an ethical outlook on the well-being of performers, seeking to keep musicians employed even though their performances have previously been sampled. He recognizes the value added by experienced session musicians, which may still matter even if the above-mentioned modern recording techniques are used. The question remains whether using live players makes an audible difference in a highly produced Zimmer or Howard score. It is a question that might strike Zimmer and Howard as audacious, and so too the dozens of orchestral performers who contributed to *TDK*. Howard's use of sequenced bassoons in the final version of 1M5 stands out as an example of a sampled part having rendered a live performer obsolete.

Primary Recurring Themes and Motifs

The following section sets out recurring themes and motifs in *TDK*. These have been subdivided into primary and secondary themes, based on their prevalence in the film and their contribution to character development and storytelling. While not necessarily an exhaustive list of each respective theme's occurrences, prominent uses of each theme and motif will be flagged.

Batflaps (for Batman)

When Zimmer was working on *Batman Begins*, he felt that there needed to be a sonic identity for Gotham and the Caped Crusader. The biggest challenge was that Batman did actually not appear until nearly one hour into the film. Zimmer says that something was needed to reassure the audience early on that this was a Batman movie. He suggested to Wesson that he should try to create the sound of wings flapping. Zimmer remembers

> ...I suggested Mel go over to the cutting room, to see what sort of thing we needed to start off with. My feeling was that it didn't even really have to be a piece of music. It just had to be something really iconic, like the flapping of ginormous wings or something. So Mel created that, and that was a good start. We put a pole in the ground with that, and decided we were going to have some of this electronic stuff.[12]

Zimmer and Wesson coined the term "Batflaps." It is interesting that Zimmer intuitively resorted to the sound of wings flapping, when the Batsuit does not really have functioning wings, certainly not ones that flap: Batman glides, he does not fly. The sound is, therefore, a conceptual abstraction that happens to work very well: the audience is unlikely to think they are actually hearing the wings of Batman. Batflaps comprises the sound of giant wings flapping followed by a low-frequency echo, dark, menacing, and suggestive of a mighty power. A timed decay on the echo gives the sound a calculated and measured feel. Batflaps may not be a musical motif in the traditional sense, but it was musically conceived by the composers and signals "Batman" effectively. Having been established in *Batman Begins*, Batflaps can allude to Batman in his absence, underline his power in his presence, and also, used more like a sound effect, amplify his strength when used in conjunction with specific actions.

At the very start of *TDK*, in 1M0 "Logo," Batflaps accompanies the Warner Brothers company logo and acts at once as Batman's calling card for viewers familiar with the previous film, as well as a primer for the film to come (Batman does not appear until reel two). Batflaps is not used at the beginning of 1M4 "Buyer Beware," when Batman imposters bust a drug deal. The audience may quickly realize that Batman would not use a weapon as crude as a shotgun. Crane's disappointed comment "that's not him" certainly helps with this impression. Importantly, the music agrees with his assessment, omitting Batflaps and the other thematic Batman elements (listed below).

In 2M16 "LSI Extraction," the motif helps the underscore convey a sense of calculated control: the audience may not yet know what Batman is up to but they are reassured that he has a plan. In its regular rhythmic nature, the motif functions as a structuring and pacing device. It also serves as a suspenseful placeholder when Lau and his security team are struggling to find the intruder who has just crashed through the window and his staying out of sight to find a good angle for attack. In 3M28 "Loud Enough," when Bruce (not Batman) and Alfred try to retrieve fingerprints from a bullet, Batflaps reminds the audience that Bruce can rely on the power of his secret alter ego in finding the Joker.

When Batman violently interrogates the Joker (5M45 "You Complete Me"), the motif reinforces the punches Batman lands. The motif hits, and significantly amplifies, each body impact. The resulting visceral force of Batman's punches is cringe-inducing and encourages the audience to feel empathetically the weight of each blow. At the same time, Batflaps is used percussively here as a musical structuring device that helps pace the scene. Music has previously been absent for some time. Alongside the Joker's Anarchy motif (see below), Batflaps works well inside the clinical and isolated interrogation room, where a more elaborate and dramatic musical solution might feel intrusive.

The rhythmic aspect of Batflaps is quoted in 5M51–52 "Hospital Bomb Scare" when, during the prolonged hospital evacuation, driving low percussion relies on a pattern very similar to that of Batflaps. It is heard in its original form when Gordon receives a text message warning him to "Watch Out!" for two officers with family members in hospital (who might therefore be after Reese). Even though Batman is not involved in evacuating the hospital, Bruce crashes his Lamborghini to save Coleman Reese from an oncoming pick-up truck. The use of Batflaps here may have felt to be conflating Bruce and his alter ego in new ways. Having a driving low percussion pattern that resembles Batflaps elegantly achieves a subtle hint at the power of the Caped Crusader without confusing him with the billionaire.

Batman Theme (BT, for Batman)

First introduced in *Batman Begins*, this theme could not be further removed from the flamboyant neo-Gothic theme in Elfman's Batman scores or Goldenthal's take on Batman with eccentric brass and a highly developed symphonic style. Zimmer himself admits that in *Batman Begins* he never established a very strong musical identity for Batman. This is firstly due to the fact that the film was an origins story and the yet-to-be-shaped character and his complicated identity were at the core of the narrative. A well-developed theme might have felt premature for the emerging character of Batman. Secondly, Zimmer adhered to Nolan's expressed desire to present a darker, more realistic take on the Batman mythology. BT is a no-frills theme for a no-frills Batman.

BT comprises two main components. The first is an agile sixteenth-note ostinato (96bpm) that traces a D-minor chord (f-A-d-A) played *detaché* in the low strings doubled with synthesizers. The timbre of this ostinato shifts flexibly, favoring the strings in some places whilst bringing out the synthesizers in others. It has a dark and sleek quality, full of sonic nuance and movement by the nature of the short note values and layered instrumentation but highly polished in the way it is edited and produced.

The second component is a two-note motif of held long notes (d'-f' doubled with the octave below, d-f), in the brass. This two-note motif is used frequently in *Batman Begins*. In *TDK* it is readily attached to Batman (for audience members who have seen the first film). The motif is played either in parallel octaves (occupying the stable first and third scale degrees) over the D-minor strings ostinato, or it splits, one voice moving down to B♭ in contrary motion over the D-minor ostinato (stable root note of D-minor to stable root and fifth of B♭-Major chord).

Although it is not particularly distinctive or memorable, the brass motif is repeated often enough in association with Batman to function well. With its sleek accompaniment, it has a distinctly masculine quality, tone being so important for the conflicted Batman character and *TDK* as a whole. What it lacks in musical sophistication and structural complexity, BT compensates for with scale and weight. Batman is a powerful superhero and BT emphasizes his strength of character as much as his physical strength. During the final showdown in the Pruitt Building (see below), the Joker confirms that he considers Batman mighty indeed when he refers to the paradoxical conflict between himself and Batman as "what happens when an unstoppable force meets an immovable object."

In 1M2 "Find the Batman," the shifting balance in the ostinato between real strings and synthesizers is easily audible: the cue starts immediately after the bank robbery sequence and accompanies a montage of Gotham's police force and politicians debating where to find Batman. As Ramirez (Monique Gabriela Curnen) mocks her colleague Wuertz (Ron Dean) for comments by the mayor (Nestor Carbonell) on TV ("hey Wuertz, the mayor says you're closing in on the Batman") the ostinato changes to a purely synthetic palette. As Ramirez then meets Gordon on the roof of the police station, strings gradually return. There is a second concurrent ostinato in the low strings here that will be addressed later.

In the ensuing 1M3 "Buyer Beware," Batman first arrives on screen taking out a group of drug dealers and some imposters. A closer look at the orchestration here reveals that certainly in the first bars the score was changed after the scoring sessions: heavy percussion in the final score does not match the orchestration. The heavy brass swell when Batman is first revealed (he grabs the barrel of an imposter's shotgun and bends it down) is written in the score but the percussion and brass stabs that follow in the recording are not notated. The BT ostinato serves as an underlying fabric here, shifting between D-minor and B♭-flat (whereby the A at the bottom of the figuration is replaced by B♭), while Batman takes out his opponents in a heavy fistfight and Crane tries to escape in a van. When all opponents are down, Batman turns away towards the garage exit ramp, which Crane's van is speeding down. The BT horn notes (d to f) briefly dominate the score, over a D-minor pedal.

In 2M16 "LSI Extraction," the BT brass motif occurs several times, here in trombones and tubas, in the context of a different ostinato. Under the topline of d to f, low brass also play D to B♭, suggesting a D-minor to B♭-Major progression (with third omitted), albeit over a D-minor ostinato in the strings, which suggests a B♭^{maj7} chord. A crescendo on D in the brass is, then, also used to prepare the moment when Batman and Lau are whisked out of the office building by a transport plane. In the closing passage of the cue, as the plane flies off toward the sunrise, the BT ostinato returns and finishes the cue.

When the Batpod deploys in 4M42, BT returns very briefly. The cue enters heavy-handedly with extremely loud low percussion that at first overpowers the ostinato. It is perhaps understandable that Nolan and the composers wished to highlight the revelation of an exciting new Batman gadget with such force. The brass motif sounds twice, the first time over a D-pedal, the second time splitting into *divisi*, with half the instruments stepping down to C♯ rather than up to F. Over the continuing D-minor pedal this results in a relatively tense $Dm^{(maj7)}$ chord. Almost immediately, the cue gets cut off as the Batpod rips off the rearview mirror of a car.

BT is clearly associated with Batman as a strong character and dependable hero. Whenever Batman loses control of his temper, BT remains silent. For example, as Batman drops Maroni off a fire escape to break his legs, there is no musical accompaniment. When he interrogates the Joker, there is a shift in the underscore when the Joker finally reveals where Rachel and Dent are held hostage (Batman goes after Rachel), but the score here comprises new material, unrelated to BT.

After a prolonged absence, BT returns near the end of 6M52 "Hospital Bomb Scare," when Bruce crashes his Lamborghini to save Coleman Reese. The two-note brass motif conveniently reference Batman *in absentia* whilst by its sustained nature and long crescendo it also conveniently builds up towards the crash as the Lamborghini approaches and intercepts the pick-up truck just in time.

Matters are more complicated when Batman tries to finally apprehend the Joker in the Pruitt Building whilst at the same time a hostage situation is unfolding on the two ferries and, as it turns out, also in the Pruitt Building. With the aid of Lucius Fox and the sonar vision system, Batman manages to neutralize the threat from the Joker's goons whilst also preventing the police SWAT teams from shooting the hostages they are mistaking for gangsters. The score here is understandably preoccupied with propelling the action forward and sustaining a high dramatic charge across various locations and character sets. Although there are moments where 6M55 "The Boats," 6M56–57a "Always a Catch," and 6M57 "Storming Pruitt Building" seem to quote BT, this happens in the context of more varied and previously unheard material, including yet another ostinato (see below). Furthermore, the action is too rapid and varied to allow time to focus on a single character, the most obvious exception being a short statement of the Joker Theme (see below) when Batman finally finds him.

The ostinato from BT gradually builds and grows, reaching into higher registers in 7M62 "I'm Not a Hero" and segues into 7M63 "A Dark Knight." These are the final moments of the film in which plot strands conclude and loose ends are tied up. The BT ostinato facilitates continuity, while the extended melody on top has a regal and dignified, perhaps somewhat elegiac quality. BT including the brass motif returns a final time under Gordon's closing monologue, right after he says, "We'll hunt him." Heavy low percussion hits assert that Batman remains a strong character and that the decision to take the blame for Dent's death is right. The second iteration of the D to F motif move to

F over B♭ on a cut to Batman racing off on his Batpod, up a highway on-ramp into the sunrise. The sync point seems somewhat heavy-handed, for all we really see is the rear wheel of a motorcycle and a dust trail. However, the weighty score is perhaps justified by the gravitas of Gordon's closing remarks. He delivers the film's title, which has been conveniently contextualized by his monologue.

"New Batman Theme," which lasts for 469 bars, is by far the longest cue orchestrated for *TDK*. It is set for strings only and remains in the key of D-minor throughout, containing long stretches of the above-mentioned BT strings ostinato. The cue was one of the additional, unnumbered cues, recorded to give Zimmer stock material from which to craft cues to use throughout the film or to add strings for balance where needed. It is therefore not surprising that BT always stays in the key of D-minor.

Joker Theme (JT, for the Joker)

> Nolan's dark star Ledger inhabits the clown prince of crime, embracing Joker's hard-R American accent, smeary makeup, puppet-master body language, freakish facial tics and brilliantly perverted logic with a ferocity that electrifies every scene he's in. Twitching with menace, Ledger generates a nearly unbearable tension in his encounters...[13]

Zimmer felt that the Joker needed a "definitive motif in direct counterpoint to Batman's" [theme].[14] Whereas BT is less than distinctive, the Joker has a very distinctive and unusual musical identity. According to Zimmer, the "sound of the Joker" was based on early photographic stills of Heath Ledger in full character make-up. Zimmer sought something "truly provocative and that people could truly hate," and decided that this could not be achieved by conventional musical means. He made the "conscious decision to go out there, to the edge." In close collaboration with Nolan, "trying to get down to the most minimal thing," Zimmer arrived at the idea of a single held tone (around d'), whose sound source is unclear, wavering in timbre and constantly shifting in micro-tonal de-tuning: "I took the idea of anarchy and [...] fearlessness. [...] What if I can define a character in one note?"

Nolan himself has identified a rock and punk aesthetic that suits the Joker. Jesse Prinz suggests that punk "intentionally violates widely held aesthetic norms,"[15] which in the case of the Joker could be expanded to violating societal norms, rules, and laws. The Joker's acts of

Analysis of the Score as Musical Text   73

rebellion may lack a clear cause, but disobedience, subversion, and non-conformity are at the core of the Joker's character.[16] JT ingeniously mirrors these character attributes and meshes well with accompanying elements of percussive riffs and electronic pulses in *TDK*. Zimmer experimented with recording different sounds, for example pencils tapping floors, razor blades scraping on a piano string, heavily distorted electric guitars and manipulated cello (played by Martin Tillman). The final sound that Zimmer settled on combines amplified and heavily processed cello paired with electric guitar played with razorblades. The resulting sound is lively, full of vibrant energy, at once gnawing, insistently controlled, but also frightfully unruly with its buzzing micro-rhythms (akin to a giant mosquito). It has an organic quality that a purely synthesized sound might not offer. At the same time, the edgy sound is off-putting in its ugliness and alarming due to its emphasis on the upper frequency spectrum. The sound does not clearly emanate from any single instrument, which makes it sound ambiguous, adding to its unsettling effect. Where it is heard in the film, it effectively announces or accompanies the harbinger of terror.

What is perhaps most remarkable about Zimmer's Joker Theme is that it accompanies this complex character with such economy: for the most part, in terms of pitch set, it comprises a single held note. However, this irreducible minimalism is counterbalanced with other complex attributes, including varied dynamic range, changing instrumentation, and evolving timbre. JT is highly versatile and it can flexibly enter and exit from amidst the sonic texture. It readily announces the Joker when he enters the scene and suggests his presence in his absence. It reflexively characterizes the Joker but it also effectively instills in the audience a sense of fear and discomfort.

The idea to use a single buzzing tone for an evil character may not be as original as it may seem: as far back as 1941 Bernard Herrmann experimented with recording humming electrical wires outside San Fernando to use for the devil's appearances in *The Devil and Daniel Webster* (original title *All That Money Can Buy*, 1941).[17] The recording technology at Herrmann's disposal was naturally less sophisticated than the resources available to Zimmer. No wonder, then, that JT is far more nuanced in its character and sonic appearance than anything Herrmann could have ever achieved.

Contrary to widely held belief, JT comprises more than a single note.[18] Zimmer himself has pointed out that JT is actually "two notes that clash beautifully," and closer listening quickly reveals that in passages of increasing dramatic tension, JT will indeed spilt into two pitches (see Figure 4.2): one that remains anchored around the starting pitch D, another that gradually rises in oblique motion above the pedal. Were the pitch of the tone simply to rise on its own, the effect might be not nearly as terrifying. It is the duality in the sound and the rising tension within that add to the overall effect.

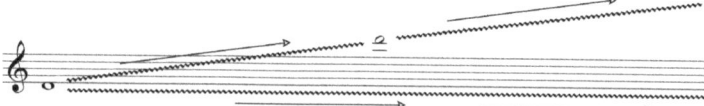

Figure 4.2. Joker Theme splits and rises

Zimmer may be right in saying "you can hear a second of this thing and know the Joker is lurking somewhere," putting the audience on edge, making them sense that something or someone unpleasant is afoot. Realistically, however, a considerable proportion of the audience might altogether fail to notice JT within the film, let alone recognize it as a musical theme. JT is markedly low-profile and is not as readily noticeable as some of the other thematic material in the film. In eschewing musical progression and development in a traditional sense, JT might be mistaken for a sound effect altogether. It is certainly the antithesis of a memorable theme.

JT enters the soundtrack very early in the film. Batflaps accompanies the Warner Brothers logo formation and the DC Comics logo is underscored with a disconcerting metallic timed ricochet on what is perhaps best described as a bow bouncing on a violin string. Menacing blue flames billow in slow motion towards the camera, the Batman logo vaguely embedded as a dark silhouette. JT enters in a slow crescendo. It acts as a sonic vector into the first scene, the cut to an office tower in broad daylight accentuated with a loud percussion thud. As the camera zooms in on the wall of windows, JT grows louder still, until it is cut off when one of the windows is shattered, glass spraying outward. To an unprimed audience, the association between the Joker and JT is not yet clear. The link soon becomes more definite when a man holding a clown mask is shown from behind, standing at a curbside and waiting to be picked up by an SUV. JT returns and grows quickly louder as the camera zooms in on the man (he is the Joker, as will be revealed later), before it is cut off again as the car stops and a bass pulse and strings take over.

For the next five minutes, as the bank robbery unfolds, the score helps propel the action forward and keep dramatic tension high. JT enters when the bank manager (William Fichtner), lying wounded on the floor, shouts, "you think you're smart, huh?" prompting the Joker to turn around and approach him. As the manager grows increasingly enraged, finally screaming, "what do you believe in?" JT morphs into the Stranger Motif (see below).

In 2M11 "Kill the Batman," the Joker interrupts a video conference between the mob bosses and Lau. JT accompanies him as he walks into the restaurant kitchen where the meeting is held. As the dialogue begins, JT recedes and when the Joker starts talking ("let's wind the clocks back a year"), it has been replaced by a low bass pulse. For the remainder of the scene, JT does not return.

When the Joker is delivered to Gamble in a zipped-up body bag (2M14–15 "Put a Smile on That Face"), JT enters ever so quietly as the bag is being placed on a table. Even less attentive audience members might subliminally feel warned that the Joker might be up to something. Moments later, he duly catches Gamble off guard when he suddenly emerges from the body bag and puts a knife to Gamble's face. The Joker Triumphant motif (see below) accentuates this moment. JT is back, much louder, more piercing in timbre. The Joker tells the first of several versions of "Do you want to know how I got these scars?" JT meanders around a syncopated bass pulse and morphs into a more aggressive tone. When the Joker quotes his father ("Why so serious?"), the tone starts to rise above a pedal on D, rising until the Joker slashes Gamble's face, when it is violently cut off by a heavy percussive hit.

Following a long dramatic build-up in 3M22 "Joker Crashes Party," during which the police commissioner and the judge presiding over the mob indictment have been killed, the Joker arrives at Bruce's fund raiser for Dent. As the lift doors open to reveal the Joker and his goons, JT is layered in with a loud statement of Joker Triumphant (see below). All music is abruptly cut off when the Joker fires a shotgun into the air and addresses the shocked crowd with faux courtesy ("good evening, ladies and gentlemen"). The Joker is looking for Dent, whom Bruce has hidden in a closet moments earlier. As he quizzes one of the party guests as to Dent's whereabouts, he is about to begin his "do you know how I got these scars" spiel. Notably, JT does not enter here, subliminally suggesting that the Joker won't go through with his story this time. Indeed, he is quickly cut off by Rachel, who steps up and interrupts him ("ok, stop!"). Now JT sets in and very gradually grows louder as the Joker approaches Rachel. The theme underlines the tension between the two characters and affirms the audience's trepidation as to what might happen to Rachel. The Joker starts telling her a new version as to how he got his scars: "I had a wife, beautiful just like you." Here, JT splits in half, its upper half rising as tension mounts. This time, the Joker's story takes longer and the rising motion subtly adapts: once the upper half has reached a certain height, it remains there and another, third layer begins rising. Effectively, there are now three simultaneous pitches. The music does not react to the punch Rachel lands in the Joker's stomach, which prompts him to say, "ooh, you got a little fight in you. I like that." To which Batman, suddenly on the scene, responds, "Then you're gonna love me," which cuts off JT. The tone returns only briefly once more as the Joker dangles Rachel in front of a broken window through which he drops her.

In 3M29 "Kitchen Timer" Bruce arrives in apartment 1502, which overlooks the street in which the vigil for the murdered commissioner is being held. The Joker has threatened to kill the mayor. Bruce discovers a number of police officers, tied up by gangsters who are now posing as them, outside in the parade. JT sneaks in and once again splits and rises. Clearly the Joker is at work here. As a gun salute is being fired, tension grows ever higher. A ticking kitchen timer that Bruce finds on a windowsill compounds this. By the time the second shot is fired, something is clearly wrong: the kitchen timer goes off and triggers the blinds to open, which results in Bruce being fired at by alarmed snipers. The third shot finally reveals the Joker himself in a police uniform and without make-up, his disfigured face looking bizarrely normal. He and his goons turn to the speaker's podium and fire at the mayor, inadvertently hitting Gordon who shields him. Joker Triumphant cuts off JT on the third shot.

4M41 accompanies an establishing shot of Gotham at nightfall when Dent is being transported in a police truck convoy. JT enters briefly, indicating that the Joker is going to try to attack the convoy and kidnap Dent. In 4M42 "Batman Down," the Joker crawls out of the 18-wheeler truck that has been flipped on its roof. JT splits rises immediately here as the Joker faces Batman approaching on the Batpod. Here, the rising line is at first markedly louder than the anchor that remains on D, paralleling the rising anxiety with the Batpod fast approaching, seemingly to hit the Joker. Stranger (see below) then gradually grows out of the D pedal and takes over just as Batman crashes his Batpod in an evasive maneuver. JT is back almost immediately, if extremely quietly and with a mellower timbre. It is steady and single-pitched now, as the Joker approaches Batman to take off his mask. Before he can do so, he is arrested by Gordon and the music segues to Harvey Dent's theme (see below).

During 5M45 "You Complete Me," JT enters as soon as the Joker teases "you're gonna have to play my little game if you wanna save one of them." He then reveals that he has not only kidnapped Harvey but also Rachel. This time, JT undergoes intensifying timbral shifts that bring out more of the upper mid frequencies in the sound. Only when the Joker is on the floor, about to say "you have nothing, nothing to threaten me with," does the tone once again split and rise, redoubling the intensification. JT once again splits into three pitches. The higher two pitches linger into the beginning of 5M46–47 "Wired," as Batman sets off to save Rachel. During the decrescendo and fade out, the timbre purifies to something more clearly akin to an electric guitar.

In the same cue, as the police and Batman race to the rescue of Rachel and Harvey, the Joker manipulates a police officer into attacking him ("Do you wanna know why I use a knife? Guns are too quick ..."), accompanied by JT: his plan is to overpower the officer and break out of the cell. Just before Rachel is killed in a massive explosion, JT returns, more quietly than before, as if to announce her death as the result of the Joker's evil plan. Similarly, as Dent lies on the ground moments later, half his face engulfed in flames, JT re-enters as if to remind the audience that this, too, is the Joker's fault. JT lingers on, very quietly and rising as the Joker now takes Lau out of his prison cell in the destroyed Major Crimes Unit.

During 6M55 "The Boats," JT rests, even though threatening to destroy two passenger ferries is the Joker's most appalling scheme yet. And yet, when he informs the passengers via intercom of his plan, the music focuses on forward propulsion and underlying tension, similar to 1M2 "Prologue," paired with an *idée fixe* for the ferries or the city's evacuation that is specific to this cue (see below).

In 7M59 "A Little Push," Batman has finally apprehended the Joker. But as he dangles upside down from the side of the unfinished building, the Joker reveals his last triumph. "I won't kill you because you're just too much fun. I think you and I are destined to do this forever." JT returns relatively quietly during the ensuing dialogue, but sufficiently gritty to cut through. When the Joker says, "Until their spirit breaks completely," JT splits and rises. The Anarchy motif enters additionally (see below) as the Joker reveals he has driven Harvey to madness. The Joker continues, "See, madness, as you know, is like gravity..." and the Stranger motif takes over, replacing JT and Anarchy. With three themes and motifs coming together, the cumulative effect is one of recapitulation and conclusion. The Joker is defeated, but he has landed one final blow to Gotham, one that proves disastrous in the scene that follows.

Joker Triumphant (Triumphant, for the Joker)

Figure 4.3 shows a short rhythmic figure that occurs throughout the film whenever the Joker strikes or is winning the upper hand. Like a sonic slap in the face, two sixteenth notes hit on a downbeat and two further sixteenth notes follow on the second eighth note of beat 2, adding to the short hacking attacks an anticipatory sense of syncopation.[19] The motif is not dissimilar to a rock riff, comprising a bass note on D with synthesizers and distorted guitars stacked on top. Heavily compressed and gated, these have a percussive and visceral attack. Each time Triumphant occurs, its distorted timbre sounds aggressive, which is further amplified by the sudden surge in relative volume of music against other soundtrack elements. After it has initially been introduced during the bank robbery, as the Joker's goons make their way downstairs into the bank vault, the motif is subsequently timed to shock and awe. With its rhythmic precision, the motif sounds assured and calculated but at the same time it sounds ramshackle and rebellious in its timbre and texture, in keeping with the aforementioned punk aesthetic. By its sound and placement in the film, it is a highly effective signifier of the Joker's triumph, however temporary, into the shortest of musical gestures.

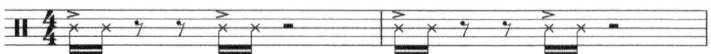

Figure 4.3. Joker Triumphant

Triumphant hits as a school bus suddenly crashes through the main doors of the bank, killing one of the Joker's goons in its path. Although the music here is rather buried under the loud sound effects (see also chapter 5), it is audible nevertheless and adds to the sonic impact of the bus. When the Joker is delivered to Gamble in a zipped-up body bag, seemingly dead, and then suddenly rises to everyone's surprise, the motif hits again. Even though we must assume the Joker would not have been killed off screen (a wasted bit of spectacle), the viewer is nevertheless invited to feel Gamble's sense of shock and fear.

A long and intense build-up (discussed in more detail below), leads to the Joker crashing Bruce Wayne's fund raiser. Triumphant heralds his arrival, which sends shockwaves through the illustrious guests. The motif is expanded to twice the length here to cherish this salient moment. After all, the Joker arriving at Wayne's penthouse constitutes a serious breach of this supposed safe haven. Ironically, the Joker never finds out Batman's alter ego identity. The Joker's arrival is a violent intrusion. Because his goons are armed, their mere arrival effectively starts a hostage situation, one that only Batman can resolve in due course.

Later, during the speech ambush, just as the Joker and his team reveal themselves and take aim for the mayor, Triumphant is truncated to a highly impactful stab of two sixteenth notes. This shortened version is sufficient to act as a musical calling card, referring back to previous occasions where the Joker triumphed. The abbreviation is well judged, because a full-length statement would overshoot here in terms of length and musico-narrative purpose.

Triumphant is heard again when the Joker violently hits Batman during their fight in the Pruitt Building, when Batman's sonar guidance system is malfunctioning and has momentarily rendered him confused. JT is again truncated here, again for lack of narrative time to fit in a full statement: Batman regains the upper hand quickly.

Stranger Motif (Stranger, for the Joker)

The Stranger Motif is named after its first occurrence in the film, just before the Joker reveals his face at the end of the bank robbery, musing, "I believe whatever doesn't kill simply makes you stranger." It comprises a long drawn-out crescendo (*p-f*) in *divisi* cellos and basses on the note D, stacked in octaves, to a leap down by a major ninth where they decrescendo back to *p* (Vc.I: d"-c', Vc.II: d'-c, Vc.III: d-C, Vc.IV: d'-c', DB: only second note on C,). Simple though it may look on the page, the effect of this motif is quite striking in the context of the passage it accompanies: paired with a revelation of the Joker's disfigured face, the downward leap is rather disorienting and helps create a moment of discomfort and perhaps fear. The relatively large leap, paired with the timbral shift in the strings from a high to low register, creates a sense of falling downwards from high above, hitting a hard and calculated surface at the bottom. There is a sense of a dizzying fall.

Throughout the film, Stranger appears in different permutations: whilst it always comprises a downward move from D to C, it contains a stack of octaves in some places but only a simple downwards step in low strings in others. The orchestration for 1M1 "Prologue" shows that Zimmer recorded at least three different versions with cellos and basses, exploring some extreme ranges to as high as D''' and as low as C,. One version in the orchestration also explores an inversion, going from unison on d *up* a minor seventh to a stacked octave on c' and c''. This version cannot be heard in the final film, perhaps omitted because its effect is quite different.

Stranger is almost drowned out by noisy sound effects when Batman fails to hit the Joker with his Batpod. The motif's crescendo here underlines the Joker's madness to stand in the way of a speeding motorcycle and inviting his opponent to run him over ("Hit me! Hit me!"). The second note of Stranger decrescendos as the Batpod skids across the tarmac and Batman tumbles to the ground,

A permutation (low strings stepping down a step) is heard after Gotham General Hospital has been blown up, coinciding with a cut to aerial footage of the demolished hospital. Here, as in the previous two instances, the motif also has a certain sense of inevitable finality, each time accompanying a conclusion or ending (the face revealed at the end of a successful heist, Batman's failure to kill the Joker, the hospital demolished).

Dangling from a rope off the Pruitt Building, apprehended by Batman, the Joker plays his last winning card:

> You didn't think I'd risk losing Gotham's soul in a fistfight with you? No, you need an ace in the hole. Mine's Harvey. [...] I took Gotham's White Knight and I brought him down to our level. It wasn't hard. See, madness, as you know, is like gravity. All it takes is a little push.

Stranger here has again been reduced to a whole step down from D to C in the basses. Swelling to fortissimo on D before stepping down to C, it adds a concluding full stop to the end of the Joker's final triumphant speech. He has driven Dent to madness and robbed Gotham of the upstanding official it so desperately needed.

Harvey Dent Theme (HD, for Harvey Dent)

Howard's Harvey Dent Theme at first attaches itself to the righteous virtues of the district attorney as opposed to his coin tossing, manipulative, and ultimately murderous alter ego. It is compelling to note that in

Nolan's adaptation Dent has already earned the nickname Two-Face long before his face is partly disfigured. The double meaning has poignant implications for the character's development: the audience is led to see early on that this ambitious lawyer and politician may have a self-serving agenda, perhaps at odds with the law. His greatest coup, rounding up and indicting dozens of mobsters, is founded on a tenuous legal detail and, ultimately, leads to the death of a judge, the commissioner, and police officers.

HD sounds assured yet inconclusive. The theme is made up of two four-bar phrases (antecedent and consequent) set in 4 at 96bpm. On the downbeat of bar one, it starts with a perfect fifth pedal in low brass (two horns, two trombones, two tubas) on C♯ and G♯ that has a stable and calm quality in the *p* dynamic it is played. On the third beat, a short tune starts on e, stated by five horns and two trombones crescendoing from *p* to *mp* over two beats. The line consists almost exclusively of half notes and descends from the downbeat of bar two via an accented passing tone (d♯) to c♯ before leaping up a perfect fourth for f# on the downbeat of bar 3. F♯ as the fourth scale degree in C#-minor over a pedal on the tonic is somewhat unstable. The melody steps back down to d♯, the second scale degree, via e on the last semiquaver of bar three (a small rhythmic variation). D♯ is another unstable non-chord tone over the ongoing pedal, that seeks resolution towards C♯. Here, it implies half cadence (masked by the pedal point). The consequent phrase brings relative stability. It starts with the same front half (e-d♯-c♯), a reiteration akin to a consolidation of the character it accompanies. But this time a more assured leap up a perfect fifth (to g♯) follows on the downbeat of bar seven, accompanied by an upward shift in the low brass, up a minor third to E. The melody now plays the major third of an E-major chord, a brighter and more stable note in this context, perhaps suggestive of the glimmer of hope for Gotham that Dent stands for. The melody then steps down a whole-tone to f♯, as the low brass jumps up a perfect fifth to B. The resulting perfect fifth between melody and bass (some inner voices have remained in B natural in oblique motion from the previous chord) brings the most stability yet and the conclusion of the consequent phrase.

The use of low brass in the early statements of HD, performed in a low dynamic and a comfortable register, lend it a markedly elegant, regal, and American sound, effectively conveying to the audience that Dent is a confident and qualified lawyer and politician. The contrast to other characters' themes is significant: HD sounds measured, reasoned, and calm. Dent is Gotham's hope, the White Knight, a balancing force. The Joker's themes are markedly more chaotic, fickle, busy, and aggressive. Batman's/Bruce's themes are more low-profile, less expressive. Incidentally, HD also contains one of the very few melodies in the entire score.

It is worth pointing out how short the tune in HD actually is. Occupying a mere eight bars and eleven successive pitches, a pitch range no larger than a perfect fifth and a rather restricted contour it is hardly a developed melody, let alone a memorable tune. It is likely that narrative time did not allow for a more elaborate theme (of the likes Howard has written for other films). Aesthetically, the use of extended melodies may have felt too melodramatic for *TDK*, imposing the kind of lyricism the film generally eschews.

HD is introduced in 1M6 "Hostile Witness," when Dent is first seen in action. 1M7 "Bank Warrants" reprises HD with Dent and Gordon meeting in his office. When Dent talks about his views on justice and vigilantism during the dinner with Rachel, Bruce and his Russian ballerina friend (1M9 "Who Appointed Batman?"), HD returns in a frailer rendition in high violin harmonics over muted violas, cellos, and harp. The lighter tone sits comfortably underneath the dialogue and also hints at a more sensitive, vulnerable side to Dent. This comes out again in 2M18 "Are You Up to It?" when the mayor challenges him. Just before, in 2M17 "Mobsters Taken to Justice," Dent has assertively indicted a large group of gangsters, with HD assuredly by his side. Here the theme is doubled in woodwinds and brass, the first three notes are elongated to half notes and the fourth note is two bars long. This drawn-out rhythmic variation, which maintains the same pitch contour, is propelled forward by a steady syncopated percussion pattern comprising "muffled" [*sic*] timpani, roto toms, big tom-toms, gong drum, and odaiko.

In 3M20–21 "Hero Without a Face," Howard's orchestrator Jeff Atmajian reminds the brass to play "Warm and noble. Always legato." Zimmer borrows HD for the opening of 3M26–27 "Lau, Watch the World Burn." This indicates that the two composers shared thematic material early on in the writing process, allowing them the swap themes for cues they were respectively responsible for. In 4M43 "Gotcha," HD accompanies the aftermath of the Joker's arrest, when Dent is feeling elated.

By stark contrast, the next time HD is heard, Dent lies in hospital the morning after his face has been burned. As grief turns to madness, a synthesized drone of two notes a perfect fifth apart grows ever louder, in a piercing and disquieting upper mid-rage. The antecedent phrase of HD is embedded therein, on high string harmonics, barely audible. As Dent then discovers his coin with identical sides (which Batman has left by his bedside the previous evening), he remembers Rachel taking the coin from him. ("You make your own luck.") Grief overwhelms him: he loses his mind, ripping off bandages from his badly burnt face.

When HD accompanies Two-Face on his murderous rampage, it is no longer the stately theme in elegant low brass. The descending three-note fragment is played in slow downward slide sounds mangled and ugly. The theme has been broken and twisted just like the character it accompanies. The man who previously stood for justice now avenges his girlfriend, the only thing stopping him from killing the coin he tosses (the burnt side says "kill"). Although the cues "Dent Kills Wertz" [*sic*] (Two-Face kills police officer Wuertz) and "Unlucky Driver" (Dent kills Maroni and his driver) use HD, they were not recorded with live orchestra. Instead, to suit Two-Face's disturbed state of mind, the theme now sounds mangled and twisted, comprising synthesized elements and remnants of recorded sounds manipulated beyond recognition. Source material for this work may have been taken from the special effects orchestrations "Long and Short Slides" and "Long and Short Slides Reverse," where nine horns, three trumpets, four trombones, two bass trombones, and strings without double bass recorded a series of upward and downward glissandi respectively across the entire ensemble at various speeds and dynamics (e.g., "gradual very slow gliss. downward"). This material could have been edited to outline the contour of the three notes at the start of HD.

At the end of 6M55 "The Boats," Dent confronts Ramirez and makes her lure Gordon's family into a trap. Suzette Moriarty's orchestration indicates a brief hushed sigh in the first violins as Gordon's wife picks up the phone (bar 97), twice on F above middle C, then once on G above, then F again, crescendoing from *niente* to *pp* each time in the short span of a bar. The final recording deviates from the score, reusing the same violin sighs on F on the cut to Two-Face and Ramirez as he says, "You didn't know what they were going to do [to Rachel]." The string section was supposed to play a variation of HD here picking up from the opening three notes of the theme, but this is omitted. However, a cluster in low muted brass with an upper structure in muted horns and trumpets, detuning downward briefly, is heard as written. The pitch bend in oblique motion over the low cluster has an effect similar to the previous murder scenes, even though Ramirez's life is spared.

7M60 "An Eye for an Eye" is perhaps the most through-composed cue in the entire score, a pained and strenuous elegy for strings, harp, and percussion. The cue unfolds in long sustained and intertwined lines, in increasingly more complex counterpoint. This cue accompanies the final standoff between Two-Face, Gordon (and his family), and Batman. Of HD, only traces are left here, notably the contour of three notes descending in stepwise motion, albeit in an altogether more conflicted context. The virtuous district attorney and his theme have been destroyed.

Secondary Recurring Themes and Motifs

Anarchy Motif (Anarchy, for the Joker)

This eerie motif appears in different guises. It is built around alternating pitches (d–c' and c–d'), a major seventh (first scale degree leaping up to the flatted seventh above), and a major ninth (the lower flatted seventh leaping to the first scale degree an octave higher, i.e., up a ninth). It is related to the Stranger motif by use of the same pitch set, but it is attached to a different aspect of the Joker's character. Repeating *ad libitum*, it has a meandering and aimless quality. It is unsettling in its unresolved tension and, in the context of where it occurs, adds to the sense of chaos and confusion.

Anarchy is first heard during a short respite in the bank robbery segment when the bank manager confronts the Joker (still masked at this point). Neither the audience nor the bank managers can ascertain the robber's intentions as he tilts his head quizzically, his terrifying clown mask hiding any facial expressions. As the bank manager explains, it seems mad to be stealing mob money when the repercussions are potentially fatal. The Joker does not agree, as he readily explains shortly after (see above). Anarchy is played here on a de-tuned and processed piano, an ugly unstable sound.

Later, during the interrogation scene, Anarchy on muted metal gongs has a meditative quality. Sparse in nature, the motif fills the aural space with ringing tensions where otherwise there would be only the oppressive silence of a tiled cell. As the Joker antagonizes Batman into a violent outburst, Anarchy calmly contrasts the aggressive madness of the Dark Knight, emphasizing how helpless he is when confronted with elusive anarchic evil. The same version of Chaos appears later as the Joker visits Dent/Two-Face in hospital and tempts him to see his point of view: "Introduce a little anarchy," he says as he pulls out a revolver and hands it to Two-Face. "Upset the established order and everything becomes chaos. I'm an agent of chaos. Oh, and you know the thing about chaos: it's fair." Anarchy thus consistently accompanies moments in which the Joker places his own fate or the fate of others in the hands of chance and luck.

Love Theme (LT, for Bruce and Rachel)

There is a subtle love theme in the form of a short chord sequence: E^+ to $F\sharp m^{7\flat 5}$ to $Am^{maj7}/G\sharp$. Performed on gentle sustained strings, this unresolved harmonic progression mirrors the unconsummated relationship between Bruce and his childhood sweetheart Rachel. Incidentally, she is the only person besides butler Alfred and Lucius Fox who knows that Bruce is Batman. Contrary to the two men, she wants Bruce to quit his superhero alter ego. LT has a suppressed yearning quality to it, due to its slow pace and long held notes in close voice leading. At the same time, the reserved mellow timbre of the strings and lack of rhythmic sub-division result in a somewhat static delivery that renders LT controlled and dispassionate, the opposite of melodramatic.

The LT is first heard in 1M5 "The New DA" (a cue composed by Howard), when Bruce watches Dent in a surveillance camera feed. Bruce tries to sound casual when Alfred asks whether he is interested in Dent's "character or his social circle," which brings Rachel into view, accompanied by LT.

In 3m20–21 "Hero Without a Face," LT appears identically (same instrumentation, same chords) when Rachel confronts Bruce on the balcony of his penthouse, accusing him of making fun of Dent during a speech at the fund raiser. Importantly, LT is not heard shortly after when Rachel and Dent have their only on-camera romantic heart-to-heart just before the Joker arrives at the party. This proves that LT specifically accompanies Bruce's and Rachel's unfulfilled relationship (she won't commit to him unless he hangs up his cape for good) and not Dent's and Rachel's actual love for each other.

LT returns at the tail end of 3M24–25 "Then You're Gonna Love Me," a Zimmer cue. Batman has saved Rachel in free fall off the building and they have crash-landed on a car. LT is virtually unchanged from before. It is worth highlighting that two composers working on separate cues and with different orchestrators nevertheless agreed on this particular chord progression, instrumentation, and specific voicing.

LT appears once again in 4M39 "Blood on My Hands," when it forms part of a progressive build-up of emotional tension between Rachel and Bruce. He is begging Rachel to be with him, promising he will give up Batman to be with her. Amidst the growing tension, Rachel snaps, "Bruce, don't make me your one hope for a normal life." When Bruce suddenly kisses her, the strings move to revolving around four repeating block chords Am, F, D, E. At this moment, Bruce actually reaches out to his love, effectively consummating their longing for each other, if ever so briefly. LT gives way to a warmer, more resolute and harmonically less complicated accompaniment.

Mourning (for Gordon and Rachel)

There is a short motif in the strings that represents mourning. Built from long held whole-note chords (the tempo is a slow 56bpm), it is first heard in the upper strings (Csus4/G, Cm/G, Dsus4/G, D/F♯), in 3M30 "Speech Ambush," when Gordon is shot by a bullet intended for the mayor. Two perfect fourths stacked on top of each other result in the second inversion of Csus4 (g', c", f "), which has an opaque sound quality, enhanced by the hollow and glassy timbre of the gentle strings. Resolving to a C-minor chord (still in second inversion, i.e., g', c", e♭"), the progression veers into a mournful direction, further emphasized by the upper two voices' ensuing descent (e♭" to d" and c" to a' respectively) in oblique motion over a g' pedal in the bottom voice. This, finally, slips down to f♯', resolving the Dsus4 chord to D in first inversion.

In 3M32B "Gordon Is Dead," the mourning lasts slightly longer when the police inform Gordon's wife of her husband death. Here, the same chord progression repeats but is then expanded. The D-major chord resolves down a perfect fifth (acting as a secondary dominant) to Gsus4, again in second inversion over D, now in the low strings. A solo cello pensively rises from among the strings, tracing the Gsus4 chord and then following the accompaniment's resolution to G-minor in the next bar with a continued upward arpeggio. The upper strings are blended with a synthesizer pad with a hollow and fragile sound. In Moriarty's orchestration, the double basses are instructed to play a low E♭ when they enter, which would significantly alter the sound and harmonic function of the resulting chord. However, it seems that this is an error: in the final recording, the lowest note in the basses under the solo cello is a G moving down to B♭. The cellos' G underneath the solo cello is not clearly audible either. The low strings move down to b♭' and the upper strings step down to a' with g' in the middle voices (violas), resulting in a *quasi* Gm$^{(add9)}$ chord in first inversion. The omission of the fifth (D) adds to a sense of incompleteness and the inversion lacks stability. The quiet dynamic, furthermore, completes a sense of hushed, defeated lament. The timbre of the elegiac strings accommodates dialogue well, which easily cuts through the music as Gordon's wife starts screaming, blaming Batman for her husband's death. This is yet another instance where editing and mixing considerations may have significantly shaped and altered the sound of the music. Such alterations are only possible if sufficient separation between the instruments has been achieved during recording through microphones positioning and layered takes.

At the end of 5M46–47 "Wired," Mourning is repeated as Alfred reads a letter (now dead) has written to Bruce. This time, the low strings remain on G, atop a drone that carries through the whole segment. We hear Rachel's words in voice-over as shots of the burning aftermath are intercut with Batman (overlooking the burning rubble), Gordon (surveying the destroyed Major Crimes Unit), and Dent (surrounded by surgeons tending to his face).

> Dear Bruce, I need to be honest and clear. I'm going to marry Harvey Dent. I love him. I want to spend the rest of my life with him. When I told you that if Gotham no longer needed Batman we could be together, I meant it. But I'm not sure the day will come when you no longer will need Batman. I hope it does, and when it does I will be there, but as your friend. I'm sorry to let you down. If you lose faith in me, please keep your faith in people. Love, now and always, Rachel.[20]

Since the letter tackles Rachel's conflicted feelings for Bruce it might perhaps have warranted LT. Instead, Zimmer and Nolan preferred to make Mourning here an elegy for both Rachel's death and the proverbial death of any prospect of Rachel and Bruce being together. The ensuing music, as Bruce and Alfred talk (and Alfred decides not to pass Rachel's letter to Bruce), the music comprises gentle strings and piano, weaving on from Mourning with similar sus4-chord resolutions and a quote from HD (three notes descending in stepwise motion).

Mourning finally returns in 7M61 "I'm Not a Hero," when Gordon rushes to check on Batman, who has fallen off a high building after killing Two-Face. The music starts just as Batman gets up. This section of the cue is basically identical to 5M46–47. Gordon summarizes the damage caused by the Joker and Batman insists, "The Joker cannot win. Gotham needs its true hero." As he turns over Two-Face's body to reveal only Dent's intact side of his face, the opening phrase of HD is heard one last time.

Scoring Techniques and Devices

James Newton Howard's cues

In terms of musical style, Howard's cues tend to speak a more traditional language, whereas Zimmer's cues are firmly grounded in a more contemporary popular idiom. Many of the cues attributed to Howard (according to the orchestrations incl. 11M5 "The New DA," 1M9 "Who Appointed Batman?," 2M18 "Are You Up to It?," and 4M40 "I Am the Batman") are generally of a smaller scale and a gentler nature (see also the table in Appendix II), which at once provides variety and contrast with Zimmer's powerful cues that surround them and also serves Harvey Dent, who at first is one of the few honest and seemingly incorruptible characters.

Howard's 7M60 "An Eye for an Eye" is an outlier because it differs from all other cues. It accompanies the final confrontation between Batman and Two-Face, who is holding Gordon and his family hostage. Howard abandons the virtuous Harvey Dent Theme, which at this point can no longer serve the character who has succumbed to raging madness. Set in D-minor, the tone of the cue is somber and dark, the ensemble instructed to play *alla Passacaglia quasi elegaic* (*sempre molto sostenuto*) by orchestrator Atmajian. The term *Passacaglia* is perhaps somewhat confusing given that the cue is set in 4 rather than the triple meter common for a dance of this type. On the other hand, the piece does have the darker tone commonly associated with a *Passacaglia*. The cue is built atop a steady *basso ostinato* played by harp, timpani, and basses. Because it does not repeat identically, it is not a true *basso ostinato*. However, there is a marked regularity to the line, with steady half-notes and frequent use of stepwise motion, recurring leaps up a minor or major third and up or down a perfect fourth. Additional strings enter gradually playing contrapuntal lines over the bass line. Over the 82 bars the cue lasts, the individual parts are layered increasingly densely, both in terms of pitch and rhythm. The music begins extremely quietly and then continues to grow in volume throughout. The rise in playing dynamic adds to a sense of intensification. In bar 75 the players are instructed, "get more intense al fine," which reaffirms the *f* stated.

In its highly contrapuntal developmental style 7M60 stands apart from the other cues in *TDK*. It is the only cue that can be described as polyphonic in the traditional sense, in stark contrast to the homophony in all other cues. There seems to have been some uncertainty on the part of orchestrator Atmajian as to how best to achieve the texture and sound that Howard intended. Perhaps the demo was indicative of a sound that was not easily achievable with a real orchestra. In the score for 7M60, he states

> Ideally this should be done on 3 Sessions: Twice with Full Strings and Once with the 28 Vc/8 CB. It must at least be done once with each of the two types of sessions!!

It is not known, however, whether the cellos and basses were overdubbed during this 28 Vc/8 CB session. In amongst the unnumbered cues, "TDK 'Passacaglia' EFX" matches cue 7M60 exactly to the note. This, however, is scored for 14 cellos and 8 basses and may have been intended as an overdub. The cue is broken up into phrases of uneven lengths (bars 1–8, 9 16, 17–26, 27–34, 35–42, 43–50, 51–54, 55–58, 59–64, 65–68, 69–72, 73–76 and 77–82) and the players are asked to hold the last note of each phrase and fade. Creating overdub recordings of these phrases with overlong endings will have created takes that could be mixed in with the *tutti* recording. Each overlong ending will have overlapped with the next phrase, adding to the dense polyphonic texture of the final cue. However, listening to the final film mix, it is not possible to determine whether these overdubs were actually used. The mix favors the upper strings throughout.

Whereas Howard's theme for Dent is melodic, none of Zimmer's themes are. There are a number of pertinent scoring techniques and devices employed by Zimmer that are exemplary of his musical language. In recent Hollywood films there is generally very little time to develop musical material in a musically coherent manner. Screen composers have always struggled with fragmentation of their music that was the result of the moment-by-moment requirements of the film they were scoring. The pace of a filmic narrative is not easily compatible with musical structure. These issues have been compounded in recent decades by technological developments in filmmaking, notably the digitalization of production and post-production. This has led to phenomena including so-called intensified continuity, short average shot lengths, and a generally accelerated visual language.[21] Flexible post-production practices are inherently incompatible with traditional film scoring methods. To succeed in this changed working environment and to serve filmic narratives effectively, composers must work flexibly and often forego considerations of purely musical development in favor of scoring solutions that optimize the relationship between music, dialogue, sound design, and moving image. These include the use of ostinato, additive layering of musical strata, and the superimposition of loud percussion hits.

Ostinati and Patterns

Zimmer himself has acknowledged that the use of ostinato played an important part in his approach to *Batman Begins* and the sequels. He has also confirmed that he is aware of the influence he subsequently may have had on contemporary film music, which in recent years has increasingly resorted to ostinati and recurring patterns. Ostinati readily provide sonic continuity and their repetitiveness conveys a sense of unity. If they comprise small note values and are rhythmically busy as a result, they can give the impression of forward momentum, impetus, and drive. Texturally and dynamically they can fluidly ebb and flow, weaving in an out of the surrounding orchestral and synthesizer texture and also the sound design. Although ostinati may restrict functional harmonic progression, they, like pedal point, accommodate dissonance and extended tonality, which may result from other parts being superimposed. Zimmer's ostinati for *TDK* mostly consist of series of sixteenth notes and sometimes eighth notes in the strings, almost always in D-minor. There are a number of ostinati that were recorded with live orchestra and can be found in the orchestrations. In many other cues, synthesizer patterns provide the underpinning ostinato instead.

One notable exception is the session score for 1M1 "Bank Robbery." Here, 127 bars of an ostinato were recorded with cellos, playing steady sixteenth notes *divisi* a major second apart on c' and d', accenting the first, fourth, seventh, eleventh, thirteenth, and fifteenth note in every bar which results in an agitated syncopated feel. Perhaps suprisingly, these live recordings are not used in the final cue: 1M1 as heard in the film does feature the very same ostinato but is performed first by a solo violin, played *detaché sul ponticello* and then taken over by a number of different sounds, including an electric guitar (or perhaps distorted cello), pulsing synthesizers, bass synths, and other synth patterns in higher registers. The note d' is always present, whereas the c' a major second below enters and exits at different points. Perhaps it was felt that an eclectic and processed blend of solo instruments and synthesizers could better convey a suitable sound for the Joker. Reserving the orchestra for Batman and Harvey Dent, generally speaking, also adds contrast to the smaller-scale forces that accompany the Joker.

1M2 "Find the Batman" accompanies a short set of sequences that summarizes the state of affairs in Gotham: the police are struggling to come to terms with Batman's role in law enforcement. Gordon hopes to work with Batman and tends to the searchlight used to summon the Caped Crusader. Ramirez visits Gordon on the roof and we learn that her mother is in hospital. This information is important to later on understand that she has betrayed Gordon for bribes to pay her mother's medical bills. Two ostinati are superimposed in this cue. The first is a sixteenth-note pattern (f'- f'-d'-d') that the violins play *staccato* for 39 bars. The pattern remains basically unaltered throughout, except in the ninth bar (labeled bar 14 in the score due to four bars' rest at the start of the score), where the patterns shifts to f♯' and d♯' to accommodate a brief tonal shift in the cellos and basses underneath. This ostinato effectively provides musical continuity and is blended with mellow synthesizers that at times dominate the texture.

The second ostinato in the lower strings enters in the latter half of the cue, playing a repeating series of four four-note figures (all eighth notes), played *legato* on the pitches c#-d-f-e, c#-d-e-f, c#-d-f-e, f-g-e-f. Half the violas and half the violoncellos double this line, which repeats identically until the end of the cue. For added intensity, the cellos split into *divisi* after eight bars, the lower half playing the same pitches but doubling up each note to sixteenth notes and *detaché*, leading to the next scene in which a drug deal is foiled by Batman imposters.

1M3 "Buyer Beware" is proof that film music does not lie, as Harry Gregson-Williams once said. When a number of Batmen interrupt a drugs deal between Scarecrow and some drug dealers, it is quickly clear that these are imposters. The music poignantly withholds any clue as to the real Batman's presence. Moments later Batman's Tumbler crashes onto the scene and underneath the loud sound effects of cars crashing and guns being shot the music is temporarily subdued. On a cut to the interior of the Tumbler, a strings ostinato enters, which will accompany Batman throughout. It is a variation of the Batman ostinato discussed above, similarly comprising a repeating series of sixteenth notes but here with an altered set of pitches: f'-a-d'-a, f'-a- d'-a, f'-a- d'-a, f'-b♭- d'-b♭, etc.). As elsewhere in the film, the ostinato here is doubled with synthesizers and the timbre frequently shifts between acoustic strings and synthesizer patterns. The heavy percussion and brass are superimposed over this ostinato and punctuate the music to close-score the ensuing fight sequence.

3M23 "Panic Room" picks up the same ostinato for a few bars as Wayne heads down into his secret basement. 4M42 "Bod Deploys" also reprises this same ostinato in the strings, with violins and violas in unison and cellos an octave below. It starts very quietly as the Batmobile reports a catastrophic damage alert and then grows gradually louder until hitting *f* by the fifth bar to match the loud percussion and brass that enter to accentuate the revelation of the Batpod. 7M62 "A Dark Knight" one last time draws on the same ostinato, if surrounded with a different strings arrangement.

In 2M10 "Move the Money," a bass synthesizer ostinato of sixteenth notes on D, accenting the first, third, and fourth beat, underpins the long held strings tones shown in the orchestration. The timbre of the bass is subtly varied. The low bass and high strings quite effectively stay out of the way of Lau's speaking voice. This is important in order to allow the audience to understand his plan to move the mobsters' money out of the reach of the police. This plan will later prompt Batman to retrieve Lau from Hong Kong.

2M13 "Trip to Hong Kong" begins with another sixteenth-note ostinato played *detaché* in the low strings (B♭-G-A-B♭, B♭-G-A-B♭, etc.) as Wayne and Alfred plan their trip to Hong Kong. The orchestration shows only strings, starting low cellos. Ambient textures and heavy low percussion that can additionally be heard in the final cue were added later. The scene segues to an atmospheric aerial shot of Bruce Wayne's yacht and a water plane landing. When the plane touches the water, the music gradually takes on a different feel, the emerging sprightly tone suitably reflecting the beautiful setting. Zimmer continues the ostinato, varying the pitches in line with chord changes whilst maintaining the overall contour.

3M28 "Loud Enough" is a re-arrangement of the same music, favoring a lower dynamic to accommodate the dialogue between Fox and Reese (who is trying to blackmail Wayne) and then Fox and Bruce when they reconstruct fingerprints from a bullet hole. It may be somewhat puzzling that the same music can accompany a leisurely boat trip in the South China Sea and a blackmail plot against Wayne. On the other hand, both scenes show Bruce plotting and preparing his next steps (the LSI extraction in the former, finding an address for the shooter who has killed two police officers in the latter).

The following cue, 2M14–15 "Put a Smile on That Face," starts with the Joker attacking Gamble. The sound palette here reverts back to familiar thematic material and textures. The ostinato from 1M1 returns in various permutations of solo strings and synthesizers. It is also underlined by a bass pulse on D in the same continuous sixteenth-note rhythm and with the same placement of accents. The second half of the cue (referred to as "Fox and Lau Meet" in Appendix II) segues back to Hong Kong, where Fox checks in at the LSI building and then meets Lau on a rooftop terrace. The ostinato Zimmer uses here is at first very similar to that in 1M3 "Buyer Beware" (see above) but then gradually recedes to give way to a syncopated mellow synth pulse on D above middle C. Low strings play long held notes underneath that trace the drawn-out minor third of the BT, subliminally reminding the audience that there is a scheme afoot. The pulsing synth ostinato facilitates forward momentum here and ensures that the scene seems to progress steadily even though the rooftop meeting is merely perfunctory, allowing Fox to plant a tracing device in the building. The synth pulse grows somewhat louder after the meeting finishes and as Fox leaves via the lobby. This segment is rather pacey and reiterates the existence of two cell phones somewhat heavy-handedly. It later transpires that the cell phone Fox has left with security can be used to jam the LSI security system; why he needs to have a second cell phone that sees him in breach of LSI security protocol is less clear: Fox refers to it as being a sonar scanning device but how exactly this device is supposed to have mapped Lau's offices when Fox has met him on the rooftop terrace is not explained. As Fox meets Wayne in a busy pedestrian area, the synth pulse segues to diegetic source music.

An intricate mesh of strings in seven parts, the violas and cellos *divisi*, forms the vibrant and textural ostinato for 2M16 "LSI Extraction." At a relatively slow 65bpm, the violins and violas play complementary combinations of sixteenth and thirty-second notes. Violins I undulate between a' and g' (two thirty-second and one sixteenth note respectively) while violins II play steady thirdy-second notes, repeating f-d'-e'-f'. Violas I play d'-a on a sixteenth and two thirty-second notes respectively, while violas II repeat a unit of a dotted sixteenth note on f followed by a (sixteenth note). Half the cellos add a figure of two sixteenth notes and one quaver on a-f-a. The lower cellos and basses underpin these polyrhythmic layers: marching basses and half the cellos accentuate every beat on D. The lower cellos also play a sixteenth-note triplet on every off-beat (e-d-f). The low strings have a strident and militaristic feel underlining a sense of aim and purpose in Batman's actions. Including the upper texture, the cumulative chord is a D-minor triad with E and G added ($Dm^{(add2, add4)}$). With accents and emphases occurring in different places in the respective parts and the dynamic never louder than *p*, the resulting sound is vivid yet static, like the hum of a cityscape, well suited to shots of Hong Kong at night.

In the beginning, the basses and cellos are virtually inaudible underneath a low synth-drone on D and an iteration of Batflaps rather loud in the mix. The horns state BT once before the ostinato recedes for a moment. The ostinato accompanies Batman's preparations to paraglide into Lau's office and kidnap the banker. It recedes briefly on the cut away from Batman (who is perched outside on an office tower facing LSI) to the interior of Lau's office (bars 12–13 in the orchestration). The ostinato then returns only gradually, building upward from the basses and cellos as Batman shoots explosive gel packs with timers across at Lau's office windows. The brief omission of the upper strings makes for a more focused and intimate sound that suits the close-up of Batman firing his charges versus the wide-angle aerial shot of previously. When the upper cellos return two bars later, they now step up to B♭ in the second bar to trace BT in the trombones and tuba atop. Moriarty's orchestration here (bar 17) wrongly shows the cellos staying on A. This appears to be an isolated error that was fixed at the session, because the orchestration correctly shows the cellos going up to B♭ in bar 39. The violas and violins remain unchanged but enter extremely quietly, almost inaudible in the final mix.

The level of separation in the sound of the different strings parts is remarkable. The sound of the lower strings in the final mix is rich and deep with a high degree of depth and perspective. By contrast, the upper strings sound close and bright without intruding on the overall mix. When audited on headphones, the upper strings sound very close and intimate, with a clear stereo separation of the first violins only on the left and the second violins only on the right. To achieve this high degree of clarity and separation Zimmer clearly has favored takes recorded with microphones in close proximity of the respective section, as opposed to stage microphones or a Decca tree perspective that would provide a roomier, more distant sound. The final mix foregoes the realistic balance of the orchestra in favor of a more manipulated and controlled sound to suit the calculated nature of Lau's impeding rendition. The careful balance between music and sound design struck in this cue will be discussed in the next chapter.

3M22 "Joker Crashes Party" introduces an ostinato that is used in several cues. It commences in the cellos when the judge slams shut the door of her car: a repeating series of sixteenth notes played *detaché* and accented as indicated in bold (**d**-A-D-A, **e**-A-D-D, **f**-A-D-A, **g**-A-**e**-A). It is noteworthy that the accented top notes of this ostinato are contained identically (pitch and rhythm) in a series of brass chords heard as early as 1M3 "Buyer Beware," albeit in an altogether different context: Batman hangs on the van Scarecrow is driving out of the parking garage. The shattering brass stabs seem to serve no particular purpose at that moment. Accented stabs on every second beat in *ff* on chords spanning two octaves (D to d). The repeating progression is Dm, A/D, Dm, A7/D with the last chord hit twice on beats three and four of the second bar. The chords are voiced in such a way that they follow a very similar top-note contour as the accented notes in the ostinato in 3M22, i.e., d-e-f-g-e. Twice more, and rather gratuitously, the same progression returns in 5M52–53 "Hospital Bomb Scare" (when the police officer calls for Davis to bring Dent down to the bus to be evacuated from Gotham General) and again at the beginning of 6M57 "Storming Pruitt Building." Right after Gordon's red team is ordered, "Go!" the brass states the progression *con forza* but, according to the orchestration, less loudly and forcefully than in the previous cues.

5M51–52 "Hospital Bomb Scare" at first uses the same ostinato as 2M13 "Trip to Hong Kong" (see above), which enters when Wayne leaves his penthouse and instructs Alfred to search for Gordon's men (apparently there are no female police officers) and their families for hospital admission (who might feel compelled to kill Coleman Reese to prevent a hospital from being blown up). This continues until the cut from Wayne's Lamborghini racing down the street to a nurse directing people in a hospital ward that is being evacuated. Here, a new ostinato starts that is a sped-up variation of the lower strings ostinato from 1M2 "Finding the Batman," played by half the violas and cellos, repeating sixteenth notes and accenting every beat: c♯-d-f-e, c♯-d-e-f, c♯-d-f-e, f-g-e-f.

The re-use of a familiar line, if in a different tempo and context, may subliminally suggest a similar predicament: just as Batman was initially needed but absent in the parking garage, so too is Coleman Reese's life being threatened here with no Batman in sight. When Reese is actually shot at, the ostinato gives way to the BT ostinato: as soon as the supposed threat becomes tangible, the music focuses on Batman rushing to the rescue. A pulsing bass synth underpins the latter part of the cue in a continuous sixteenth note pattern that weaves in and out of the mix.

The lower line of the "Hospital Bomb Scare" ostinato reappears in 6M56–57a "Always a Catch," where it continues throughout the entire cue, growing more and more intense. It is also the main building block for 6M57 "Storming Pruitt Building," which culminates in the final standoff between Batman and the Joker.

A final new ostinato prepares and accompanies the lead up to the ferries segment. It is a repeating short figure of four half notes, dovetailed with itself in two octaves, with a yearning and reaching quality

(D-d-c♯-d, d-d'-c♯'-d') in a variable tempo between 90.4-99.7bpm. This ostinato is first heard right after Coleman Reese has read out a message from the Joker on the news instructing Gotham's citizen's to evacuate the city ("Explosion Aftermath" in Appendix I). There are striking similarities between this "Boats" ostinato and Anarchy, the Joker's motif of chaotic mischief. Both are recurring four-note motifs. Both start with a large leap. The respective second halves are only slightly different: the leap down a minor seventh C to D followed by a leap up a major ninth C to D was described above. The semitone steps D to C♯ to D in the "Boats" ostinato are similar in terms of pitch class but hold significantly more tension and more energy than Anarchy. The Joker's evil challenge, threatening to blow up two passenger ferries but giving the passengers a morally impossible choice to blow up one another to save themselves, is his darkest scheme yet. As a warped mutation of Anarchy, the "Boats" ostinato effectively mirrors the level of escalation at hand.

Fox arrives at the Wayne Enterprises Research and Development department after a security breach has been reported there and he discovers the sonar scanning system Bruce has installed. The 4-note "Boats" figure plays six times here in a score segment that was not orchestrated separately. The musical material was most likely lifted from takes of 6M55, which features the same material (strings, brass, timpani) and this same fragment as repeating ostinato. 6M55 "The Boats" combines the 4-note figure as an ostinato with the Batman ostinato (see above).

Interestingly, the next two cues ("Sonar System" and "Unlucky Driver") are also compiled from different cues and feature musical material heard previously in different contexts. The music is relatively quiet here compared to the dialogue, possibly to allow the audience to better follow what is being said. It also makes sense to insert two relatively low-profile cues here before 6M55 "The Boats," which is of a much grander scale.

Additive Layering and Dramatic Pacing

Most action sequences in *TDK* last several minutes and require prolonged dramatic support. Audiences can tire quickly and the effectiveness of even the most visceral audio-visual spectacle can rapidly wear out. Music in this context is often called upon to keep the audience engaged and to keep adrenaline levels high. The composer may pick up on selected actions and incidents, perhaps synchronizing these with a particular musical gesture for added impact and emphasis. In longer action sequences, it can be equally important, however, to uphold tension in a more sustained fashion while effectively tracing shifts in the narrative and dramatic contour. In order to achieve this, Zimmer relies on compatible musical layers that can be liberally added, subtracted, and recombined. In almost every cue, an ostinato will provide at least one of these musical layers. Octave doublings can thicken a texture. Additional elements may include complementary textures in other instruments, superimposed brass swells, synthesizer parts, and ambient sound design. The adding and removing of component parts leads to a relatively fuller or sparser musical canvas, which, combined with dynamic changes, can help pace and sustain a long action scene.

One notable exception is the truck chase sequence that begins with an aerial shot of Gotham by nightfall (accompanied by a short appearance from JT) and ends when the 18-wheeler truck is flipped on its head. Nolan and his sound design team must have felt so confident about the effectiveness of this segment that it is left un-scored, apart from a brief musical interjection when the Batpod is revealed.

Bank Robbery

The bank robbery sequence that opens the film has been labeled "Prologue" in the orchestrators' score, even if, narratively speaking, it is not a prologue but part of the main body narrative. The segment simultaneously serves a number of functions. It is a character exposé for the Joker and introduces his four themes and motifs that will accompany him throughout the film. The segment also lays the groundwork for a major plot strand: the Joker meddling with the mob's affairs and upsetting the criminal balance of power in Gotham. Finally, the sequence sets the gritty and realist tone for the film.

Throughout the bank robbery, music is closely shaped to fit the picture. A ricocheting violin pattern starts in accented sixteenth notes (on d'), which is a reduced variant of the ostinato described above, with the same accents. A low percussion hit marks the cut to a shot of the Joker from behind, standing at the curbside. JT gradually fades up, then gets cut off, when an SUV pulls up. JT and the violin are replaced by low bass synth and new string sound playing the sixteenth-note ostinato (c' and d'). Music accommodates the dialogue between the gangsters inside the SUV and the two who have zip-wired onto the bank's roof. When the bank robbery takes its course, only the low pulsing bass remains prominent for a short while. As gunshots are fired and the goons are shouting, this occupies the upper frequency range of the soundtrack. The higher strings ostinato returns gradually after a cut to the gangsters on the roof, one of whom is intercepting the silent alarm call. Zimmer very carefully finds short moments where music can come to the foreground. For example, as one of the gangsters heads down to the bank vault, Triumphant is stated four times (and rather loudly) but it is slotted into a moment of relative silence in the soundtrack. The interplay of dialogue, sound design, music, and visuals is very carefully crafted. The musical texture shifts readily and frequently. Even on repetitive patterns, gradual dynamic changes and filter sweeps create a sense of constant development and forward movement.

Zimmer is able to significantly ramp up dramatic tension when required. When the bank manager intervenes and starts shooting at the robbers, dissonance mounts in the score. A hectic timpani pattern underpins the upward rise of JT, paired with an overall rising dissonant texture. The gunshots almost seem integrated in the percussive palette here. The music poignantly cuts back just before the bank manager screams, "Do you have any idea who you are stealing from?" Only a much quieter remnant of the aforementioned ostinato and some soft and extremely high aleatoric strings remain to perform a decrescendo. Music closely traces the rise and fall in adrenaline levels as experienced by the gangsters here.

The sound shifts into a more synthetic realm now, as the Joker is framed from the front for the first time (still wearing a clown mask) and the bank vault is broken open. A subtle time lapse is woven into the next segment, cutting from the bank vault opening (which is celebrated with Triumphant)[22] to bags full of cash being dragged into the main hall. This must be quite some time later, given the amount of money and the number of bags.

Music never stops for the entire six minutes of the bank robbery. And yet, the score subtly weaves in and out of the soundscape and flexibly comes to the foreground or recedes to the background. Zimmer's technologically enabled approach allows him to adjust readily to the dramatic pacing of this sequence. Whereas a film score in the past would routinely be brought up or down in the overall sound mix, depending on what other elements had to be accommodated (dialogue, sound design), Zimmer's approach is far more sophisticated. Instead of adjusting music purely by volume, he opts for subtle timbral adjustments from harsh and cutting to mellow and smooth (by use of high-cut filters, drive filters, distortion effects, addition and subtraction of layers). Given the fast-paced continuity of the underlying ostinato, these shifts can take place almost instantaneously and nevertheless appear to have musical context. This aspect of Zimmer's approach is scoring by production rather than composition and the techniques involved (mixing, editing, coloring) have a lot in common with DJing. The ostinato-driven sixteenth-note pulse of the score in this segment ensures that a constant pulse is maintained throughout. Zimmer achieves an extremely wide textural and timbral breadth and depth through additive layering of synthesizer parts, manipulated strings, cello and guitar parts. By the time the Zen-like gongs of the Anarchy motif arrive (when the Joker dances quizzically around his last remaining ally before he gets hit by the bus), this is an unsettling respite from five preceding minutes of action. The Joker is about to leave when the bank manager calls, "You think you're smart, huh..." JT supplants much of the rhythmically driven texture now and gradually crossfades into Stranger. The moment when the Joker's disfigured face is finally revealed is one of the more obviously constructed ones: the crescendo in the strings is very loud and Heath Ledger's voice sounds uncomfortably close and artificially bass-heavy when he says, "stranger." This manipulation effectively adds to the shocking impact of his face.

Joker Crashes Party

3M22 "Joker Crashes Party" accompanies a scene that dramatically escalates the Joker's actions. He crashes Bruce's party figuratively when he murders the judge who presides over the mob hearings (with a car bomb) and the police commissioner (with acid in his whiskey). He then actually crashes Bruce's fund raiser for Dent.

The cue starts just after Ramirez has informed Gordon of the Joker's intended next targets. As Gordon gives her instructions ("Seal the building. No one in or out until I get there."), ambient rumbling mask the entrance on an eighth-note synth pulse on low D at the tempo of 93.63BPM.[23] By narrative ellipsis, we cut immediately to Gordon arriving at Commissioner Loeb's office and two police officers arriving at the judge's home. The unpitched ricocheting violin pattern returns briefly here, recalling the very beginning of the film prior to the bank robbery. Another plan of the Joker is underway. Gordon tells the commissioner a threat has been made against his life and the judge is instructed to get in her car and leave. Meanwhile, Rachel is talking with Dent at Wayne's fund raiser, which briefly suspends the build-up that has been set in motion. Two pianos and harp at a low dynamic enter, adding color to *con sordino* strings and sustained synthesizer pads, none of which encroach on the dialogue but are able to fade in and out very subtly.

The bass pulse returns just as the judge is shown getting in her car. When she slams the door shut, visibly annoyed by the inconvenience of having to leave her home, another ostinato commences (described above), played by half the cellos and doubled on a muted bass synthesizer. The dynamic is very quiet to start (*pp* in the cellos) and then grows increasingly louder. After six bars, cut to Dent, who asks Rachel to respond to his proposal to marry him. Upon the next cut, back to the commissioner's office (he is about to take a sip from his drink), the upper strings begin building up harmonic tension, which leads to Gordon shouting, "wait" realizing too late that the drink may be poisoned.

To Rachel's horror, Wayne renders Dent unconscious to take him to safety. As he grips Dent in a chokehold from behind, the music rises noticeably in volume. The basses and remaining cellos start accenting beats 1 and 3 on D. The cellos and synth ostinato are now doubled in the violas. The texture grows ever thicker and louder. The upper strings and horns pick up the accented notes from the ostinato and harmonize these (i-V-i-V^7). Growing louder and louder to a *ff* across the whole ensemble, the ostinato finally leads to three loud statements of JT as the elevator doors to the penthouse open and the Joker and his gang arrive. The concluding hit to the cue is a shot fired from the Joker's pump gun into the ceiling.

Zimmer most effectively manages to trace the dramatic trajectory of this segment, which is not an easy task, given that the action involves multiple disparate locations and characters. Conceptually, Nolan likes to raise the stakes by intercutting several discrete but simultaneous settings (the judge dying, the commissioner dying, Dent in protective custody, the Joker crashing the party). We see the same narrative strategy applied in later segments. For the composer, the challenge is to help bring unity to the segment and to help channel the affect into one singular sense of escalation.

Wired

5M46–47 "Wired" starts with a brief aggressive passage that mirrors Batman's state of mind. As he rushes past Gordon out of the interrogation room and to what he thinks is Rachel's rescue, a bass figuration in C-Phrygian stomps in an irregular pattern of alternating 3/4 and 5/8. The cue has been built up to with JT. On the cut to Rachel tied to a chair in a large warehouse, the same ostinato as in 3M22 returns, though this time in G-Minor. It makes sense to re-use this ostinato as the segment it accompanies is structured, very similarly to 3M22, as a sustained dramatic build-up that leads to the death of the Joker's victim(s) and the failure of the police and Batman to intervene. The economical re-use of musical material also ensures coherence across prolonged passages of the score.

As Harvey wakes up and hears Rachel scream via radio and responds, "Rachel?" the ostinato is also picked up by the violas, an octave higher. As before in 3M22, a piano part enters both times when Dent talks to Rachel. Although it plays a different topline here, the use of piano to accompany dialogue between Dent and Rachel is congruous with the shift in texture amidst a surrounding dramatic build-up used in 3M22. When Dent falls over and oil spills, the ostinato returns accompanied by a strong crescendo in the brass.

On the cut to Batman racing through Gotham on the Batpod, the ostinato has shifted to C-minor. Although the C-minor chord as such could be interpreted as the subdominant chord of the G-minor, it soon transpires that the cue has permanently shifted key centers by direct modulation. The next cut returns to the Joker and Stephens (Keith Szarabajka) in the interrogation room. The ostinato drops out completely for a few bars, with only a held C in the low strings and synth with a low mellow drum pulse underpinning the Joker's dialogue (he is manipulating Stephens into attacking him, which leads to him gaining the upper hand and breaking out of the interrogation room). While the Joker speaks, the low strings pick up the ostinato again, gradually getting louder (the orchestration instructs "slow build!"). JT rises from amongst the texture and provides a forward trajectory as before, rising slowly and continuing across the next cut, to an inmate collapsing in the holding cell. The following cut shows Batman on the Batpod, still racing down the street, the revving engine tracing rising pitch of JT in similar motion. The score here effectively performs two tasks: providing continuity and keeping the tension high.

The Joker is holding Stephens hostage and another officer shouts, "What do you want?" upon which the ostinato drops out and so too JT. The Joker responds with fake innocence, "I just want my phone call." Cut to Dent lying in the spilled oil and Rachel talking over the radio. Only a low C in the strings and the aforementioned mellow drum pulse remain. This becomes a moment of relative calm before action erupts again. As the Joker places his call, a cell phone rings in the collapsed inmate's abdomen. The ostinato returns gradually but is drowned out by the shocking impact of the huge explosion that destroys the police station (only the Joker remains standing). Stomping brass play a rising line in half notes that take the score to a higher dramatic plane. Gone is the ostinato. These last few moments of the sequence are about creating a sense of the inevitable. The explosion in the police station must not detract from the ongoing threat of imminent death for either Rachel or Dent. Brass swells pulse in and out from underneath high strings stabs. Here, Zimmer runs into trouble for once, because he has to raise the dynamic and overall density of texture for the requisite visceral impact of the moment. However, Rachel is still talking to Dent on the radio and her voice simply wouldn't be heard if the music were not, exceptionally, dipped down in volume, a copout Zimmer so ingeniously avoids in previous cues. As a compromise, only the upper strings are dipped (which is possible because stems were recorded) and the low brass and percussion can remain relatively loud. It is a well-established scoring concept that spoken dialogue can be treated as part of the music texture in terms of frequency range and that surrounding musical texture can remain relatively loud so long as it stays out of the way of the dialogue in terms of frequency range.

The music cuts completely as Batman breaks open the doors to the place where Dent is held. Rachel has just professed, amongst all the drama, that, "yes," she wants to marry Dent. It is poignant that the next word we hear is Dent screaming, "no," not in response to her but in realizing that Batman has inadvertently chosen to save him, not Rachel. It is not at all clear why Dent assumes that the police will be unable to save Rachel (which indeed they are... for no clear reason). JT simmers relatively low in the mix until a massive explosion puts an end to the segment.

Hospital Bomb Scare

At the beginning of 5M51–52 "Hospital Bomb Scare," a pulsing bass synth bridges the transition from the previous cue (5M50 "This Is My City"). Bruce and Alfred are watching Coleman Reese on television (and so, too, is Gordon, elsewhere) who is about to reveal Batman's true identity. Suddenly, the Joker phones in and threatens to blow up a hospital if Coleman Reese is not dead within 60 minutes. The orchestration shows low brass and strings in parallel fifths meandering forth in small intervals and at relatively low dynamics. It is important that the audience can follow the Joker's threat because this sets the premise for the mayhem that ensues. Gordon is shown shouting instructions at his men, to evacuate hospitals, and to take Reese into protective custody. A timpani roll marks the end of this preliminary section, the last strike hitting the cut to Bruce getting underway to protect Reese. The above-mentioned 5M51–52 ostinato sets in, quiet at first. Right away, it is accompanied by a strident electronic rhythm reminiscent of Batflaps, giving the music a strong forward drive. A drawn-out line in the brass is similar to BT but progresses differently. It is daytime, after all, and in *TDK* Batman does not operate by day (in *The Dark Knight Rises* he does).

The development of the score now follows a familiar pattern. The ostinato is gradually doubled in octaves to increase dramatic tension. The driving rhythm grows heavier, the brass moves into upper registers and louder dynamics. Drum hits are superimposed (see also below). There is a brief halt on the cut to the interior of Gotham General and a nurse asks the police officer guarding Dent's room for help. It is important that the audience is allowed to notice this because the officer abandons his post, leaving Dent unguarded (so the Joker can gain access to his room).

After only two bars' pause, the ostinato is back. When shots are fired at Reese, the BT ostinato weaves into the already dense texture. Although Batman is not around, the use of his ostinato is nevertheless justified because Reese remarks, "they're trying to kill me," and Gordon flippantly responds, "well, maybe Batman can save you," not realizing that Bruce/Batman is indeed on his way to the rescue.

Inside the police SUV that is transporting Reese, Gordon, and another officer, the music temporarily simmers down to a quiet synth pulse and a low-profile tune in the low strings (D-C-A-B♭-C-G). Batflaps sounds briefly as Gordon receives a text message informing him to watch out for police officers with family members in hospital. On the cut back to the interior of Gotham General, where the police officer is now looking for his colleagues with whom he has lost radio contact, a driving sixteenth-note bass synth takes over.

As the officer enters Dent's room, this synth briefly crossfades into the minor second ostinato from Figure 11 before getting cut off by a very loud statement of JT as the Joker shoots the police officer. Remarkably, the "Hospital Bomb Scare" cue is over long before the hospital actually gets blown up. Then again, once the hospital is fully evacuated, the threat is diminished.

The Boats & Storming Pruitt Building

6M55 starts as Maroni's car crashes. For twelve bars, the music cycles through a repeating chord progression (Dm, Dm/F, B♭, Gm) and layers the Batman ostinato with the "Boats" ostinato. A timpani roll and crescendo demarcates the end of four bar phrases. After the third phrase, the music breaks down to near silence on a cut to the interior of one of the ferries whose engines are failing.

The orchestration here shows the strings play tremolo at *pp* and in the overall mix they are barely audible. Ambient rumblings weave in and out and add to the ominous effect of sudden relative silence. When a detonator is revealed, the ambient texture swells up almost imperceptively, making the revelation all the more daunting. A few low drum hits, very quiet, are added here. These are not shown in the orchestration and thus were likely added later. As the Joker starts speaking over the intercom, a steady sixteenth-note synthesizer pulse sets in. When the Joker says, "each of you has a remote," the mangled voices from the cell phone feeds Fox is monitoring briefly form what sounds like a crunching percussive eighth-note pattern that is low-pass filtered to be constrained to low mid-range frequencies.

Fox locates the Joker and Batman rushes off on the Batpod, which predictably prompts the BT ostinato to return (bar 64 in the orchestration). In a somewhat unusual variation, the accompaniment in the basses moves down a semitone (D to D♭ rather than up a minor third as so many times before). In the orchestration it states D to C♯ but this is an enharmonic misspelling, given that the chord progression is clearly D-minor to B♭-minor over its third (B♭/D♭), correctly spelled out in the 2nd cellos which play the Batman ostinato. This ostinato soon recedes (as the civilians on the ferry start arguing) and in its absence it transpires that the semitone undulation in the low strings is derived from the 4-note "Boats" ostinato (see above).

Dent confronts Ramirez. The mangled brass cluster that is heard as he knocks her unconscious provides the segue point from 6M55 to 6M56–57a "Always a Catch." The ostinato from 5M51–52 returns and continues throughout the entire cue, growing more and more intense through an increasing number of stacked octaves, layers of synthesizers, and subtle percussion. Low brass enters as Gordon gets frustrated, arguing with Batman as to how best to tackle the hostage crisis in the Pruitt Building.

On a cut back to the interior of the civilian ferry (where a ballot is taking place), strident low string stabs in a quarter note pulse commence. As before during the "Wired" and "Hospital Bomb Scare" sequence, Nolan presents disparate settings and scenarios in parallel. The score is tasked to help keep up a sense of increasing urgency even when the different narrative strands unfold at a different respective speed. The music here is close-scored in that the orchestration matches the final recording exactly in terms of bar numbers and score layout. For example, when Batman takes off to fly over to the Pruitt Building and Gordon threatens to shoot him, a momentary triumphant interjection in strings and brass is spelled out in the written orchestration.

The music becomes quite reiterative with the strings ostinato repeating over and over and percussion and brass rising and falling in amongst the surrounding texture. The reason such continuity music works here is that there is so much going on in the film: the frantic back-and-forth cutting between Batman, the clowns in the Pruitt Building, Fox at the sonar system, Gordon on the roof, his SWAT teams storming the building, and his wife calling to say she has been kidnapped.

At the end of 6M56–57a, the ostinato of 1M1 "Bank Robbery" returns very briefly (accented sixteenth notes on c' and d'), underlining the fact that the Joker has once again swapped targets (the clowns are in fact his hostages). 6M57 "Storming Pruitt Building" starts with the gratuitous brass fanfare described above. This reprise seems to serve no narrative purpose other than adding weight to the SWAT team attack. This time, a loud explosion curtails the second phrase of the fanfare. The 5M51–52 ostinato returns again, the frantic busy-ness of the score adding to the dizzying pace of the editing. This cue remains close-scored and the detailed score layout (including precise adjustments to the tempo here and there and frequent meter changes) matches the scene. JT is heard twice in what would be bars 31–32 in the orchestrated score. However, as before, JT is played by synthesized elements and instruments recorded outside of the orchestral sessions. The orchestrated score here tapers down to a much-reduced texture of un-pitched percussion and a D-pedal in the low brass.

Bars 37–45 in the orchestrated score are marked "Heroic." Indeed, a fanfare-like line in the brass stands out as Batman fights the SWAT to prevent them from attacking hostages in clown masks. The written line opens with a rising fourth and moves sequentially down. However, in the final mix there is a counter-line in the horns that is not spelled out in the orchestrated score but appears to have been added after the fact.

The score breaks down to quiet textures of strings and synthesizers again on the cut to the ferries where the final tally from the ballot is being announced. Back in the Pruitt Building, the tempo of the music goes down from 104.5bpm to 76bpm. The same sixteenth-note ostinato is now 25% slower. Remarkably, this is not immediately obvious when heard in context. It certainly does not detract from the cue's effectiveness. Perhaps the slower tempo allows for the ostinato and surrounding texture to have a steadier and more measured feel, underlining Batman's strength and resolve. Indeed, he is winning the upper hand and a bright and very loud statement of the BT (Dm to B♭ with D rising to F in the topline) celebrates his triumph when he finally manages to incapacitate the SWAT team. Amidst the sustained audio-visual barrage of the last ten minutes, only this heavy-handed musical gesture can crank the musical impact up a proverbial notch. It is perhaps the least subtle of musical moments in the entire score.

For the remainder of the cue, the situation once again escalates as Batman now faces the Joker in a final fight. The challenge here is one of collapsed scale: Where Batman moments ago faced many opponents he now only faces one (with three dogs that are bothersome but hardly dangerous). To prevent a sense of anticlimax, Nolan cuts back to the prisoners' ferry. Here, in a moment of tense calm, the soundtrack simmers down to near nothing. The prisoners' leader takes matters into his hands and this short passage is enough of a respite to make the ensuing final fight between Batman and the Joker feel relatively exciting once again.

The 10-minute passage comprises the longest sustained action sequence in the film and is a rather exhausting *tour de force*. Zimmer's method of creating flexible and combinable musical layers allows him to sustain even the longest action sequences. He shows meticulous judgment in gauging the required tone and intended level of dramatic charge for a sequence. Some of the material may seem overly repetitive but this is a creative choice that is congruous with Zimmer's preferred idiom. The iterative nature of much of the music, resulting from extensive use of ostinato and other looped elements, not only lends continuity to the juxtaposition of otherwise disjointed settings in action-laden passages. More broadly, the musical material also imbues a sense of unity across the whole film, which, regardless of how one might feel about the music in and of itself, is an important function narrative film music must serve.

Swells, Thuds, and Bangs

Low percussive beats, heavy drums hits, dark rumbling textures (including Batflaps) and sudden brass crescendos permeate the score.

These musical elements are interjected frequently as scoring devices that serve a number of functions. They are firstly used to lend more visceral impact and emphasis to key moments, most effectively in abovementioned passages where the audio-visual canvas is already quite densely populated. They secondly help delineate musical structure (end of phrases, end of cues, transition to new section, etc.) and narrative structure (hit a cut to a different scene, hit a gun shot, the impact of a fist, etc.). In this respect, they are akin to punctuation in written language, fulfilling the functions of commas, full stops, and exclamation marks. They also help characterize Batman as a powerful and masculine hero. Whereas the percussive hits are inherently instantaneous and best applied to hit a specific moment, swells in the brass are durational and gestural (akin to hand gestures during a speech) and used to lead up to an action (Batman preparing to take-off, the Joker arriving, and so on).

Brass swells abound in the score and reliably serve to prepare on-screen actions. This tried and tested method allows the composer to help facilitate directionality in the filmic narrative and propel key actions forward. For example, Zimmer prepares Batman's take-off in the Hong Kong sequence with a strong and dissonant crescendo in the brass, which then immediately breaks into a more percussive and pattern-based accompaniment upon take-off. The technique maintains currency throughout the film. There is obvious resemblance between these purely functional swells and BT, which in itself is a two-tone brass motif, and crescendos on the first note and decrescendos on the second. Such similarities usefully further musical homogeneity.

Thuds and Bangs

The heaviest percussion is clearly reserved for Batman. The aforementioned Triumphant is a syncopated riff (first heard during the bank robbery sequence) that has a hard percussive attack but occupies only the upper middle frequencies, not the bottom lower end where heavy percussion resides. The affective properties of the riff signal the Joker's evil and anarchic character. By contrast, Batman is larger than life and requires mightier, darker musical forces.

From the first time he appears in the parking garage, heavy percussion abounds in the cues that accompany Batman. Sometimes the lines between Batman and Bruce Wayne are blurred. For example, when Bruce's "alibi" for his sudden trip to Hong Kong is revealed, heavy percussion in 2M13 "Trip to Hong Kong" is used simply to make the revelation seem more meaningful. In many cues, the low percussion that accompanies Batman has been added after the scoring sessions and is therefore not showing in the orchestrations. For example, the percussion in 2M14–15 "Put A Smile on That Face" (transition to Hong Kong) is not in the score.

Occasionally, Zimmer will ask pitched instruments to join the percussion for hits. In 3M24–25 "Then You're Gonna Love Me," the strings are asked to aleatorically play "any note" in *f* to double a percussion impact when Batman appears. Howard uses a similar technique in his cue 2M18 "Are You Up To It." He calls for a massive hit when the corpse of a Batman imposter hits the mayor's office window. On the downbeat of bar 10 in the orchestration, Howard asks for snap pizzicato in the strings and dense clusters in the brass, percussion, and piano, all in *ff*. A written instruction adds "Huge Orchestra Hit (includes following samples): VL Orch Perc, Orch Percuss, Big Bangs, King Kong Orch Hits, Dino Orch Hits, A Big Hits, MV Metal 1&2." Violas and lower cellos play a note behind the bridge that they sustain for several bars longer, gradually decrescendoing. They are reminded in writing, "this should not be pretty." There is nothing subtle about these heavily constructed moments where musical texture is momentarily punctured by sheer mass and volume.

At times, the high level of emphasis seems excessive, erring on the side of redundancy in the interest of spectacle. When the Batpod is revealed for the first time (presumably a key moment for invested fans), 4M42 "Pod Deploys" starts with very loud taiko hits that only compound the loud sound effects and impressive visuals already present. Elsewhere, the music goes to the opposite extreme by not hitting a moment where this might be expected. In 4M42b "Batman Down," the final crash of the Batpod is left un-hit. Instead, the noise of the crash itself acts as the impact sound that cuts off the music.

Batflaps is inherently percussive. In the interrogation room sequence, this is used to good effect to amplify a sense of anger and aggression in Batman's reaction to the Joker's manipulative monologue.

> We wanted to be very edgy, very brutal. We wanted it to be the point at which Batman is truly tested by the Joker and you see that the Joker is truly capable of getting under everybody's skin.[24]

The interrogation between Batman and the Joker was shot with minimal lighting, the desk lamp visible in the shot being the actual sole source of light in the first part.[25] Nolan takes realism to another level here by relying solely on the dialogue track recorded on set (as opposed to re-recording passages in ADR as would be common practice). The harsh lighting, bleak color palette, and thorough minimalism of the setting frame the claustrophobic effect of this scene.

When the Joker subsequently manages to enrage Batman to the point where he is giving in to sheer brutality (and employing interrogation methods that amount to torture), Batflaps coincides with powerful body impact sounds. The motif provides a downward expansion of the impact sounds into a frequency range that is pure depth and weight. The percussive decay on a timed delay also prolongs the impact, sounding almost akin to a timed echo of the body impacts themselves. It is intriguing to hear Batflaps used in this way here, given that it was originally devised to foreshadow Batman's existence (in the early part of *Batman Begins*). Here, now, it acts as an amplifier of Batman's anger and as a sonic extension of the unrestrained brutality this evokes.

5

ANALYSIS OF THE SCORE AS PART OF THE SOUNDSCAPE

This chapter discusses the score in the context of dialogue, production sound, sound design, and ambient music design. The exceptionally nuanced relationship of music and sound design in *The Dark Knight* is the cumulative result of a creative vision shared by the key contributors, realized through an intensely collaborative creative process, and facilitated by sound and music technology. Another look at the conceptual and creative process involved in the making of *TDK* highlights planning and practical decisions made during pre-production, production, and post-production. The concept of "Total Soundtrack Composition" helps appreciate aesthetic, qualitative, and technical overlaps between music and sound design in the sonic territory they share.[1] An exploration of the technical process of ambient music designer Mel Wesson shows how his work blurs the lines between music and sound design, bridging gaps and pushing respective boundaries. Analyses of selected key scenes then dissect the relationship and sonic interplay of music and other soundtrack elements. These analyses ask, "What do I hear of what I see?" and "What do I see of what I hear?" as well as assessing the role and function of music in amongst other soundtrack elements.[2]

It is important to keep in mind the limitations of viewing and hearing *TDK* outside the cinema environment. Most home cinema systems simply cannot rival the speaker setup, dynamic range, and frequency range of sound systems in state-of-the-art cinemas, let alone IMAX cinemas. Since the cinematic viewing and listening experience can no longer be replicated, for the purpose of study, the UK Blu-ray release was used, which offers excellent sound quality and large dynamic range. Good quality headphones can be useful when trying to hear nuances in the soundscape. However, even the best headphones are limited in the extreme low- and high-end of the frequency spectrum. Furthermore, when auditing the stereo conversion of a surround mix, one does not get a true impression of the original soundtrack as heard during the initial release. These limitations of access and reproducibility aside, *post hoc* observations can generally provide only limited insight into the underlying processes. Access to creatives involved in production and post-production through firsthand interviews and third party sources has therefore proven highly valuable.

A More Realistic Soundtrack

According to sound mixer and sound recordist Ed Novick, Chris Nolan paid close attention to sound recording and sound post-production, in pursuit of his vision of heightened realism. He was keen to capture production sound during shooting, if only as a basis "upon which post-production can build."[3] During location scouting he always had a member of the sound team present to help identify potential challenges. He carefully planned ahead to mitigate noisy locations and to work around reflective surfaces (sound/visual). He shot with sound in mind, tried to provide sound-friendly camera and microphone setups, and had lapel microphones fitted in the Batman suit and on the Joker. Novick points out that most of the dialogue heard in the final mix was recorded on set, which is highly unusual for sci-fi action films where dialogue is often re-recorded in post-production.[4] He remembers that Nolan's insistence on practical effects (as opposed to CGI) posed challenges to on-set recording, in terms of location noise, moving cameras, and loud IMAX cameras, which all had to be negotiated to capture usable production sound.

It is all the more interesting to note, then, that despite this purist striving for realism during production, a flexible combination of production sound, sound design, music, and so-called ambient music elements were later called upon to take the soundtrack to a more constructed affective plane. Drawing on his sound team to make the soundscape of his film an extension of the visual aesthetic of heightened reality,[5] Nolan judiciously balances subtlety and mainstream spectacle. The interplay of sound and relative silence, the intricate sonic attributes of selected sound effects and their relative volume in the soundtrack are all carefully devised. The fluid interplay of music and sound design is as fascinating as the use of ambient music design that pushes the composed musical score into the realm of sound design. *TDK* eschews the gratuitous redundancy of film sound elements that can be readily observed in other sci-fi action films released around the same time. For example, in action sequences of Michael Bay's *Transformers* (2007), music routinely adds to an already overloaded soundtrack, with little effect. J. J. Abrams makes striking use of beautifully crafted sound effects in *Star Trek* (2009) but nevertheless draws somewhat heavy-handedly on Michael Giacchino's orchestral score to highlight key moments.

Collaborative Creative Process: Total Soundtrack Composition

> I love working with Hans because he approaches music in a similar way that I approach sound effects in that everything is music to him. All sound is music.[6]
> Richard King, *TDK* supervising sound editor

In the realm of sound film, there have always been sonic and conceptual overlaps between music and sound effects. Traditionally, these two elements were treated as discrete elements and their respective creative gestation took place in relative isolation. Mutually unaware, the composer and the sound design team would devise ideas that might clash in the final dub. At the point of dubbing, film composers would habitually bemoan the loss of one cue or another or that their music fell victim to the sound effects track, invariably the result of uncoordinated planning.

Figure 5.1 illustrates the shared sonic territory and conceptual overlaps between qualitative attributes in music and sound design. Not only do both elements share key qualities that are consciously considered during their respective creation. They also inhabit the same physical medium and aural space when delivered to the audience. Every film composer and every sound designer will be able to conceive of their respective output in the terms listed here (the list is not exhaustive).

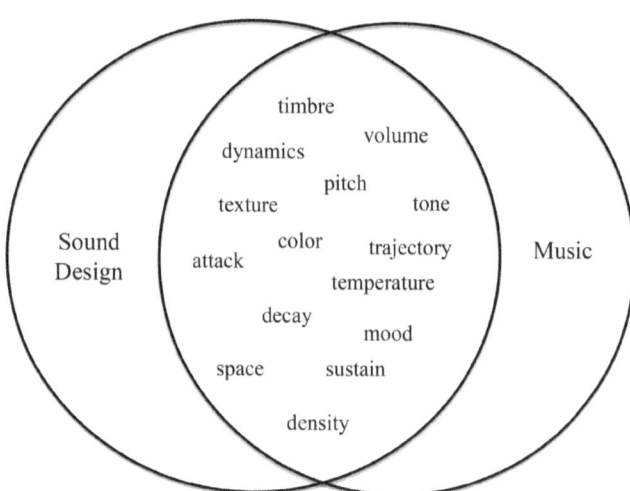

Figure 5.1. Shared sonic territory and conceptual overlaps between music and sound design

In the area of film sound, the day-to-day workflows and user interfaces have been transformed by emerging technology. A dialogue between composers and sound designers may not be newly available but it has certainly been facilitated by digital technology both parties use. Recent Hollywood (sound) film production has increasingly relied on digital technology, which has made workflows more efficient and, crucially, cheaper. Filming on digital media and digital sound recording has made non-linear and digital post-production possible: virtual editing, sound editing, and mixing. Nolan has resisted the industry's drive towards digital media,[7] and there are others advocating to save 35mm and 70mm film.[8] Nevertheless, Nolan has readily adopted, and adapted his working methods to, other technological innovations such as the large-frame IMAX film format, extensive use of green screen, and digital surround sound.[9]

The use of digital sound recording, editing, and mixing has particular implications for the place and placement of music in the soundtrack. Emerging sound technology allows for the exploration of ever wider dynamic and frequency ranges, at an unprecedented level of clarity and nuance. Music on digital soundtracks resides in the same sonic sphere as sound effects. Increasingly sophisticated soundtracks put music under threat of being drowned out (volume levels) or crowded out (soundscape too busy) because sound designers hope to explore the sonic possibilities of the digitally enabled soundtrack to the fullest extent possible. Film composers' traditional, linear approach to film scoring has been rendered incompatible with the prevalent mode of sound film post-production. To the extent music and sound effects share sonic qualities and attributes, these can be designed to the same affective end, if the respective creative teams coordinate their creative effort. Zimmer has always shown sensibility for close-scoring and intricate engagement with the narrative, dialogue, and sound design: on *Rain Main*, aiming for a "full sonic experience," Zimmer collaborated with the sound design team musically to match the tuning of car tires on a bridge. There are some enjoyably subtle musical transitions in this road movie, for example on a cross-fade from a driving segment to Hoffman staring at a washing machine in a laundromat. Dropping the melodic topline and lowering the relative volume of the accompanying percussion, Zimmer is able to shift musical gears fluidly and seamlessly deliver the viewer from the preceding montage segment to the next dialogue scene.

In recent decades, Zimmer has continued to champion collaboration. Sound designer and supervising sound editor Richard King notes that on *TDK* he and co-composers Zimmer and Howard collaborated closely:

> I always try to hear early versions of the music, and conversely if I have an idea of how something is going to sound, I'll make it available to the composers. Chris wanted the temp mix to be a very close template of what the final mix would sound like. We worked very hard on the temp, for which we had sampled versions of the final score assembled by the music editor, Alex Gibson, which would eventually be recorded with an orchestra. Once I heard the music mock-ups that Hans and James had composed, I was able to then go back and make sure the frequencies and textures we were using didn't clash with the music. But that barely happened at all. I think they got a sense from the temp dub and early sound demos what we were up to, and we got an idea what the music would be doing, and both the music and sound effects evolved from there. [...] It was worked out early on in Chris' head where sound effects were going to rule, where music was going to rule and where they would work together.[10]

Just because discrete creative filmmaking areas use the same technology, this does not automatically mean people communicate. They still have to *choose* to communicate. Zimmer actively pursues a creative dialogue between the music and sound team. In the case of *TDK*, this dialogue was put on course and supervised by Nolan himself who brought his own authorial vision to the table, if not the technical facility to undertake the work himself.[11] Because Zimmer and his team were involved in *TDK* from the early conceptual stages (pre-shoot) until the very last post-production stage (the dub), novel creative opportunities and affective possibilities arose for the relationship and combination of music and sound design.[12] This sustained collaborative and experimental approach potentially unlocks a richer and more varied sound palette. The creation of sonically conceived music and musically conceived sound design requires their respective creators' mutual awareness of each others' creative vision and process, as well as narrative intentions. The explorative, speculative, and experimental approach to music (including ambient music design) and sound design in *TDK* lead to a soundtrack whose component parts are at times unrecognizable as purely music or purely sound effects. The end result is less predictable than many of its contemporaries and avoids clichés. Where music meets sound design, *TDK* presents compelling creative solutions that push the boundaries of conventional film scoring.

King's quote above indicates that Nolan had an overriding vision for the soundtrack of his film and King has stressed this elsewhere when he explained that, "Chris is the grand orchestrator of where sound effects play, where music plays and where there's silence."[13]

Ambient Music Design: Pushing Boundaries, Building Bridges

> One of the things you need to realize about these *Dark Knight* movies and *Inception* as well: we work in a very different way than other people where Richard [King] and I work really closely together. There's another […] person there, Mel Wesson … Richard, Mel and I are forever crossing the lines of what are sound effects and what is music.[14]
>
> Hans Zimmer

Mel Wesson has worked with both Howard and Zimmer on numerous projects, credited as ambient music designer. Asked what contribution he made to *TDK*, Wesson responds,

I spent the initial months creating sounds and grouping them in moods and characters, things like "Oxides," "Rage," "Chaos," "S-Laughter." I've always found it easier to collate sounds in terms of food groups rather than just "Pulses," "Percussion," "Underscores," etc., and anyway, that would've been a little unimaginative! An amount of this material first saw daylight in The Prologue. That was invaluable in terms of recognizing at an early stage how far this movie differed tonally from [*Batman Begins*]. As the team came together over at Remote Control I joined them and began putting ideas together through the reels; these went either directly to the mix or via Hans and James to brighten their days! [...][15]

Wesson occupies a creative niche that few film composers have explored as yet. His contribution as ambient music designer provides layers of musically conceived sounds created through synthesis or the digital manipulation of recorded acoustic sounds, crafted with an ear for their sonic and affective qualities. Wesson provides textures that can easily fade in and out of the soundscape. Wesson's work has been facilitated by remarkable advances in digital sound technology, both at the stage of recording, production, and reproduction: only in recent years has film sound technology become nuanced enough to accommodate ambient music design in all its subtleties.

To manipulate sounds, Wesson uses Metasynth, a Mac-based sound design and music production tool. Metasynth was developed by U&I Software co-founders Eric Wenger and Edward Spiegel and first released in 1999. The company's self-proclaimed mission is "to provide creative artists with tools that encourage discovery and liberate them from the constraints of traditional software and techniques. Our applications provide environments that nourish creativity and exploration by providing both paradigm-breaking functionality and aesthetically inspiring user-interfaces that are themselves works of art."[16]

Traditional music production tools, including their digital emulations, commonly affect standard parameters such as pitch, dynamic range, frequency range, timbre, and reverberation. Digital tools have opened up possibilities to manipulate sounds at sample-level and to apply distortion, time-stretching, and audio-quantization. Groundbreaking developments in music synthesis in the 1980s and '90s brought about new virtual tools for manipulating sounds in the realm of select aspects such as harmonics, formants, and physical modeling. Effects plug-ins that perform any of the aforementioned functions have commonly been embedded within standard software sequencers. Their user interface tended to be modeled after hardware equivalents (buttons, turning knobs, faders) or offered numeric input methods. Other softwares offer fewer pre-set user interfaces to allow creative practitioners to focus on their aesthetic intuition. The Max/MSP software by Cycle '74 offers an interactive visual environment that allows composers to create and patch modules for a wide range of creative outputs.[17] The software is widely used by composers of so-called electroacoustic music and perhaps works most effectively in a live performance environment. The sophisticated and comprehensive nature of the range of Max/MSP's abilities means it is not the most user-friendly.

This is where Metasynth offers "paradigm-breaking functionality." Its unique interface is highly visual and offers new ways of manipulating sound. It is split into discrete editing sections and divides different sets of parameters into so-called rooms. The software allows access to sound properties of a chosen sound source (including recorded sounds) through pixels, colors, even scanned images (through spectral analysis).[18] Metasynth requires no notation, no MIDI, no samples, thus liberating the user from the counter-intuitive strictures and limitations of standard music production tools and manipulations.

The Metasynth user is able to shape sounds through visual manipulations and then aesthetically judge the result. This process innovation facilitates product innovation: users can focus solely on sonic qualities and attributes that they wish to alter and, when working in the context of film scoring, evaluate the outcome in terms of its narrative, emotive, and visceral effect and suitability. A unique user interface in this context facilitates a novel creative process, which in turn leads to musical outcomes that are completely different from those devised by more traditional means. If the ambient music designer is able to focus on his or her craft purely in terms of sound and sonic qualities, and less in terms of traditional music-only parameters, overlaps emerge between his or her creative outlook and that of sound designers, both at the technical but, more so, the conceptual and aesthetic level. As a result, music and sound design grow ever closer together and fascinating sonic and affective possibilities arise.

Reflecting on his craft, Wesson is mindful of the need to customize his approach to each respective project:

> So much of Hans's world, well, James Newton Howard's world for that matter, is an orchestral world. Everything I do has to live with that so you can't go off on crazy tangents and create what we jokingly call "pigs in space" which is when we end up with something that sounds like it's a crazy sci-fi movie, which *Inception* kind of was in some ways. That's quite an important thing: to try and keep those sounds grounded in an organic sense and maybe in some ways also—

not so much to question what that sound is, but to accept it without really realising that you've accepted that it is part of that score. It's not sticking out and waving. "Oh, that's an electronic part of the score." It has to sit in with everything else and you have to believe it belongs there. I think that's a very important part of everything that we do.[19]

Wesson joined Zimmer during pre-production of *Hannibal* (2001) to record location sounds and later use these as a basis for ambient music design. For example, he fed a photograph of Anthony Hopkins as Hannibal Lecter into Metasynth to use the spectral analysis for sound manipulation. Even if the end result of Wesson's work is hardly recognizable as to its original source, Wesson nevertheless finds unique solutions for each film. He will start forming and shaping sounds from recorded source material and gradually refine a sonic palette for the respective film at hand. Asked where he draws the line between music and sound design, Wesson explains,

> I wouldn't differentiate between [music and sound design] sonically, but I'd say there's a dividing line in whether you're being figurative or abstract in the way you use sound. The priority for my work is with the score, what I do has to have some musical sensibility, whether it's playing a supportive, colorist role or driving the structure from which a cue is built up. I always work with the sound design team in mind though. You have to be aware of what those guys are up to, and it doesn't help if there's half a dozen things all doing the same job at the dub, you need clarity, and everything has to be focused.

Given that his contribution to the soundtrack resides in the sonic overlap of pure music and pure sound design, Wesson stays involved in the creation of the final soundtrack during the dubbing process, fully aware that he may need to alter, edit, or cut out parts of his work during the dub, where final decisions are made about the placement and balance of dialogue, sound design, music, and ambient music design.

> The final dub is open season for sound, but aside from fixes or specific requests my role morphs into more of a 'doctor on call' situation. It's often the first time everything comes together as a whole [...] I don't get too protective about my work though; if something doesn't make it to the cut it's for a reason and I'd sooner hear one sound cut through and have an effect on an audience than have a wall of mush that does nothing. It's the end result that counts.

Wesson has described in detail how for a scene in *The Dark Knight Rises*, there were a large number of options available. For the fight between Bane and Batman in which Bane breaks Batman's back, Zimmer composed a cue of quasi-aleatoric high strings and pained brass sighs, which were recorded during the scoring sessions. There was a clean ADR recording of Bane's voice (Tom Hardy) as well as draft sound design stems (a waterfall, impact sounds of clanking metal and thudding fists, room sound of the cavernous space in which the fight takes place). Wesson used Metasynth to design one track of strings and brass, mangling the original recordings beyond recognition. He also created a second track of low rumblings and textures. In the final mix of the film, no purely orchestral elements were used. Bane's voice is eerily foregrounded and remarkably dry amidst unnaturally reduced room ambience. In this particular segment, Wesson's ambient tracks are used subtly but do not stand out.

Interplay of Music and Sound Design: Key Scenes

Bank Robbery: Sonic Clarity and Artifacts

The flexible balance of music elements, sound design, and dialogue in this opening segment allows for an exciting soundtrack that can quickly shift and react to the fast-moving on-screen action. Ambient music design provides added atmosphere and builds bridges where music alone might stand out as heavy-handed and sound effects might seem out of place or affectively fall short of the required impact. This complementary interplay of three sonic elements creates a soundscape of rare fluidity and impact.

A loud thud coincides with the cut to the daytime exterior of an office tower and the Joker Theme (JT) grows louder. A ticking noise that resembles a ticking clock accompanies this and through fast rhythmic subdivision helps imbue JT with a sense of forward drive. The ticking also subliminally underlines the calculated nature of the Joker's scheme. Nondescript traffic noise is faintly audible but there is also a low-frequency rumbling underneath, almost inaudible but present nevertheless. This may be a low synthesizer, or, more likely, an ambient music design element that balances the texture of JT. The low rumbling remains in the mix until the SUV pulls up at the curbside and the overall texture shifts to a more distinct guitar and synth sixteenth-note pattern.

When the two clowns zip-wire across to the roof of the bank building, extremely loud drums pierce the mix. In these early shots, the mix of music and sound design flexibly accommodates dialogue where it occurs. The interior of the SUV is left rather quiet to allow the audience to hear the three clowns talking about the Joker, which is crucial to establish the character. The sound of guns being loaded and prepped is prominent in the upper frequency register, but sits well above the frequency of the speaking voices and therefore does not get in the way. A sub-bass pulse enters as the clowns get out of the SUV, which, at least on headphones, is quite intrusive. As the bank robbery gets underway, the gunshots are once again extremely loud.

The ensuing bank robbery is fast-paced yet nuanced. The soundtrack contains several artifacts that add to the affective impact of specific moments but do not emanate from an obvious diegetic source. A high-pitched rising sound enters as one of the clowns begins to distribute hand grenades among the hostages. The sound stops abruptly on the cut to the two clowns on the roof, just before one shoots the other. When, shortly after, one clown reaches the bank vault, a spooky low swoosh sound emerges from the musical textures. This sound is clearly not part of the natural soundscape in the bank vault but it effectively attenuates the swirling movement of the camera and places added emphasis on the huge vault door that the clowns must presumably break open to get to the money.

It is remarkable how comfortably music and sound design coexist during the robbery: even though both elements rely heavily on high-pitched sounds, the balance and mix of the elements is carefully refined to find space for both. The clown in the vault starts drilling into the door and the motor sound of the power drill remains in the soundtrack, if more quietly, even after the cut back into the main hall where a clown is beating one of the hostages. Yet the drill noise is then cut off violently when the bank manager suddenly fires his pump gun, another gunshot that is very loud. This sets off a cacophonous wall of noise in the soundscape that is underpinned by filtered timpani hits and punctuated by further gunshots. The noisy wall of sound rises up sluggishly and underlines the rising tension as the clowns scramble to evade the bullets fired at them. An oddly artificial sound that sounds like an airlock closing in a sci-fi film cuts off this rising texture, metallic, mechanical, and seemingly not belonging to the soundscape of the location. Perhaps such an otherworldly sound was needed to effectively cut off most of the music and make way for the bank manager to shout, "Do you have any idea who you're stealing from?" Only high dissonant strings remain.

Relative calm ensues for a short while. One clown seeks reassurance from the other ("He's out, right?"), only to be shot at with the manager's last round when he gets up. As the other clown in turn shoots the bank manager, his semi-automatic gun purrs gently, in marked contrast to the guns heard thus far. The low sub-bass pulse returns and JT rises in volume out of the mix of the ongoing sixteenth-note ostinato. Music now provides continuity as two clowns finally open the vault door. When one clown recalls the Joker's plan that he should kill his partner once he had performed his part of the heist ("The boss said I should take him out") the calculated ticking returns briefly. The gun that kills this clown again shoots relatively quietly. A highly stylized hollow and metallic swoosh links a brief shot of the Joker (still in clown mask) up in the main hall back to a reverse shot from inside the vault of the remaining clown opening the vault door. If this is a sound effect, the placement is unrealistic because the audience would not hear the vault door before the cut inside the vault. More likely, this is an effect that Wesson helped devise, one that resembles the sound of a large metallic door opening but that is used musically, as a percussive crescendo (like a timpani or cymbal rolls) to connect two discrete visual settings and facilitate the segue between them. The source and level of realism of the sound here is, then, less important than the conceptual congruity between what is happening at this moment (the vault door is being opened) and what is heard in the score (metallic door-like sound used as percussive linkage).

When the last clown standing has the sense to hold the Joker at gunpoint (although he also does not know his boss is standing before him, as evidenced by the use of third person address: "I'm bettin' the Joker told you to kill me as soon as we loaded the cash."), the musical texture recedes and mellows. The Anarchy motif is heard for the first time here, accompanied by low ambient rumblings and a busy but relatively quiet high metallic sound, akin to rain hitting a metal roof or brushes hitting metal pots. Even though the Joker is being threatened, the music helps give the impression that he remains calm and in control. Anarchy here supports the baffling continuation of the Joker's plan, which his opponent clearly does not foresee: a school bus crashing through the front door that hits and kills him.

The build-up to the bus crashing into the building is traced with another artificial sound evoking a machine or motor powering up (alongside an upward swoosh). Again, this sound effect cannot reasonably emanate from the school bus, which is firstly outside and therefore would not sound so close and which, secondly, would not be accelerating so briefly to gather enough speed to crash successfully through the doors. Once again, this is most likely a musically conceived sound effect devised by Wesson. A hollow click cuts the texture on a downbeat just before the bank manager says, "You think you're smart, huh?"

In the build-up to the revealing of the Joker's face, JT cross-fades at pitch to the top note of the Stranger motif (it helps that this entire segment is scored in D-minor). For a brief moment, only Stranger can be heard besides the Joker's spoken dialogue. His voice on the word "stranger" is eerily guttural and bass-heavy. As he rushes off immediately after, a loud metallic pang with an overlong bright long reverb tail traces his departure, the bank manager staring after him in shock. JT fades back in and so too the sub-bass pulse and sixteenth-note strings patterns.

When the departing bus pulls the trigger of the grenade the Joker has placed in the bank manager's mouth, an unsettling momentary silence (only an extremely quiet and fading ticking continues) makes the audience fear the grenade might explode. It comes as a relief to the audience, and so too the bank manager, when the grenade only emits a harmless green smoke.

LSI Extraction: Impact and Weight

This segments starts on the cut to a helicopter shot of Hong Kong at night, the camera circling around an office tower lit in eerie blue. Bruce Wayne is perched on a ledge near the roof, wearing a modified Batman suit. The ostinato described in the previous chapter accompanies this opening shot. Batflaps weightily punctuates and suggests a tempo in the veil-like strings texture that, although it is in itself rhythmically busy, lacks a clear demarcation of beat and forward movement. A medium high unpitched percussion pulse provides added rhythmic pace and links together the repeated hits of Batflaps. The Batman Theme furthermore announces the presence of Batman.

As the camera narrows in on Batman, the strings fade out first and then the rhythmic pulse almost immediately after. The strings ostinato has been used mainly to help smooth the transition into this sequence from the early establishing shots to the ensuing core action. Batflaps, which occupies mostly the lower end of the frequency spectrum, remains louder for longer, while the sound design now dominates the upper frequencies. Batman is readying some sort of gadget. The sounds that accompany the preparation are beautifully nuanced, comprising high melodic clicks and pings. A dial that seems to set a timer makes a prominent metallic ticking sound. The aforementioned low contrabass and cello ostinato enters underneath and the frequency of the low strings elegantly stays out of the way of the sound design. The strident feel in the music highlights the calculated nature of Batman's action, even if his plan is unclear as yet. It soon becomes apparent that Batman has readied some sort of rifle whose charging and firing introduces whines and hisses to the soundscape that sit comfortably above the low strings. As Batman fires his projectiles, which hit another building and apparently carry timed detonators, the gadget's sounds remain prominent in the mix, with music providing impetus and flow underneath. It may have been important to Nolan and his sound design team that these gadgets have a lively and prominent sound to render them more believable. Given that the scene is taking place at night, it is difficult to see the gadgets very clearly so sound design helps render their physicality. The continuing ostinato circumscribes the bi-chord harmony of BT, reminding the audience of Batman's presence when the camera focuses temporarily on Lau in his office.

When the power is cut in Lau's office, the two combined strings ostinati (low strings and upper texture combined) cut out and only Batflaps remains, stealthy and threatening. Lau's security detail is suddenly on high alert but clearly have no idea what is about literally to hit them or where the suspected intruder might be lurking. As the security guards scramble to make sense of the sudden power cut, Batflaps ebbs away and for a brief moment low ambient textures paint a disquieting low veil. This cross-fades into a dissonant brass crescendo on the cut back to Batman standing on the roof ledge, ready to jump. The brass grows extremely loud up until the moment Batman jumps, upon which loud and busy percussion sets in, accented with further brass stabs and swells. The contrast between the guards frantically rushing around looking for an intruder and Batman's measured and calm actions could not be starker. The music seems to want to leave no one in doubt that Batman is powerful and in charge and that his plan, whatever it may be, will succeed.

On the cut back to Lau, both strings ostinati are back, accented with Batflaps. This reiteration may seem less than inspired musically, but the identical repetition of musical ideas helps provide continuity amidst the sequence's fast pace. All rhythmic momentum in the soundtrack suddenly dissipates on the next cut to Batman in flight. Only the sound of his cape flapping in the wind can be heard for a few seconds.

This momentary near-silence makes Batman's landing and the ensuing fighting seem that much more impressive. This is a technique that is used more extensively during the truck chase (see below).

Another dissonant brass swell crescendos and peaks as Batman crashes through one of Lau's office windows. The glass shatters with a bright and crunchy splash that suggests a heavy object has hit a fragile surface. It is interesting to note that the breaking glass is so loud in the mix that it covers up the first downbeat of the percussion-driven cue that accompanies the fight that follows. The cue comprises heavy percussion and brass stabs, timed carefully to surround the many body impacts and fight sounds. Batman lands a punch that is markedly bass-heavy and sounds powerful as a result. In fact, in the mix, his punches are louder than the gunshots fired at him a few seconds later.

When Batman seemingly falls down in a hail of bullets, the music swells and then halts (cut to an ambulance arriving), but Batflaps sets in immediately, suggesting quite clearly that this segment is not yet over and dispelling any fear that Batman might be seriously hurt. Soon after, Batman attacks again and takes out Lau's last men standing. The music now is continuously frantic, mirroring Lau's panic at being dragged by his feet by Batman.

As several times elsewhere in the film, the police arrive too late to be helpful and they look on helplessly as Batman drags Lau towards the windows. The rigged charges explode outside and rip open the corner of Lau's office. The BT motif is stated but is re-harmonized to move from D-minor to D♭-Major, which prevents it from sounding too familiar or overly conclusive. After all, Batman's mission is not yet accomplished. Fast-paced percussion in triple meter continues as Batman sends out a blinking light beacon. The percussion now shifts into the upper frequencies, seemingly by use of filters and effects processors rather than different instrumentation. The rhythmic pulse has a synthetic quality about it and might in fact be wholly synthetic at this point. The brass crescendos on D until an airplane appears and picks up the blinking beacon to whisk Batman and Lau out of the LSI Building. The music here is the same as can be heard at the beginning of the closing credits and lends the moment a triumphant air. Music takes over the soundscape and all sound design disappears until the cross-fade to Gotham by daylight is completed and Gordon finds Lau on the police station's doorstep.

Truck Chase: A Less Redundant Soundscape

> Chris [Nolan] decided to play the scene with sound effects and no music for the most part, which is rare for a scene like this, so it's been a great opportunity for [...] me to look at the sequence, and say, "What tonalities and textures will do some of the work music would normally do? There's a lot of gunfire, so what kind of frequencies, pitches and sounds can we highlight in the gunfire? What kind of odd sounds can we throw in?" It's been a really fun scene to work on. A huge amount of recording was done for this sequence, from diesel trucks to a wide variety of weapons.[20]
>
> Richard King

The truck chase is an important scene in *TDK* in several ways. It takes place immediately after the halfway point of the film, exactly in the middle of its 150-minute running time. Thompson has conclusively described the mid-point of a Hollywood film as a moment of key significance for the filmic narrative.[21] The chase leads to a significant escalation of the stakes: the Joker finally gets arrested at the end of this action-laden sequence. The segment also features spectacular action, including the revelation of Batman's motorcycle, the Batpod, and vehicular destruction on a scale seldom seen on film. The flipping of an actual 18-wheeler truck was certainly unprecedented. Nolan's decision to rely on sound effects for this scene rather than music shows assured judgment in terms of balance and tone, giving this segment a serious and mature feel. By contrast, a chase at the beginning of *The Avengers* (2012, dir. Joss Whedon) features a tunnel chase that is very similar in setup but could not be more different in its excessive execution.

The truck chase segment starts when a convoy of police cars and two armored vehicles (one of them transporting Dent) drive through downtown Chicago, a helicopter noisily flying overheard. JT fades in and gradually supplants all other sounds. This provides a moment of calm that provides and effective contrast to the noisy action to come. One is reminded of observations David Sonnenschein has made on *Terminator 2: Judgment Day* (1991), explaining the challenge in action films to make "everything seem loud."[22] In order to retain a high level of sonic impact, the contrast between loud and soft, high and low, and harsh and mellow timbres can effectively be utilized. In *T2*, a compelling example is the iconic moment when the Terminator shoots his frozen T1000 opponent. Just before the shot is fired, the entire soundtrack goes silent, making the gunshot seem that much more impactful by

contrast.
 The same principle is applied at the start of the truck chase. Trouble starts when a loud truck horn blares and attracts the attention of an officer manning a roadblock. When the officer is shot by the Joker from within the driver's cabin, this is so shocking it requires no added musical marker such as Triumphant that was heard during the bank robbery and will return in later scenes. The use of Triumphant here would potentially disrupt the gradual build-up in tension (the Joker is after Dent) and might also lessen the impact of musical material later in the segment. When the police convoy reaches a burning fire engine that blocks their way, they decide to head to an underpass that leads in the same direction (Lower 5th, "Exit down, exit down."), which is exactly what the Joker wants them to do. JT rises as the convoy heads underground but then gradually fades out in volume. It begins to mesh with the sound of car engines, and sneaks out under the loud helicopter passing above. By the time a large garbage truck pulls up beside the first police cruiser, JT has exited and only sound design remains.
 The following minutes are sonically dense and frantic. A wonderfully rich array of sound effects brings to life the various vehicles caught up in the chase between the garbage truck (used to shove police cars out of the way), and an 18-wheeler truck (that the Joker and his goons ride on), police cars, and quite a number of civilian cars that get shoved out of the way. The number of potential casualties is staggering and the material damage done is severe. In the absence of music that might typically accompany this type of chase, the sound design here can be more fully realized and more fully fleshed out. The various vehicles have markedly different engine sounds. They approach, recede, and crash with a wide range of noises. Soon gunshots join the collection of sounds, rhythmically subdividing the soundscape, as do concrete pillars flying by in between the fast-moving vehicles.
 Amongst the chaos, Nolan finds subtle ways to escalate the action further, even with a humorous touch: when the Joker's semi-automatic weapon and his pump gun have both failed to penetrate the armored vehicle that carries Dent (the weapon's respective firing and bullet impact sound distinctly different), Dent seeks reassurance inside the vehicle from his guard, who promises the Joker is, "going to need something a lot bigger to get through this." As if on cue, the Joker pulls out a bazooka. This he fires twice at the police cruiser ahead of the armored vehicle, before a low thud draws his attention: Batman arrives on the scene with the Tumbler. The sound is certainly not motivated by anything that is happening on-screen or elsewhere in the diegesis at this point. It does, however, effectively cut through the busy soundscape

and plausibly prompts the Joker to turn his head.

The Tumbler is Nolan's version of the Batmobile. The vehicle seen in this segment is a composite of real car and miniature scale models but, crucially, not CGI. In the absence of music, and with fun shots temporarily suspended, the soundtrack is filled with the detailed and complex engine roars, whirrs, bleeps, and buzzes that comprise the sound of the Tumbler. Batman then stops the garbage truck cold in its tracks, taking out a major obstacle. Having been briefly distracted by Batman's arrival, the Joker now readies his bazooka for a third shot, this one aimed straight at the armored truck that carries Dent. The intercutting between the Joker aiming, the armored truck racing past behind concrete columns opposite, and the Tumbler in pursuit, is classic Hollywood continuity editing, albeit at a dizzying cutting speed.[23] The soundtrack is truly remarkable here in that the engine noises of the various vehicles cumulatively keep rising higher and higher, the rise ramped up more steeply when Batman engages a rocket engine to jump into the bazooka's path. The Joker fires and for a fraction of a second there is silence, making the impact on the Tumbler seem that much more destructive.

Everything grinds to a halt upon the huge explosion that catastrophically damages the Tumbler. Once again, the soundtrack benefits from brief silences to help amplify the impact of the sound effects that follow. Here, the Tumbler spins and flips and a group of homeless people look at the wall of flames approaching, in a few seconds' silence before the Tumbler explodes through a concrete barrier. Near-complete silence ensues, allowing for a cut to the interior of the Tumbler where alarms are going off. Batman works the computer system for reasons as yet unclear. Meanwhile, the Joker chases the armored truck back to street level, himself now driving the 18-wheeler truck. His frantic remarks ("I like this job, I like it.") provide welcome comic relief.

Back inside the Tumbler, Batman initiates an eject sequence that for the first time reveals the Batpod, a motorbike. The front wheels spinning faster and faster until the Batpod finally breaks free and emerges from the wreckage of the Tumbler, the board computer chimes, "Goodbye," before the score enters for the first time in minutes. There is nothing subtle about this music entry: a massive hit on low drums, BT and Batman ostinato in familiar fashion bludgeoning the moment as if to declare triumphantly that Batman is still standing and ready to take on the Joker once more. Bringing in music at this point raises tension even higher and introduces another affective plane that the chaotic soundscape in the preceding chase segment has not reached. From a narrative viewpoint, the music here also sounds mark-

Analysis of the Score as Part of the Soundscape 129

edly more controlled, strident, and assertive, mirroring qualities of Batman that sound design alone could not highlight as expressively. Whilst the music entry is therefore well motivated dramatically and narratively, the music exit potentially risks withdrawing dramatic tension when in fact it still needs to be maintained. Nolan and his team place the music-out point with good judgment: the music does not stop immediately on the cut away from the Batpod but instead carries on a little further, until rear mirrors are mysteriously ripped off civilians' cars, observed from inside one of the cars, and the Batpod's sonic identity is ramped up high enough to mask the music's exit. As a result, there is no obvious loss in overall soundtrack volume. The sounds of the Batpod and its impacts as it damages civilian cars are as loud and as widely spread in the frequency range (low engine, high glass impacts) as the music just prior.

The following passage once again contains no music and the sound design alone attenuates impacts and breakages (crashing of the police helicopter, Batpod racing through a shopping mall). When the Tumbler crashes through glass doors, an unusually low bang precedes the sound of glass splinters, adding to the sense of weight and heft in the sound. By use of the Shepard tone effect, the engine sounds of the Batpod keep on rising and rising.[24] Batman takes on the 18-wheeler truck, spanning a rope across the street to stop it (a strategy whose effectiveness the Joker's goons have proven on the police helicopter moments prior). When the 18-wheeler truck is stopped and flipped on its long axis, the sound design again dips to near silence for a second, from which low metallic groans rise (the heavy truck flipping) followed by a shattering impact. This moment is all the more effective because it is seemingly unmitigated and realistic. All sound effects here were post-synced: Nolan's special effects team had to carefully plan how to make the truck actually flip. They used hydraulic pistons underneath the chassis, which rendered the location sound unusable. The overall effect is nevertheless spectacular, wholly without the use of music.

The score only re-enters once the Joker stumbles out of the truck and confronts Batman. JT gradually grows out of the silence, even though the Joker is hardly in control at this moment. Low drum hits and Bartók pizzicato in the low strings accentuate the passage in even rhythmic intervals. The volume and pitch of JT rise higher and higher and cross-fade to Stranger when Batman crashes the Batpod rather than hitting (and killing) the Joker.

Interrogation Room: Back to Basics

> The scene starts between Gary Oldman [as James Gordon] and Heath with the lights out, and [director of photography] Wally Pfister literally just lit the scene with the desk lamp, the table lamp, and nothing else. And then when the lights come on, Batman is revealed, and the rest of the scene plays out with a massive overexposure. He overexposed like five stops, I want to say, and then printed it down to bring some of the color back in. But it's this incredibly intense overhead light, which let us move in any direction. We had a handheld camera and shot however we wanted, be very spontaneous.[25]

The interrogation room scene is a prolonged encounter between Batman and the Joker. The late Heath Ledger's outstanding performance shines brightly in this bare and stark environment. With no other distractions, the conflict between the two characters takes center stage. Nolan takes a *cinéma vérité*-style approach to the scene, relying on limited lighting, handheld camera, and few visual or sonic distractions. However, it is compelling that the soundtrack in the most intimate environment is more manipulated and layered than might meet the ear at first. At the start of the scene, the footage is markedly dark and the room tone reflects the Joker's measured voice. It is a beautiful moment of relative silence, with surrounding ambience barely audible in the background: hints of an air vent, noises from elsewhere in the building almost drown in the underlying white noise floor. As soon as Gordon leaves, bright overhead lights switch on accompanied by a high-pitched buzz of the fluorescent bulbs, in sonic parallel with the uncomfortable shift to brightness. The Joker does not flinch when the bright lights come on, but his eyes zip back and forth quizzically before Batman slams his head onto the desk from behind.[26] The impact of the Joker's head coincides with a loud statement of Batflaps, which compounds a sense of raw aggression and the force of impact also emphasizes Batman's overpowering presence in the room. The next hit on the Joker's right hand is accompanied by another statement of Batflaps, again, very loud. The echoing decay of the sound extends the sonic duration of each impact by several seconds. Even though there is nothing subtle about Batflaps in terms of relative volume and sonic heft, it may quite possibly go unnoticed by the average audience member. Because this musically conceived sonic logo doubles up as sound design and coincides with on-screen actions of body impacts, it is rendered less noticeable, functioning perhaps more at the subliminal level.

The high-pitched sound of the fluorescent bulbs continues. Even though the ensuing scene may appear to be unscored on first listening, low undulating ambient textures commence when the Joker starts talking to Batman. Of indistinct pitch, these meander in the lower frequency range and shroud the Joker's monologue in a spooky veil. The ambience is of a mellow and rounded timbre and effectively stays well out of the way of the spoken word. The upper frequencies in the Joker's speaking voice (plosives and sibilants) are attenuated by close microphone proximity, wall reflections of the cold concrete and glass surfaces in the room, and the suggested relative silence that encloses the two characters.

When the Joker tells Batman, "Don't talk like you're one of them. You're not. Even if you'd like to be," the Anarchy motif starts in a gentle, quiet, gong-like timbre and repeats at pitch seven times before moving up an octave and slowing to a halt. The Joker leans back and announces, "See, I'm not a monster. I'm just ahead of the curve." This prompts Batman to erupt in renewed anger, and Batflaps stomps out Anarchy, underpinning the loud metallic sound of the table and chairs being shoved about. The second impact, also doubled with Batflaps, is even louder, of the Joker being slammed against a tiled column. This second iteration of Batflaps decays and gives way to ambient silence not heard since Gordon left the room. This momentary respite gives rise to JT as the Joker explains that Batman has to play his "little game if you wanna save one of *them*." He reveals that he is not only holding Dent hostage but also Rachel. JT grows louder and louder and, tellingly, the impacts that follow are not accompanied by Batflaps: Batman has lost control of the situation, no longer has the upper hand, and his overt brutality no longer has the desired coercive effect. JT rises in pitch as the Joker explains where Dent and Rachel are and Batman must listen. As he storms out, the next music cue commences ("Wired").

Stylized Madness

The Joker manages to escape from jail by blowing up the MCU. Gordon realizes too late that he has been played. The Joker drives off in a convoy of police cruisers, presumably driven by his goons. The sound of sirens blaring meshes with the atmosphere of the moment (alarm and destruction all around) but quickly cross-fades to a low ambient drone that provides a welcome respite from the high-frequency sounds of the high-energy action just prior. The Joker sticks his head out of the cruiser's window and enjoys the breeze in his hair, shakes his head as if to shake off the pain and stress he has just escaped. This brief moment is heavily constructed but also eerily beautiful, accompanied only with low ambient rumbling in the soundtrack. The film here attains a lyrical or, as *New York Times* film critic Manohla Dargis has called it, operatic quality. She remarks,

> ...it is hard not to fall for a film that makes room for a shot of the Joker leaning out the window of a stolen police car and laughing into the wind, the city's colored lights gleaming behind him like jewels. He's just a clown in black velvet, but he's also some kind of masterpiece.[27]

Moments later, Dent wakes up in hospital, half his face covered in gauze, and discovers his lucky coin, which Batman has left on his nightstand. Subdued room ambience and Dent's unsteady breathing are the only sounds present. A high-pitched synthesizer sound playing two notes a perfect fifth apart in a glassy hollow timbre grows increasingly louder and intrusive, as if gnawing away at Dent's sanity. He groans when he almost touches the left side of his face and remembers that he is injured. As he then picks up his lucky coin, the horror of the previous night is coming back to him, flashback of Rachel holding the coin, his recollection of all that has happened. The antecedent phrase of the Harvey Dent Theme (HD) plays in high strings harmonics. As he turns the coin over, a low mellow drum hit pushes aside all other sounds except the high-pitched fifth, which now grows ever more prominent. The attenuation of upper mid-range frequencies makes this sound very uncomfortable to listen to, an area in the frequency spectrum that in high-volume mixing one would normally try to restrain quite carefully. In putting emphasis on this very area, the audience is made to feel uneasy and perhaps empathize with Dent as he goes mad with pain, sadness, and rage. The use of only the high-pitched synth in lieu of Dent's screaming and shouting (which is visible but not audible) makes this moment all the more poignant. The sudden cut to a news broadcast makes for a harsh contrast to something seemingly more trivial. Instead, this introduces into the next major set piece, the hospital bomb scare.

CONCLUSION

Amidst too many commercially driven films whose main draw is gratuitous spectacle (and that have put many scholars off taking recent mainstream Hollywood film music seriously), *The Dark Knight* is an outlier with an intelligent script, investible characters, stunning photography, and a carefully balanced composite soundtrack of sound design, music, and ambient music design in fluid interplay.

TDK stands apart from a relatively homogenized body of Hollywood films and film music therein that can so readily be observed today. Such sameness is often the result of fiscal pressures, risk-averse creative thinking, and commercial competition in the marketplace. Hans Zimmer stresses that those working on a Hollywood film set out with the greatest creative integrity and the best of intentions. Everyone wants to make the best film they possibly can, which, Zimmer admits, does not necessarily prevent a disappointing end product. To be sure, there are many Hollywood films where all the component parts have fortuitously aligned to produce a well-wrought film, but on these commercially driven projects, numerous factors influence aesthetic considerations and creative choices that are ultimately settled between filmmakers and executives rather than composers.[1]

TDK proves that where working conditions and creative process are altered, new possibilities arise. The deeply technical nature of filmmaking has always been an obstacle to directors who must rely on technology by necessity but may struggle to channel their ideas using that same technology as a tool. Christopher Nolan embraced and transcended cutting-edge technology to realize his vision. He guided his vast team with an assured hand, nevertheless allowing a constructive creative dialogue. He challenged his sound team to negotiate noisy IMAX cameras during shooting, pushed his special effects team to find a way to flip an 18-wheeler truck, and insisted that action sequences be created with minimal use of CGI.

Aware of the narrative and affective potential of music, he worked closely with the composers and sound design team, planning the score holistically as one storytelling tool among others and treating music as far more than a purchasable commodity. Zimmer, Howard, and Wesson embraced the opportunity to join the filmmaking process early on. Their creative process was enabled by improved fiscal and logistical conditions that nurtured an experimental, flexible, and open-ended workflow. The composers were invited, willing, and able to continue to develop and continually revise their respective musical contributions as the film took shape throughout post-production. With the typical barriers to a rewarding scoring process—lack of time and money—lowered, the composers were encouraged to explore a closer and more organic relationship with film. The placement of music in the film, the interplay of music and sound design and the use of ambient music design (a novel third strand, pushing the notion of what is music and what is sound design) were ingeniously handled, as has been shown.

Prevalent creative practice has shaped the nature of recent Hollywood film music. Conditions can require or render obsolete, help construct or destruct, starve or nourish original film music. *TDK* is evidence that where the detrimental impact of poor communication and financial pressures is lessened, compelling results can emerge. At first, Nolan alone may have felt inspired to turn the struggle of Batman and the Joker into far more than a comic book movie, but he worked with his co-writers, producers, visual and sound teams, including music, in a collaborative creative process that led to one of the most critically acclaimed, best-loved, and most commercially successful films (and film scores) of all time.

NOTES

Introduction

[1] Composer Jeff Rona points out that a former assistant of his once worked with Howard for five years but felt he never truly got to know his quiet boss.

[2] With over 1.7 million "likes" on his official Facebook page at the time of this writing. https://www.facebook.com/hanszimmer (13 August 2015). By contrast, James Newton Howard had just over 55,000 "likes."

[3] His Q&A at the Royal College of Music's Amaryllis Flemming Concert Hall in October 2013 attracted a capacity crowd, unprecedented for a composer visit that was closed to the public. In the days prior, the RCM box office was inundated with ticket requests from fans. At the 7th Krakow Film Music Festival in 2014, Zimmer was the only guest guarded by a personal bodyguard.

[4] See for example Erik Heine, *James Newton Howard's* Signs: *A Film Score Guide* (Lanham, MD.: Scarecrow Press, 2016).

Chapter 1

[1] The following overview of Zimmer's career is based on conversations held in person in August 2013 at his apartment in London, a masterclass held at the Royal College of Music on 30 October 2013, and an interview between Zimmer and Simon Greenaway (director of ASCAP London) on 27 September 2014 at the MOS in Kraków, Poland.

[2] Anon. "Ex-Partner Hits Zimmer With $10 Million Lawsuit." Text. *Billboard*, December 8, 2003 http://www.billboard.com/biz/articles/news/1474061/ex-partner-hits-zimmer-with-10-million-lawsuit (13 January 2015).

[3] The studio's resistance seems odd considering that, five years prior, Basil Poledouris had made extensive use of a Russian-style male choir in John

McTiernan's commercially successful *The Hunt for Red October* (1990) and delivered a score that was musically rather more daring than Zimmer's would turn out to be. David Sonnenschein undertakes a fascinating comparison of the two films in terms of their respective attitude toward the respective Cold War parties and the corresponding sound design. See Sonnenschein, D. *Sound Design: The Expressive Power of Music, Voice and Sound Effects in Cinema.* Studio City, CA: Michael Wiese Productions, 2001.

[4] Zimmer says, "There are very few films that I work on these days where I don't write the music first."

[5] Burlingame, Jon. "20 Billion-Dollar Composer: For Hans Zimmer, 'The Real Risk Is Playing It Safe.'" *Variety*. http://variety.com/2014/music/features/20-billion-dollar-composer-for-hans-zimmer-the-real-risk-is-playing-it-safe-1201173698/ (27 September 2014).

[6] Previn, A. *No Minor Chords: My Days in Hollywood.* New edition. London/New York: Bantam Books, 1993.

[7] The author has argued elsewhere that these changes have demanded new approaches to film music. Hexel, V. "Understanding Contextual Agents and Their Impact on Recent Hollywood Film Music Practice." Ph.D., Royal College of Music, 2014. http://ethos.bl.uk/OrderDetails.do?uin=uk.bl.ethos.606560 (23 January 2015). Bordwell highlights that the language of Hollywood films, too, has undergone remarkable changes over the years, in Bordwell, D. *The Way Hollywood Tells It: Story and Style in Modern Movies.* Berkeley/Los Angeles: University of California Press, 2006.

[8] Information about Remote Control Productions is collated from firsthand accounts from a number of colleagues who have worked with RCP; from stories shared by industry insiders at ASCAP and elsewhere in Los Angeles; and from reports by the author's former student Nathan Stornetta, who at the time of this writing worked for RCP.

[9] In 2013, Zimmer launched a second company, Bleeding Fingers Inc., in partnership with SONY/ATV, to provide stock music for U.S. television programs.

[10] Burlingame, Jon. "20 Billion-Dollar Composer: For Hans Zimmer, 'The Real Risk Is Playing It Safe.'" *Variety*. http://variety.com/2014/music/features/20-billion-dollar-composer-for-hans-zimmer-the-real-risk-is-playing-it-safe-1201173698/ (27 September 2014).

[11] Eshkeri during his keynote address on 6 November 2009 at the Film Music Conference at the University of Leeds, School of Music.

[12] Though not talking about this particular film, Rebecca Morellato, Senior Vice President of Film Music Production at Fox, explains that studios will rarely take "a $100m+ risk" with a relatively unknown composer.

[13] Given the somewhat limited nature of his involvement in *TDK* and the scope of this book, Howard's biography here is condensed. For a more detailed biographical overview, see Heine, *James Newton Howard's* Signs: *A Film Score Guide*.

[14] *Defiance* (2008, original score), *Michael Clayton* (2007, original score), *The Village* (2004, original score), *My Best Friend's Wedding* (1997, original

musical or comedy score), *One Fine Day* (1996, original song, for the song 'For the First Time'), *Junior* (1994, original song, for the song 'Look What Love Has Done'), *The Fugitive* (1993, original score), *The Prince of Tides* (1991, original score).

Chapter 2

[1] For an interesting visual history of Batman, see Matthew K. Manning and Matt Forbeck, *Batman: A Visual History* (London: Dorling Kindersley Ltd, 2014) and also Matthew K. Manning and Robert Greenberger, *The Batman Vault: A Museum-in-a-Book with Rare Collectibles from the Batcave*, Spi edition (Philadelphia, PA: Running Press, 2009).

[2] Roger Ebert, "The Man Who Laughs Movie Review (1928)," http://www.rogerebert.com/reviews/great-movie-the-man-who-laughs-1928 (13 August 2015).

[3] Manning and Forbeck. *Batman: A Visual History*, 44.

[4] For an amusing compilation of some of Robin's exclamations see http://www.bat-mania.co.uk/trivia/holyrobin.php (14 December 2014).

[5] Manning and Forbeck, *Batman A Visual History*, 182.

[6] Manning and Greenberger, *The Batman Vault*, 41.

[7] Will Brooker, *Hunting the Dark Knight: Twenty-First Century Batman* (London/New York: I. B. Tauris, 2012), x.

[8] Ibid., 1.

[9] His score for the prior analyzed in J. K. Halfyard, *Danny Elfman's Batman: A Film Score Guide* (Lanham, MD: Scarecrow Press, 2004).

[10] "Nolan Directing Batman Begins Sequel | Movie News | Empire," http://www.empireonline.com/news/story.asp?NID=19241&page=7 (2 July 2015).

[11] http://www.boxofficemojo.com/alltime/weekends/ (13 August 2015).

[12] http://www.boxofficemojo.com/movies/?id=darkknight.htm (12 August 2015).

[13] http://www.rottentomatoes.com/m/the_dark_knight/ (13 August 2015).

[14] http://www.imdb.com/title/tt0468569/ (13 August 2015).

[15] http://www.metacritic.com/movie/the-dark-knight (13 August 2015).

[16] Peter Bradshaw, "The Dark Knight," *Guardian*, July 25, 2008, sec. Film, http://www.theguardian.com/film/2008/jul/25/actionandadventure1 (13 August 2015).

[17] Roger Ebert, "The Dark Knight Movie Review & Film Summary (2008), http://www.rogerebert.com/reviews/the-dark-knight-2008 (13 August 2015).

[18] All Batman films to date have had the coveted PG-13 rating, which ensures the widest possible audience reach including, crucially, the lucrative quadrant of teenaged male viewers.

Marvel Comics film adaptations and franchises (selection):
X-Men: *X-Men* (2000), *X2: X-Men United* (2003), *X-Men: The Last Stand* (2006), *X-Men Origins: Wolverine* (2009), *X-Men: First Class* (2011), *The Wolverine* (2013), *X-Men: Days of Future Past* (2014), *X-Men Apocalypse* (2016); Spider-Man: *Marvel's Spider-Man* (2002), *Spider-Man 2* (2004), *Spider-Man 3* (2007), *The Amazing Spider-Man* (2012), *The Amazing Spider-Man 2* (2014); Thor: *Thor* (2011), *Thor: The Dark World* (2013), *Thor: Ragnarok* (2017); Iron Man: *Iron Man* (2008), *Iron Man 2* (2010), *Iron Man 3* (2013); Hulk: *Hulk* (2003), *The Incredible Hulk* (2008); The Avengers: *The Avengers* (2012), *Avengers: Age of Ultron* (2015); Captain America: *Captain America: The First Avenger* (2011), *Captain America: The Winter Soldier* (2014), *Captain America: Civil War* (2016); *Guardians of the Galaxy* (2014), *Ant-Man* (2015), *X-Men: Apocalypse* (2016); *Ant-Man* (2015).

DC Comics film adaptations (selection): Superman: *DC Comics' Superman* (1978), *Superman II* (1980), *Superman III* (1983), *Superman IV: The Quest for Peace* (1987), *Superman Returns* (2006), *Man of Steel* (2013); Batman: *Batman* (1989), *Batman Returns* (1992), *Batman Forever* (1995), *Batman & Robin* (1997), *Batman Begins* (2005), *The Dark Knight* (2008), *The Dark Knight Rises* (2012), *Batman v Superman: Dawn of Justice* (2015).

[19] Cooke devotes an entire volume to sequels in C. Jess-Cooke, *Film Sequels: Theory and Practice from Hollywood to Bollywood* (Edinburgh: Edinburgh University Press, 2009).

[20] "Movie Franchises—Box Office History—The Numbers," http://www.the-numbers.com/movies/franchises/ (1 April 2015).

[21] J. Wyatt, *High Concept: Movies and Marketing in Hollywood* (Austin: University of Texas Press, 1994), 104.

[22] Tom Hoover, *Keeping Score: Interviews with Today's Top Film, Television and Game Music Composers* (Boston: Course Technology, 2010), 15.

[23] Halfyard, *Danny Elfman's Batman: A Film Score Guide*.

[24] Gary Collinson, *Holy Franchise, Batman!: Bringing the Caped Crusader to the Screen* (London: Robert Hale Ltd, 2012).

[25] Ibid., 105.

[26] Neil Jeffries, "Empireonline Reviews | Reviews | Empire," *Empireonline.com*, accessed December 15, 2014, http://www.empireonline.com/reviews/reviewcomplete.asp?FID=131928.

[27] See also "Don't Be Afraid of the Dark Knight | Variety," http://variety.com/2008/film/news/don-t-be-afraid-of-the-dark-knight-1117988395/ (1 April 2015).

[28] Brooker, *Hunting the Dark Knight*, 17.

[29] R. Reynolds, *Super Heroes* (London: B.T. Batsford, 1992), 44.

[30] Brooker makes the compelling point that by the time *TDK* was being promoted – and on the back of the remarkable commercial success of *Batman Begins*, Nolan's name was attached to the film for the purpose of advertising and branding, arguably more so than to acknowledge his actual role as author. Will Brooker, *Hunting the Dark Knight*, 7.

[31] Ibid., 49.

[32] Compare the blatant product placement in *Skyfall* (2012) (Audi, Bollinger, Heinecken, Omega watches, and others) or *Jurassic World* (2015) (Starbucks, Mercedes, Ben & Jerry's, Samsung, Brookstone, and others).

[33] See "Prince's Batman Soundtrack Is Not the Embarrassment It's Reputed to Be · We're No. 1 · The A.V. Club," http://www.avclub.com/article/princes-ibatmani-soundtrack-is-not-the-embarrassme-86404 (2 April 2015).

[34] G. Boucher, "Christopher Nolan on 'Dark Knight' and Its Box-Office Billion: 'It's Mystifying to Me,'" *Los Angeles Times*, October 27, 2008, online edition, http://herocomplex.latimes.com/2008/10/27/christopher-nol/ (20 September 2014).

[35] B. Isaacs, *Toward a New Film Aesthetic* (New York/London: Continuum International Publishing Group Ltd., 2008), 8.

[36] Wyatt discusses product differentiaton in Hollywood films in Wyatt, *High Concept*, 99.

[37] "Behind-the-Scenes: Truck Flip Sequence in The Dark Knight—Cinemablography," http://www.cinemablography.org/blog/behind-the-scenes-truck-flip-sequence-inthe-dark-knight (2 April 2015).

[38] For a fascinating discussion of the cinematography of *TDK*, see "The ASC—American Cinematographer: Batman Looms Larger," http://www.theasc.com/ac_magazine/July2008/TheDarkKnight/page1.php (1 April 2015).

[39] Denby complains that some of the most interesting dialogue scenes are truncated in favor of gratuitously long action sequences: D. Denby, "PAST SHOCK 'The Dark Knight' and 'WALL-E.,'" *New Yorker*, July 21, 2008, http://www.newyorker.com/arts/critics/cinema/2008/07/21/080721crci_cinema_denby?currentPage=all (2 April 2015).

[40] Compare K. Thompson, *Storytelling in the New Hollywood: Understanding Classical Narrative Technique* (Cambridge, MA: Harvard University Press, 1999), 20.

[41] For a detailed overview on cohesion devices in Hollywood films, see D. Bordwell, *The Way Hollywood Tells It*, 41–43.

[42] Compare Wyatt, *High Concept*, 16.

[43] White et al. undertake a multi-angle philosophical and psychological dissection of Batman in M. D. White, R. Arp and W. Irwin, eds., *Batman and Philosophy: The Dark Knight of the Soul*, (Hoboken, NJ: John Wiley & Sons, 2008).

[44] M. Dargis, "Showdown in Gotham Town," *New York Times*, July 18, 2008, online edition. http://movies.nytimes.com/2008/07/18/movies/18knig.html?pagewanted=all (14 Setpember 2014).

[45] T. Docherty, "Introduction," in *Postmodernism: A Reader*, ed. T. Docherty, (Routledge, 1992), 1–31; quoted in Isaacs, *Toward a New Film Aesthetic*, 61.

[46] J. F. Lyotard, *The Postmodern Condition: A Report on Knowledge* (Minneapolis: University of Minnesota Press, 1984); quoted in Isaacs, *Toward a New Film Aesthetic*, 69.

[47] Applying Reynolds's generic list of features that define the superhero for reference: R. Reynolds, *Super Heroes* (London: B. T. Batsford, 1992), 16.

[48] T. McGowan, "The Exceptional Darkness of The Dark Knight," *Jump Cut: A Review of Contemporary Media*, Spring 2009.

[49] Reynolds, *Super Heroes*, 19, describes how Gotham is generally assumed to represent New York and that "Gotham" is in fact simply another name for it, randomly chosen from a phone book by Batman writer Bill Finger.

[50] However, key scenes, including the explosion that kills Rachel and the final stand-off with Two-Face, were shot on location at London's Battersea power station.

[51] S. Bunch, "MOVIES: Gotham City's War on Terror—Washington Times," July 18, 2008, http://www.washingtontimes.com/news/2008/jul/18/gotham-citys-war-on-terror/?page=all (1 April 2015).

[52] McGowan, "The Exceptional Darkness of The Dark Knight."

[53] Dana Stevens, "No Joke," *Slate*, July 17, 2008, http://www.slate.com/articles/arts/movies/2008/07/no_joke.html (2 April 2015).

[54] Brooker, *Hunting the Dark Knight*, 200–201.

[55] Ip points out that "the use of torture and coercion in *The Dark Knight* is uniformly ineffective." J. Ip, "The Dark Knight's War on Terrorism," SSRN Scholarly Paper (Rochester, NY: Social Science Research Network, September 1, 2011), 5.

[56] White, Arp and Irwin, *Batman and Philosophy*, 7–8.

[57] S. Treat, "How America Learned to Stop Worrying and Cynically ENJOY! The Post-9/11 Superhero Zeitgeist," *Communication and Critical/Cultural Studies* 6, no. 1 (2009): 103–9.

[58] Dargis, "Showdown in Gotham Town." (28 September 2014).

[59] G. Boucher, "Christopher Nolan on 'Dark Knight' and Its Box-office Billion: 'It's Mystifying to Me, '" *Los Angeles Times* (October 27, 2008), online edition, http://herocomplex.latimes.com/2008/10/27/christopher-nol/ (28 September 2012).

[60] McGowan, "The Exceptional Darkness of The Dark Knight."

[61] "The Dark Knight : The Joker Theme—YouTube," https://www.youtube.com/watch?v=ho8Nm1HyOAs (30 March 2015).

[62] D. Morgan, *Knowing the Score*, 12.

[63] http://www.raindance.org/site/picture/upload/image/general/movies/dark_knight,_the_production_notes.pdf, 8-11 (accessed 16 December 2014; site removed as of 2 April 2015).

[64] See Collinson, *Holy Franchise, Batman!*, 146. Also "In Conversation With Christopher Nolan," http://www.empireonline.com/interviews/interview.asp?IID=763 (2 April 2015).

[65] The resemblance is striking: https://www.youtube.com/watch?v=uUFklia47WM (15 December 2014]

[66] Stevens, "No Joke."

[67] Brooker, *Hunting the Dark Knight*, 17.

[68] Reynolds, *Super Heroes*, 24.

[69] On the "Curse of Batman" see http://www.theguardian.com/film/2008/nov/03/dark-knigh-stuntman

dark knight shooting (13 August 2015).

[70] http://edition.cnn.com/2008/SHOWBIZ/Movies/01/22/heath.ledger.dead/index.html?eref=yahoo (12 August 2015).
[71] http://www.nydailynews.com/news/jack-nicholson-warned-heath-ledger-joker-role-article-1.340786 (12 August 2015).
[72] "Empireonline Reviews | Reviews | Empire," *Empireonline.com*, http://www.empireonline.com/reviews/reviewcomplete.asp?FID=134520 (13 August 2015).
[73] Dargis, "Showdown in Gotham Town."
[74] Ebert, "The Dark Knight Movie Review & Film Summary (2008)."

Chapter 3

[1] "SoundWorks Collection—The Sound and Music of The Dark Knight Rises," http://soundworkscollection.com/videos/darkknightrises (30 March 2015).
[2] See also electronic composer Wendy Carlos on the effort involved in programming expressive performance parameters into early synthesizers in R. Lack, *Twenty Four Frames Under: Buried History of Film Music* (London: Quartet Books, 1997), 313–314. Carlos about her work on Disney's *TRON* and the use of synthesizers to supplant the symphony orchestra therein: R. Moog, "Wendy Carlos & Michael Fremer Reveal the Secrets Behind the Soundtrack of TRON," *Keyboard*, 1982.
[3] Each sampler offered 16-bit, Twenty-four-voice polyphonic, up to 32MB internal RAM and cost $4,500 in 2015 money. So-called voices in music technology terms refer to the number of individual sounds or notes a device can play back simultaneously. Twenty-four-voice polyphony means the device can play 24 notes at the same time.
[4] "Media Adventures," http://www.soundonsound.com/sos/oct02/articles/hanszimmer.asp (24 March 2015).
[5] If readers will pardon the pun, given the composer's and the author's German origin: *Arbeitsbeschaffungsmaßnahme* (ABM) was a popular German government subsidy scheme in the 1990s to create jobs in times of high unemployment rates.
[6] "Roger Sayer," http://www.templechurch.com/whos-who/roger-sayer/ (25 March 2015).
[7] Zimmer's 2002 studio setup outlined in "Media Adventures."
[8] On the author's most recent visit to Hans Zimmer's apartment in London on 10 September 2013.
[9] See also "Interview: Mark Wherry, Man Behind Hollywood's Digital Musical Instruments, Hans Zimmer Collaborator—Create Digital Music," http://createdigitalmusic.com/2012/10/interview-mark-wherry-man-behind-hollywoods-digital-musical-instruments-hans-zimmer-collaborator/ (31 March 2015).

[10] "ROLI—Products—The Seaboard," https://www.roli.com/seaboard/ (30 March 2015).

[11] "Hans Zimmer On Scoring Batman | Interviews," *Empireonline.com*, http://www.empireonline.com/interviews/interview.asp?IID=1532 (24 March 2015).

[12] "Media Adventures" (op. cit.).

[13] "The Dark Knight : The Joker Theme—YouTube."

[14] Jon Burlingame, "20 Billion-Dollar Composer: For Hans Zimmer, 'The Real Risk Is Playing It Safe,'" *Variety*, http://variety.com/2014/music/features/20-billion-dollar-composer-for-hans-zimmer-the-real-risk-is-playing-it-safe-1201173698/ (27 September 2015).

[15] "Dear Guitar Hero: Johnny Marr Talks Guitars, 'Inception' Soundtrack, Working with John Frusciante and More | Guitar World," http://www.guitarworld.com/dear-guitar-hero-johnny-marr-talks-guitars-inception-soundtrack-working-john-frusciante-and-more (1 April 2015).

[16] See http://www.imdb.com/name/nm0863415/ (7 June 2015).

[17] The author's former student Daniel Elms heard this anecdote first-hand and in turn shared it with me on 11 September 2013.

[18] During a talk at the Royal College of Music on 13 November 2013.

[19] Burlingame, "20 Billion-Dollar Composer."

[20] At a panel discussion on 28 September 2014 in Kino Kijów, Krakow, Poland.

[21] Composers frequently work closely with filmmakers from an early conceptual stage on art films, avant-garde films, and documentaries. It is the commercial nature of Hollywood filmmaking that has often precluded such early engagement and Zimmer's approach thus constitutes process innovation towards a more holistically collaborative creative process. Composer Philip Glass usefully contrasts his approach (get in early) to Godfrey Reggio's *Koyaanisqatsi* (1977) with the approach (get in late) routinely taken by composers in the "traditional filmmaking process." See Philip Glass, *Word Without Music* (New York: Liveright Publishing Company (a division of W. W. Norton & Company, Inc.), 2015), 323.

[22] "Interview: Mark Wherry, Man Behind Hollywood's Digital Musical Instruments, Hans Zimmer Collaborator—Create Digital Music."

[23] Patrick Russ at an NYU Conference: Music and the Moving Image, 2014.

[24] Klaus Badelt interviewed on 10 November 2011 by Skype.

[25] M. Schelle, *The Score: Interviews with Film Composers* (Beverly Hills, CA: Silman-James Press, 2000), 183.

[26] During a talk at the Royal College of Music on 13 November 2013.

[27] During the same talk on 13 November 2013.

[28] Howard also refused to be interviewed about *TDK* during the author's research for this book.

[29] Schelle, *The Score*, 177.

[30] Hans Zimmer On Scoring Batman in an interview with Owen Williams, http://www.empireonline.com/interviews/interview.asp?IID=1532 (4 Feburary 2015).

[31] "Interview: Hans Zimmer and James Newton Howard on The Dark Knight's Score | FirstShowing.net," http://www.firstshowing.net/2008/interview-hans-zimmer-and-james-newton-howard-on-the-dark-knights-score/ (31 March 2015).

[32] https://www.youtube.com/watch?v=a9PyX_uiiPA (13 January 2015).

[33] http://thefilmstage.com/news/james-newton-howard-passes-on-dark-knight-rises-cliff-martinez-scoring-winding-refns-only-god-forgives (13 January 2015).

[34] http://www.youtube.com/watch?v=pefwLO6cixo (31 March 2015).

[35] "James Newton Howard All Access 360—YouTube," https://www.youtube.com/watch?v=pefwLO6cixo (31 March 2015).

[36] "Spectrasonics News—James Newton Howard," https://www.spectrasonics.net/news/news-content.php?id=46/%255D (31 March 2015).

[37] "JNH Studios | Nonzero \ Architecture," http://nonzeroarch.com/create-capture/jnh-studios (31 March 2015). The same company designed and built Zimmer's RCP facilities in the same area of western Los Angeles.

[38] "Spectrasonics News—James Newton Howard."

[39] Schelle, *The Score*, 326.

[40] Ibid., 328.

[41] Ibid., 324–325.

[42] Ibid., 331.

[43] Ibid., 324. Heine (2016) has discussed the fleeting moments of melody and stratification in Howard's score for *Signs*.

[44] James Newton Howard in C. Reynolds and M. Brill, "On the Art and Craft of Film Music: A Conversation with James Newton Howard," *Hopkins Review* 3, no. 3 (2010), 331.

[45] "Spectrasonics News—James Newton Howard."

[46] Reynolds and Brill, "On the Art and Craft of Film Music," 338.

[47] "James Newton Howard All Access 360—YouTube."

[48] Reynolds and Brill, "On the Art and Craft of Film Music," 334–336.

Chapter 4

[1] The cue sheet is available to PRS members and online account holders at http://apps.prsformusic.com/wacs/Detail.aspx?node=ProductionDetails&title=dark+knight&year=2008&cue=A&ex=False&page=0&sdir=asc&scol=title&bro=&dfr=&dto=&tot=1&id=159677122&row=1 (7 April 2015).

[2] See "James Newton Howard Collection." http://www.usc.edu/libraries/finding_aids/records/finding_aid.php?fa=0075#adminInfo (7 April 2015).

[3] http://www.lornebalfe.com/listen/film/ "Gotham Towers" (30 July 2015).

[4] Wuertz's name is misspelled in the spotting notes and the orchestrator scores.

[5] The track can be heard at "JW Media Music—Music Search/Download—Search/Download" http://www.jwmediamusic.com/music/search.php?start=2140&library=Beatbox (7 April 2015).

[6] The piece can be heard at http://m.unippm.co.uk/en/Browse/Labels/CD%20Listing/CD%20Details/Track%20Details.aspx?cdId=1486&wId=136363 (7 April 2015).

[7] Photographs of the shoot can be found at "Pipes & Drums of the Chicago Police Department," http://pdcpd.org/batman.htm (7 April 2015).

[8] "The Dark Knight—Box Office Data, DVD and Blu-Ray Sales, Movie News, Cast and Crew Information—The Numbers," accessed April 10, 2015, http://www.the-numbers.com/movie/Dark-Knight-The#tab=summary; "Imdb Dark Knight," http://www.imdb.com/title/tt0468569/business?ref_=tt_dt_bus (10 April 2015).

[9] Described in A. Copland and V. Perlis, *Copland: 1900 Through 1942*, 2nd ed. (London: Faber and Faber, 1987), 299.

[10] The extent to which Zimmer's scores are produced towards a larger-than-life aesthetic becomes strikingly obvious at live performances of his music. At a concert-screening of *Gladiator* in the Tauron Arena in Kraków in August 2014, the large symphony orchestra, including a large number of percussionists, failed to deliver the highly polished and impactful sound one remembers from the recorded score.

[11] To paraphrase Zimmer at a scoring session in 2014, "more is more."

[12] "Hans Zimmer On Scoring Batman | Interviews." *Empireonline.com*, http://www.empireonline.com/interviews/interview.asp (17 December 2014).

[13] Hugh Hart "Review: Joker Plays the Wild Card in Dazzling Dark Knight." WIRED, July 16, 2008, http://www.wired.com/2008/07/joker-jousts-mi/ (3 August 2015).

[14] http://majorspoilers.com/2009/05/22/the-dark-knight-the-sound-of-anarchy/ (16 December 2014).

[15] Jesse Prinz, "The Aesthetics of Punk Rock," *Philosophy Compass* 9, no. 9 (2014): 583–593.

[16] See also Johan Kugelberg, *Punk: An Aesthetic* (New York: Rizzoli International Publications, 2012) and compare to the viral promotional campaign for *TDK* in which the Joker defaced a Gotham newspaper: http://www.whysoseriousredux.com/joker/thehahahatimes1.htm (17 April 2015).

[17] See Smith (2002), 86–87.

[18] When the author interviewed Ramin Djawadi, an RCP composer, via Skype on 3 August 2010, Djawadi noted that Zimmer had managed to give Batman a two-note theme in *Batman Begins* and now he had "brought it down

to one" note for the Joker. "Where do you go from here?" he marveled. Internet fan forums are filled with comments on the Joker Theme being a one-note theme.

[19] I am grateful to Prof. David Burnand for the "sonic slap in the face" analogy.

[20] From the *TDK* shooting script, http://www.joblo.com/scripts/The_Dark_Knight.pdf (16 April 2015). Words underlined as per the original.

[21] Compare D. Bordwell, "Intensified Continuity Visual Style in Contemporary American Film," *Film Quarterly* 55, no. 3 (2002): 16–28; D. Bordwell, *The Way Hollywood Tells It* and K. Thompson, *Storytelling in the New Hollywood*.

[22] This exact same riff can be heard in Harry Gregson-Williams's score for Tony Scott's *Unstoppable* (2010) in the cue "The Stanton Curve." In fact, the entire cue closely resembles Zimmer's bank robbery cue, including similar production and scoring techniques employed, the same sound palette, and even a statement of the Triumphant motif. Gregson-Williams was based at RCP when scoring *Unstoppable*.

[23] As specified in the orchestration. BPM tempo markings with fractions are fairly common in film music because synchronizing music to picture can require minute tempo adjustments to reach a solution with the most musically sensible hit points.

[24] G. Boucher, "Christopher Nolan Revisits His Favorite Scene in 'Dark Knight,'" *Los Angeles Times*, October 28, 2008, online edition, http://herocomplex.latimes.com/2008/10/28/christopher-n-1/ (20 August 2015).

[25] Ibid.

Chapter 5

[1] The author first presented this concept in a conference paper at the Music and the Moving Image Conference at New York University, Steinhardt School of Music, New York, NY, on 1 June 2014. An extended 90-minute talk explored the concept in more detail, drawing on findings collated during research for this book, at SoundTrack_Cologne 11, Cologne, Germany, on 22 November 2014.

[2] Chion suggests these questions, among others, as part of an audio-visual analysis in M. Chion, *Audio-Vision: Sound on Screen* (New York: Columbia University Press, 1994).

[3] "'The Dark Knight' (Pt.2)—Exclusive Interview with Sound Mixer Ed Novick | Designing Sound," http://designingsound.org/2008/07/the-dark-knight-pt-2-exclusive-interview-with-sound-mixer-ed-novick/ (28 January 2015).

[4] For example, the team at Skywalker Sound, responsible for the soundtrack of *TRON: Legacy* (2010, dir. J. Kosinski), explain in a sound panel how they had to re-record much of the dialogue between Sam Flynn (Garrett Hedlund) and Quorra (Olivia Wilde) due to a noisy shooting environment. http://soundworkscollection.com/videos/tronlegacysoundshow (10 August 2015). Start watching ca. 17 minutes in.

[5] Nolan describes the level of diegetic realism in *TDK* as "heightened reality" in G. Boucher, "Christopher Nolan on 'Dark Knight' and Its Box-Office Billion: 'It's Mystifying to Me,'" *Los Angeles Times*, October 27, 2008, online edition, http://herocomplex.latimes.com/2008/10/27/christopher-nol/ (23 June 2015).

[6] "The Sound and Music of The Dark Knight Rises—Hans Zimmer & Richard King - YouTube." https://www.youtube.com/watch?v=fvqwyKw-WOj4 (9 June 2015).

[7] "Quentin Tarantino, Chris Nolan & J.J. Abrams Save Film From Extinction," http://www.cinemablend.com/new/Quentin-Tarantino-Chris-Nolan-J-J-Abrams-Save-Film-From-Extinction-66537.html (8 June 2015).

[8] http://www.savefilm.org/ (8 June 2015).

[9] See a fascinating article about the filming of *TDK* at "The ASC—American Cinematographer: Batman Looms Larger," http://www.theasc.com/ac_magazine/July2008/TheDarkKnight/page1.php(23 June 2015).

[10] "Batman Rides Again: The Dark Knight | Mixonline," http://www.mixonline.com/news/films-tv/batman-rides-again-dark-knight/369207 (2 April 2015).

[11] Some directors, including John Carpenter, Clint Eastwood, and Tom Tykwer compose their own music.

[12] The novelty addressed here is the combination of music and sound design through creative collaboration and to an affective end. Chion notes that even some decades ago, Hollywood soundtracks in pursuit of spectacle had already begun exploring affective qualities in sound design (alone) for added effect. In M. Chion, *The Voice in Cinema* (New York: Columbia University Press, 1999), 54.

[13] "The Sound and Music of The Dark Knight Rises—Hans Zimmer & Richard King—YouTube."

[14] Ibid.

[15] http://designingsound.org/2008/08/the-dark-knight-pt-4-exclusive-interview-with-ambient-sound-designer-mel-wesson/ (24 January 2015).

[16] "Welcome to U&I Software," http://www.uisoftware.com/PAGES/uimain.html (11 June 2015).

[17] "Cycling '74: Makers of Max," https://cycling74.com (11 June 2015).

[18] "An Introduction to Metasynth—Tuts+ Music & Audio Tutorial," http://music.tutsplus.com/tutorials/an-introduction-to-metasynth--audio-2425 (11 June 2015).

[19] This and all the following Wesson quotes from his talk at the Royal College of Music on 13 November 2013. It is interesting to note that Wesson's

work on Howard's *Snow White and the Huntsman* (2012) and the recent *Hunger Games* films has gone un-credited.

[20] "Batman Rides Again: The Dark Knight | Mixonline."

[21] On the "mid-point" in Hollywood films see K. Thompson, *Storytelling in the New Hollywood*, 31.

[22] D. Sonnenschein, *Sound Design: The Expressive Power of Music, Voice and Sound Effects in Cinema* (Studio City, CA: Michael Wiese Productions, 2001), 128.

[23] Compare, for example, the climax of *Back to the Future* (1985) when Marty McFly races towards City Hall in the DeLorean.

[24] See https://www.youtube.com/watch?v=IlWKCRI1sBI (16 June 2015) for a discussion of the Shepard tone.

[25] G. Boucher, "Christopher Nolan Revisits His Favorite Scene in 'Dark Knight,'" *Los Angeles Times*, October 28, 2008, online edition, http://herocomplex.latimes.com/2008/10/28/christopher-n-1/ (22 June 2015).

[26] Reviewing this moment frame-by-frame reveals that Heath Ledger anticipates the head slam by a fraction of a second, squinting as if in pain and gearing up for being pushed from behind. This will almost certainly go unnoticed by the casual viewer.

[27] M. Dargis, "Showdown in Gotham Town" (op. cit.).

Conclusion

[1] A recent very public rant by director Josh Trank against 20th Century Fox Studios is a good example. He complained that a year prior to the release of his *Fantastic Four* (2015), he had cut a version of the film he feels the fans would have loved. Fox then allegedly had the film re-cut several times without Trank's involvement, resulting in a version he disapproves of (and that flopped spectacularly at the box office). http://www.hollywoodreporter.com/news/fantastic-four-blame-game-fox-814764 (17 August 2015).

APPENDIX I

SPOTTING NOTES

The following table lists all music cues in the order they appear in the film. Where applicable, the cue names have been taken from the full orchestrations (see below). For cues that were not recorded live, and therefore are not included in the orchestrations, cue names have been collated from unofficial online sources and corroborated against the actual film. Where no cue name is stated, the music entry is diegetic, for example, the string quartet in Wayne's restaurant. Composer initials next to the cue title indicate the composer responsible for each cue respectively. This was determined by reference to the orchestrations or by deduction from other context. Music entry ("MX IN") and music exit point ("MX OUT") were determined by ear. Since some entry and exit points are extremely subtle (and hard to hear despite the increased sonic clarity of the Blu-ray format used for screenings), timings given are approximate. The timings are stated in hours:minutes:seconds and based on relative time elapsed based on the regions-free 2-disc Blu-ray edition of *TDK*, released in December 2008 by Warner Home Video. The "duration" column indicated cue duration in minutes and seconds.

Cue Name:	Logo
Music In:	00:00:00
Visual:	CUT to Legendary Pictures Card
Music Out:	00:00:30
Visual:	CUT to LS of EXT office building
Duration:	30"
Description:	Ambient textures. Batflaps

Appendix I

Context: A blue tinge, dark tones, and foreboding soundscape set the tone for the film. This continues with a reveal of the DC Comics logo, followed by the Batman emblem flying toward the camera out of blue flames. It finally covers the whole frame before a CUT to a MLS of skyscrapers in Gotham.

Cue Name: Bank Robbery (1M1 Prologue)
Music In: 00:00:30
Visual: CUT to LS of EXT office building
Music Out: 00:06:01
Visual: Click of grenade latch
Duration: 5'31"
Description: JT, Triumphant, Stranger, Anarchy
Context: Establish the Joker, introduce the mob as a potential threat.

Cue Name: Find the Batman (1M2)
Music In: 00:06:07
Visual: CUT to MLS of school bus leaving bank
Music Out: 00:07:55
Visual: Scarecrow gets out of van
Duration: 1'48"
Description: BT strings, synth pattern, low strings ostinato
Context: Gotham is suffering from crime, needs a hero to help. Police officer Ramirez's mother is in hospital (dangling cause: She betrays Rachel and Dent because she needs the money offered to her).

Cue Name: Buyer Beware (1M3)
Music In: 00:08:05
Visual: Dogs barking
Music Out: 00:10:35
Visual: "I'm not wearing hockey pads."
Duration: 2'30"
Description: BT, rumblings, swells, brass stabs, heavy low percussion once shooting starts.

Context:	Batman returns and tells his imposters to cease and desist. This scene ties up a loose plot end from previous film (the Scarecrow is defeated).

Cue Name:	The New DA (1M5) [*sic*: 1m4 "Dirty Cash" omitted in the final film]
Music In:	00:13:14
Visual:	"I am, closely." (Harvey Dent on surveillance screen)
Music Out:	00:14:00
Visual:	CUT to INT of courtroom
Duration:	46"
Description:	Love Theme. Strings and piano, more acoustic sound.
Context:	Harvey Dent is introduced, Wayne's interest in Rachel highlighted, and Alfred advises Wayne not to push his limits.

Cue Name:	Hostile Witness (1M6)
Music In:	00:14:05
Visual:	"Where were you?"
Music Out:	00:15:38
Visual:	CUT to Rachel and Harvey walk & talk
Duration:	1'33"
Description:	HD
Context:	Dent's theme established and he is shown as a competent DA and tough guy who can handle an attack.

Cue Name:	Bank Warrants (1M7)
Music In:	00:16:51
Visual:	"I've put every known money launderer in Gotham behind bars…"
Music Out:	00:19:20
Visual:	CUT to INT restaurant
Duration:	2'29"
Description:	Regal, stately horns, then build, woodwinds, timpani during conversation between Gordon and Dent. The cue then continues on segue to the Wayne Enterprises boardroom where Lau and Fox are wrapping up a business meeting.

152   Appendix I

Context: Dent's relationship with Gordon is established. Dangling cause: Gordon has a special unit, many of whose members Dent investigated when he was in the Internal Affairs department. Later in the film, during the Joker's reign, it turns out that a number of Gordon's team are corrupt and helping the Joker. Second dangling cause: Gordon calls Dent 'White Knight' but Dent says "I heard they have another name for me down there at the precinct" (which Gordon doesn't confirm at this point, but it later turns out Dent's nickname is Harvey Two-Face). Elsewhere, Wayne requests an improved suit from Lucius Fox to protect him against dog bites.

Cue Name:	String quartet
Music In:	00:19:20
Visual:	String quartet in Wayne's restaurant
Music Out:	00:20:00
Visual:	CUT to later the same evening (four of them at the table)
Duration:	40"
Description:	Diegetic string quartet

Cue Name:	Who Appointed Batman? (2M9)
Music In:	00:20:35
Visual:	"All of us."
Music Out:	00:21:40
Visual:	CUT to INT kitchen (mob bosses meeting)
Duration:	1'05"
Description:	HD in high string harmonics. Very subtle.
Context:	Dent outlines his view on Batman and vigilanteism and makes the comparison between having a single guardian of law and order with the suspension of democracy and establishment of a single ruler in ancient Rome in times of threat. Rachel warns that such actions can lead to the likes of Julius Caeasar suspending democracy but then never to abdicate. [NB: Rachel knows that Wayne is Batman, Dent does not.] Dent concedes, "Okay, you either die a hero or live long enough to see yourself become the villain." This statement sets up the

end of the film when Batman takes the blame for killing several police officers to stops the truth about Dent / Two-Face from coming out in order to preserve public morale.

Cue Name:	Move the Money (2M10)
Music In:	00:22:00
Visual:	CUT to: Bank raids
Music Out:	00:23:08
Visual:	SEGUE on Joker's laugh and entrance
Duration:	1'08"
Description:	Low rumblings and patterns, understated tension.
Context:	Lau's plan is to move the mob's money to Hong Kong.

Cue Name:	Kill The Batman (2M11)
Music In:	00:23:08
Visual:	Joker laughs and enters the room
Music Out:	00:26:20
Visual:	CUT to EXT LS of Gotham by night
Duration:	3'12"
Description:	JT, Music continues as low ambient rumbles once JT recedes while Joker speaks. Ambient music continues very quietly.
Context:	The Joker gets involved, threatens Lau, sides with the Mob against Batman. This scene highlights the Joker's unpredictable and murderous ways. Gamble threatens Joker.

Cue Name:	Trip To Hong Kong (2M13)
Music In:	00:28:40
Visual:	"Can you think of an alibi?" then CUT to EXT of ballet
Music Out:	00:29:38
Visual:	CUT to INT Gamble's place
Duration:	58"
Description:	Very different flavor to the other cues. More colorful, more musical.
Context:	Wayne travels to Hong Kong to retrieve Lau.

Cue Name:	Put A Smile On That Face [NB: the orchestrator's score, this cue is labelled 2M14—15 but starts in bar 53. This first half does not use live orchestra. The second half does but this accompanies the meeting between Fox and Lau.]
Music In:	00:29:38
Visual:	CUT to INT Gamble's place
Music Out:	00:31:44
Visual:	"Make it fast."
Duration:	2'06"
Description:	On cut to Gamble hitting pool balls, Batflaps, spooky low ambience, JT layered in, but very low in the mix, ticking ... tension, then massive hits when Joker turns out to be alive (Triumphant motif), pulsing.
Context:	The Joker kills Gamble, having been challenged by him during the mob briefing.

Cue Name:	Fox and Lau Meet (bar 56 onwards in the orchestrator's score of "Put A Smile On That Face" (2M14–15)
Music In:	00:31:44
Visual:	CUT to EXT Hong Kong by day
Music Out:	00:33:30
Visual:	Lucius exits the office tower lobby
Duration:	1'46"
Description:	Strings ostinato, brass, low percussion, then continuity pattern, low undulating brass lines, and ambience.

Cue Name:	Background Source Music
Music In:	00:33:35
Visual:	Lucius meets Wayne in public place
Music Out:	00:34:00
Visual:	CUT to EXT Hong Kong by night
Duration:	25"
Description:	Diegetic music through PA system
Context:	Mobile phone ringing during lunch only fulfils function of explaining that Fox has two phones = need not pick up his phone from the security desk.

Cue Name:	LSI Extraction (2M16)
Music In:	00:34:00
Visual:	CUT to EXT Hong Kong by night
Music Out:	00:37:50
Visual:	Segue to Lau being discovered unconscious outside the police station
Duration:	3' 50"
Description:	BT, Batflaps, ambience, brass swells, then low ostinato

Cue Name:	Mobsters Taken to Justice (2M17)
Music In:	00:39:30
Visual:	After Gordon says "Lau stays"
Music Out:	00:40:15
Visual:	CUT to INT of courtroom, charges are being read.
Duration:	45"
Description:	HD variation with brass and ostinato
Context:	Just after the cue, Joker's calling card in judge's folder = threat = dangling cause.

Cue Name:	Are You Up to It? (2M18)
Music In:	00:41:20
Visual:	"The public likes you"
Music Out:	00:42:10
Visual:	CUT to INT of ballroom
Duration:	50"
Description:	HD in high harmonics and synth, massive shock when the Batman imposter's corpse hits window
Context:	The mayor explains that, for the time being, Dent is the only one upholding justice and that the mobsters will be in jail only for as long as no negative press, any dirt comes up about him. This conversation sets up why Batman must take blame for police officers' deaths later and Dent's transformation to Two-Face must not be known by the public.

Cue Name:	String quartet
Music In:	00:43:40
Visual:	CUT to reception at Wayne's penthouse
Music Out:	00:44:00
Visual:	Stops when helicopter arrives

Duration: 20"
Description: Diegetic string quartet at reception

Cue Name: A Hero Without a Face (3M20–21)
Music In: 00:45:05
Visual: Wayne's speech
Music Out: 00:46:22
Visual: CUT to Gordon
Duration: 1'17"
Description: HD regal brass, mellow, segues into conversation with Rachel
Context: Wayne tells Rachel Gotham needs a "hero with a face."—Dangling cause: when Dent literally loses half his face in the fire later and then consequently turns evil.

Cue Name: Joker Crashes Party (3M22)
Music In: 00:46:40
Visual: CUT to Gordon arriving at the Commissioner's office
Music Out: 00:49:10
Visual: Joker arrives: "Good evening, ladies and gentlemen."
Duration: 2'30"
Description: Pulsing, meandering. Intercuts between Rachel/Dent and commissioner/judge—builds up to judge's and commissioner's death and Rachel answering to Dent's proposal. Triumphant motif as Joker arrives.
Context: Judge and commissioner are killed. Gordon thinks of the commissioner's glass as being source of his DNA on the calling card that has been found (see above) too late to stop him from drinking poison. Dent proposes to Rachel and she does not answer (dangling cause).

Cue Name: Panic Room (3M23)
Music In: 00:49:40
Visual: Wayne preps to intervene
Music Out: 00:50:10
Visual: "You gotta be kidding."
Duration: 30"
Description: Similar to Hong Kong segment

Context: Wayne comes close to revealing his hidden lair when he reveals a hidden door in front of a couple kissing in the hallway. The girl comments, "You've got a panic room," indicating she has not caught on.

Cue Name: Then You're Gonna Love Me (3M24–25)
Music In: 00:50:20
Visual: Rachel steps in
Music Out: 00:53:20
Visual: CUT to jail cells
Duration: 3'
Description: Rising JT, timbral shifts
Context: First face-to-face encounter between Batman and the Joker. Batman saves Rachel.

Cue Name: Lau, Watch the World Burn (3M26–27)
Music In: 00:54:00
Visual: Dent arrives to interview Lau
Music Out: 00:56:15
Visual: Batman takes fingerprints
Duration: 2' 15"
Description: HD, low profile tension, then shift into JT on CU of Joker's face after Alfred delivers his line.
Context: Gordon has picked up an intact bullet that sat atop the newspaper announcing the mayor as the next target. Alfred tells the story of the bandit who did not value precious stones and with this analogy tries to put the Joker's madness in context.

Cue Name: Loud Enough (3M28A)
Music In: 00:56:15
Visual: Segue to Wayne's layer
Music Out: 00:59:28
Visual: CUT to helicopter shot of street parade
Duration: 3' 14"
Description: Batflaps
Context: Batman fires bullets into blocks of concrete to reassemble a fingerprint. The whole process is forensically ridiculous.

Cue Name: Balmoral
Music In: 00:59:28
Visual: CUT to helicopter shot of street parade
Music Out: 00:59:39
Visual: CUT back to Wayne's lair
Duration: 14"
Description: Diegetic source cue
Context: Police band marching in Chicago streets

Cue Name: Loud Enough (3M28B)
Music In: 00:59:39
Visual: CUT back to Wayne's lair
Music Out: 01:00:00
Visual: CUT to CU of parade
Duration: 31"
Description: BT. Drone, then brass, Batflaps as Wayne ascends with the elevator (on motorcycle)

Cue Name: Balmoral
Music In: 01:00:10
Visual: CUT to CU of parade
Music Out: 01:00:49
Visual: CUT to INT Wayne walking down corridor
Duration: 39"
Description: Diegetic source cue

Cue Name: Kitchen Timer (3M29)
Music In: 01:01:17
Visual: Camera sweeps past police officers in CU
Music Out: 01:02:15
Visual: Shooting at bandstand
Duration: 58"
Description: Similar to bank heist: rising JT, big hits on gun shots. Triumphant on shots fired at bandstand.
Context: The Joker's goons have taken the police officers' uniforms. It is perhaps rather implausible that the fingerprints Wayne has discovered lead him to this apartment that just so happens to oversee the parade route.

Cue Name:	Speech Ambush (3M30)
Music In:	01:02:28
Visual:	CUT to CU of Gordon down
Music Out:	01:02:40
Visual:	CUT to Dent walking
Duration:	12"

Cue Name:	Dent to Van (3M32) [sic]
Music In:	01:02:40
Visual:	CUT to Dent walking
Music Out:	01:03:19
Visual:	Dent drives off in ambulance
Duration:	39"
Description:	At first high strings (adagio), then undulating synth and brass as Dent gets into ambulance, string glissando, brass clusters, blends with diegetic sirens.
Context:	Dent takes law-enforcement into his own hands in questioning the injured criminal who is wearing a nametag that reads "Rachel Dent." This means she is likely to be the next victim.

Cue Name:	Gordon is Dead (3M31)
Music In:	01:03:19
Visual:	CUT to Gordon's apt
Music Out:	01:04:00
Visual:	CUT to nightclub
Duration:	41"
Description:	Strings, mournful cascading suspensions. Mourning motif.
Context:	Gordon's wife blames Batman ("You brought this craziness on us!"). Her son looks up at Batman, lurking in the shadows.

Cue Name:	Nightclub
Music In:	01:04:00
Visual:	CUT to INT nightclub.
Music Out:	01:04:38
Visual:	CUT to INT Rachel's office in police station
Duration:	38"

160　　　　　　　　　　Appendix I

Description:　Loud diegetic source music
Context:　Batman seeks out Maroni.

Cue Name:　I Don't Know Anything (4m37–38)
Music In:　01:04:38
Visual:　CUT to INT Rachel's office in police station
Music Out:　01:08:25
Visual:　CUT to INT Wayne's apartment
Duration:　3'47"
Description:　Ambience very subtly sneaks in as Dent tries to convince Rachel to seek safety. Twisted brass as Dent interrogation gets increasingly tense.
Context:　Dent ask Rachel to hide in Wayne's apartment. ("The Joker's named you next.") Dent then interrogates the fake police officer. The intercutting between Dent and his prisoner with Batman and Maroni is an interesting stylistic device. Batman breaks Maroni's leg to find out where the Joker is, overstepping a boundary. Maroni explains that the Joker has no rules and that the only way to get him to show himself is for Batman to reveal his true identity.—Stopping Dent from nearly killing his prisoner ("His name is Schiff. What do you expect to learn from him?"), Batman warns Dent that he must not be seen to be a vigilante himself. ("If anyone saw this, everything you have achieved would come undone.") This perpetuates the notion that Two-Face's identity cannot be revealed later. Batman instructs Dent to hold a press conference ("Gotham is in your hands now.") suggesting that he is giving up the cape.

Cue Name:　Blood On My Hands / The Outcast (4M39)
Music In:　01:08:25
Visual:　CUT to INT Wayne's apartment
Music Out:　01:10:40
Visual:　As Alfred and Wayne walk through the bare lair
Duration:　2'15"
Description:　Strings, open chords, mellow, markedly more acoustic oboe and flute, then less and less music.

Context:	Rachel to Wayne: "If you turn yourself in, they're not going to let us be together." Wayne and Alfred destroy evidence of Batman "He can be the outcast, he can make the choice that no one else can make; the right choice." Alfred tells Wayne to endure, to stop being Batman, even though people will hate him for it.

Cue Name:	I Am the Batman (4M40)
Music In:	01:10:49
Visual:	At Dent's press conference
Music Out:	01:14:30
Visual:	CUT to EXT police convoy
Duration:	3'41"
Description:	HD. Low strings, brass, piano come in when Rachel and Alfred talk. End on low drone tonic on CUT. As Rachel tries to convince Dent to stop pretending he is Batman: Love Theme. He explains this is his one chance to lure out the Joker.
Context:	Dent: "The night is darkest just before the dawn—I promise you, the dawn is coming." He is indirectly speaking to whoever Batman is, encouraging him to continue. By turning himself in, he frees Wayne to continue his work. Alfred: "Perhaps both Bruce and Mr. Dent believed Batman [is] something more than a hero ..."—Terse cello as Rachel pleads with Dent to stop the acting. 1:14:19 coin revealed to have two identical sides. This undermines everything virtuous Dent stands for. Rachel to Dent (who is being driven off in an armored police truck): "You make your own luck."

HALFWAY POINT

Cue Name:	Truck Convoy (4M41)
Music In:	01:14:35
Visual:	MLS of helicopter and police convoy
Music Out:	01:15:28
Visual:	On first impact
Duration:	53"
Description:	JT, rising and rising.

Context: Quite subtle and low-profile music entry of mostly JT and some surrounding atmosphere.

Cue Name: Pod Deploys (4m42)
Music In: 01:19:06
Visual: Batpod revealed
Music Out: 01:19:37
Visual: CU of Batpod, camera chasing
Duration: 31"
Description: BT, heavy percussion, synth, rhythmic pattern

Cue Name: Batman Down (4M42b)
Music In: 01:21:51
Visual: MLS of Joker getting out of wrecked truck
Music Out: 01:22:45
Visual: Joker held at gunpoint by Gordon
Duration: 54"
Description: Rising JT, permutation of Stranger.
Context: Batman won't kill the Joker. But Gordon is alive and arrests the Joker.

Cue Name: Gotcha (4M43)
Music In: 01:22:50
Visual: Joker held at gunpoint by Gordon
Music Out: 01:23:24
Visual: CUT to jail, Gordon back at work
Duration: 34"
Description: Thuds, then HD in low strings.
Context: Dent gives a brief brief press statement: "I expected Batman to do the right thing: saving my ass!"—As Dent then drives off, he announces he his heading to see Rachel. ("I gotta date with a pretty upset girlfriend.") CUT to detective Ramirez in CU, with an odd, foreboding look on her face. This plants the notion that she has betrayed Dent.

Cue Name: Gordon Returns Home (4M44)
Music In: 01:24:38
Visual: CUT to Gordon's wife opening the door

Music Out: 01:25:33
Visual: CUT back to jail.
Duration: 55"
Description: Music very low in the mix
Context: Gordon returns home and his son asks him, "Did Batman save you, daddy?" Then phone rings: Harvey Dent never made it home.

Cue Name: Interrogation
Music In: 01:27:18
Visual: Lights on
Music Out: 01:28:18
Visual: Interrogation begins
Duration: 1'
Description: Batflaps, big drum thuds on each hit! Then ambience, very quiet in the mix. Anarchy
Context: Batman effectively takes interrogation into his own hands and the police do not intervene despite his brutal methods.

Cue Name: You Complete Me (4M45)
Music In: 01:28:18
Visual: Interrogation begins
Music Out: 01:30:36
Visual: Joker hits the floor
Duration: 2'18"
Description: Anarchy. Timbral shifts. Suddenly loud Batflaps as Batman interrupts Joker when he reveals that he has abducted Rachel too. JT, rising, growing increasingly intense.
Context: Joker to Batman: "Tonight you're gonna break your one rule." The Joker, harbinger of chaos and anarchy and Batman, the vigilante tied by his self-imposed rules and morals, clash philosophically. It is only after "You're gonna have to play my little game," that Batman realizes Joker has abducted Rachel too. As Batman then loses control, the Joker reminds him, "You have nothing, nothing to threaten me with." The Joker gives Batman a choice whom to save. The terms of the game presuppose that the police (who will try to save

the other one) will fail. This incompetence of law enforcement is already indicated when they rely on Batman to conduct the Joker's interrogation to get results!

Cue Name:	Wired (4M46)
Music In:	01:30:36
Visual:	Joker hits the floor
Music Out:	01:37:00
Visual:	CUT to Alfred reading letter
Duration:	6'24"
Description:	Big tutti, low percussion, heavy brass, strings and percussion ostinato. Continuity and tension music that connects Dent, Rachel, the Joker tricking the cop to attack him (at which point JT is laid over the continuity cue). Loud build when police station explodes. In the aftermath, JT again.
Context:	Rachel and Dent are tied up in two different locations, wired to oil drums rigged with explosives. Dent topples over, falls into a puddle of spilled oil, which will soon ignite, burn, and disfigure his face. As the Joker aggravates a police officer, glass splinters behind him foreshadow that he will win the ensuing fight. ("I just want my phone call.") The phone call the Joker places blows up the police station. Rachel dies in the first explosion: The Joker has told Batman the correct locations but swapped who is where. As a result, Batman inadvertently saves Dent. The Joker abducts Lau from the destroyed police station. Beautiful, almost poetic shots of the Joker enjoying the breeze in the wind as he drives off in a police cruiser. Poetic shots of fire fighters in the smoldering ruins are a striking visual allusion to 9/11.

Cue Name:	Aftermath (4M47)
Music In:	01:37:00
Visual:	CUT to Alfred reading letter
Music Out:	01:39:19
Visual:	"We burned the forest down."
Duration:	2'19"
Description:	Dark ambient drone, sparse strings, cello mournful,

	piano. Mourning motif. This cue provides a soothing and contemplative contrast to the action-laden section that preceded it. Ends on a dominant chord (V), creating a sense of withheld resolution.
Context:	Rachel's letter is read out in voice-over. She chose to marry Harvey. Wayne, who has not seen the letter, says to Alfred: "I was meant to inspire good, not madness," and, "She was going to wait for me, Alfred." Alfred chooses not to reveal what Rachel has written in her letter. This sets up his and Wayne's falling out in the *The Dark Knight Rises*. When Alfred tells Wayne how he caught the aforementioned bandit, who was hiding in a forest in Burma: "We burned the forest down." = A disproportionate and overwhelming response where the means are not justified by the end. This dialogue raises the question at what cost one should pursue justice.

Cue Name:	Harvey Two-Face (5M48–49)
Music In:	01:39:20
Visual:	Dent discovers his coin
Music Out:	01:41:50
Visual:	Gordon leaves Dent's room
Duration:	2' 30"
Description:	High tone that gets increasingly louder as Dent's grief turns to madness. Then HD on piano, subtle strings doubling, dark undulating terror in low brass. Big sluggish build on Dent's disfigured face.
Context:	It is important to show Dent as giving in to his grief, in a mad frenzy, to help explain how the Joker can tip him over the edge and turn vengeful. Also, in his frenzy, he rips off the gauze covering his facial injury and physically turns into Two-Face. Gordon acknowledges in conversation that Dent is refusing skin grafts or painkillers. Asked by Dent, screaming, "say my name!" Gordon responds: "Two-Face, Harvey Two-Face," upon which Dent's new face is revealed to Gordon, first off-camera, his reaction is one of shock, then visible to the audience.

Cue Name:	This is My City (5M50)
Music In:	01:42:10
Visual:	CUT to limousine arriving at harbor
Music Out:	01:44:08
Visual:	Joker places phone call
Duration:	1' 58"
Description:	Clicking semiquavers, then low-end strings and heavy impacts, intercut with Wayne Enterprises employee on TV threatening to reveal Batman's true identity.
Context:	Joker burns Lau on top of his share of the mafia cash: "It's not about money; it's about sending a message. Everything burns."

Cue Name:	Hospital Bomb Scare Pt.1 (5M51–52)
Music In:	01:44:08
Visual:	Joker places phone call
Music Out:	01:47:37
Visual:	Joker visiting Dent
Duration:	3' 28"
Description:	Synth pulsing as the Joker calls in to the TV station: Announces if Coleman Reese is not dead within the hour he will, "blow up a hospital." There is a percussive element in the ensuing cue during the hospital evacuation that is strikingly similar to Batflaps. Triumphant when Joker shoots police officer.
Context:	Joker wants Coleman Reese killed so he cannot reveal the true identify of Batman. Wayne intervenes and saves Reese's life.

Cue Name:	Hospital Bomb Scare Pt.2 (6M52b) [*sic*]
Music In:	01:47:37
Visual:	Joker visiting Dent
Music Out:	01:51:27
Visual:	On car crash
Duration:	3' 50"
Description:	Triumphant. As Joker calms Two-Face down. Musically, same approach as during Bank Robbery: On "introduce a little Anarchy," gongs are back (Anarchy motif). Wayne drives his Lamborghini in the way of a

Spotting

	pick-up truck that is to ram the police car transporting Reese. Anarchy back as Joker talks to Dent: "Introduce a little anarchy."
Context:	Wayne saves Reese whilst the Joker colludes with Dent/Two-Face.

Cue Name:	Explosion Aftermath [cue number not known]
Music In:	01:53:00
Visual:	CUT to Gordon reacting to the sound of the explosion: "That's Gotham General."
Music Out:	01:55:00
Visual:	Segue into Wuertz at bar
Duration:	2'
Description:	Stranger: Loud basses downward step, then very subtle low ambience, eerie tension, gradually, after TV announcement: "The bridge and tunnel crowd is in for a surprise."—Basses and cellos continuity on CUT to sniffer dog on bridge, harmonized (pedal moves to bVI). The music very quiet as Two-Face arrives ... high string tones, falling gliss. Close-scoring as Two-Face speaks.
Context:	Gordon instructs his team not to tell anyone that Dent is missing. ("If anybody asks: we got him out!") This later enables him to lie about Dent's fate. The Joker makes non-descript threat against city via TV news: "Everybody get out!" But he announces that bridges and tunnels are out of bounds and creates mass panic. A supposed break-in at Wayne Enterprises' R&D unit reveals Batman's new sonar system.

Cue Name:	Dent Kills Wertz [*sic*] (cue number not known)
Music In:	01:55:00
Visual:	Segue into Wuertz at bar
Music Out:	01:55:46
Visual:	On gunshot and CUT to Wayne's R&D unit
Duration:	46"
Description:	HD twisted and mangled
Context:	Dent kills Wuertz

168   Appendix I

Cue Name:	Sonar System (cue number not known)
Music In:	01:55:46
Visual:	On gunshot and CUT to Wayne's R&D unit
Music Out:	01:57:52
Visual:	CUT to EXT Falcone gets in his car
Duration:	2'06"
Description:	Synth pulse, forward propulsion, turns into familiar Batman motifs. Then semitone down on CUT to LS of bridges. Gordon is discussing situation (incl. Dent's disappearance) with the mayor. When mayor asks, "How long can you keep this quiet?" Percussive synth gets louder, tension rising, no answer.
Context:	Fox objects to the sonar system on ethical grounds. At what cost to civil liberty should one spy on the city's population? Fox gives an ultimatum: "I will help you this one time. But as long as this machine is a Wayne Enterprises, I won't be." Wayne tells him to type his name into the system when he is done. Gordon, meanwhile, discusses with the mayor the evacuation of prisoners by use of one of the commuter ferries.

Cue Name:	Unlucky Driver [cue number not known]
Music In:	01:57:52
Visual:	CUT to EXT Maroni gets in his car
Music Out:	01:59:13
Visual:	On gunshot (Two-Face shoots the driver)
Duration:	1'21"
Description:	Medium-low strings ostinato throughout conversation. Twisted version of antecedent of HD (intonation off, etc.). On the crash post gunshot once again no music.
Context:	Maroni blames Detective Ramirez for Rachel's death. Two-Face kills Maroni.

Cue Name:	The Boats (6M55)
Music In:	01:59:17
Visual:	As Maroni's car flips and comes to rest
Music Out:	02:03:50
Visual:	CUT to EXT Pruitt Building
Duration:	4'33"
Description:	Basses and cellos semitone undulation, big percussion

	hits, call and response, octaves; ambience, very quiet at first, 1:55:38 when one of the ferries' captains hears about the rigged charges below deck, a low thud accents the revelation. At 1:56:00, as Joker speaks, pulsing starts, BT brass and strings as Batman seeks out Joker.
Context:	The Joker explains he has given each ferry a remote to blow up the other boat. Through triangulation, Batman has found the Joker's location in the Pruitt Building. Dent uses Ramirez to lure Gordon's family into a trap. He then knocks her unconscious. Batman liaises with police over strategy how to take out the Joker. Dilemma: Will the ferries blow each other up? Or will the Joker blow up both? Batman goes in to confront the Joker.

Cue Name:	Always a Catch (6M56–57a)
Music In:	02:03:50
Visual:	CUT to EXT Pruitt Building
Music Out:	02:06:00
Visual:	CUT INT Pruitt Building
Duration:	2'20"
Description:	When Batman says, "I need five minutes alone," big chords, continuing ostinato
Context:	Batman interferes with the police raid on the Pruitt Building. Complicating action: Gordon's wife calls to say she's in trouble. ("He has the kids!") Batman realizes that the actual hostages and the clowns (the Joker's goons) have swapped masks and costumes.

Cue Name:	Storming Pruitt Building (6M57)
Music In:	02:06:00
Visual:	CUT INT Pruitt Building
Music Out:	02:09:50
Visual:	CUT INT ferry
Duration:	3'50"
Description:	Triumphant motif when the Joker becomes visible. Big fanfare for Batman triumphant when he rounds up the police officers who are about to attack whom they think are the Joker's goons.

Context: The police once again seem incompetent. Batman and Joker begin final fight.

Cue Name: Give It To Me (7M58)
Music In: 02:09:50
Visual: CUT INT ferry
Music Out: 02:13:20
Visual: Joker dangling
Duration: 3'30"
Description: Cue segues, picks up from "The Boats" cue earlier. Ramp up high strings: Stranger motif.
Context: "And here we go." Nothing happens. The clock ticks past midnight = the Joker fails.

Cue Name: A Little Push (7M59)
Music In: 02:13:25
Visual: Joker still dangling
Music Out: 02:15:22
Visual: CUT to industrial ruins
Duration: 1'57"
Description: High synthesizer tone at first, as Joker speaks, horn lines weave in: "You're just too much fun." As he says, "we're destined to do this forever," JT back. One last triumph. Anarchy back to reveal his "ace in the hole.—Mine's Harvey." Big build to the end of this monologue (Stranger).
Context: Final setup: "I took Gotham's White Knight and brought him down to our level. See, as you know, madness is like gravity, all it takes is a little push."

Cue Name: Eye For An Eye (7M60)
Music In: 02:16:15
Visual: As Two-Face talks to Gordon
Music Out: 02:20:30
Visual: On Gordon running down stairs
Duration: 4'15"
Description: Basses in linear developmental continuo based on HD. Strings go gradually higher and higher, denser in texture. Massive BT hit 2:19:59 when Batman shoves

Spotting 171

Context: Two-Face off Gordon's son. Batman falls, strings fall in pitch also, solo cello as Batman turns face, HD gentle.
Two-Face: "You think I wanna escape from this? There is no escape from this." The only morality in a cruel world is chance. Batman: "You were the best of us. [The Joker] wanted to prove that even someone as good as you could fall." Dent shoots at Batman.

Cue Name: I'm Not a Hero (7M61)
Music In: 02:20:30
Visual: On Gordon running down stairs
Music Out: 02:24:00
Visual: Gordon's monologue
Duration: 3'30"
Description: 2:22:16 Batman resolute: "I killed those people." His music back. BT, rousing build, gradually growing in texture.
Context: "You'll hunt me, condemn me, set the dogs on me because that's what needs to happen because sometimes the truth isn't good enough." Meanwhile, Fox destroys the sonar system.

Cue Name: A Dark Knight (7M62)
Music In: 02:24:00
Visual: Gordon's monologue
Music Out: 02:24:28
Visual: On CUT to black
Duration: 28"
Description: BT
Context: "He's a silent guardian, a watchful protector—a Dark Knight."

Cue Name: Closing Credits (compilation)
Music In: 02:24:32
Visual: Title Card "The Dark Knight"
Music Out: End
Visual: Fade to black
Duration: Approx 8'

APPENDIX II

ORCHESTRATIONS

           Cue #: 1M1
        Cue title: Prologue 10.02 Meeting
      Composer: HZ^1
   Orchestrator: Not known
Instrumentation: 0, 0, 0, 0, – 0, 0, 0, 0, – divisi vc 1, 2, 3, 4 (likely 28 cellos session, see also below), db^2
Starting Tempo: 96bpm (steady)
         Length: 151 bars (numbered 182–333)
          Notes: This score provides elements for the "Bank Robbery" opening. It is interesting that the composer has called this "Prologue" when the bank robbery actually functions as an essential main body plot point (the

---

[1] Composers key: Hans Zimmer (HZ), James Newton Howard (JNH), Lorne Balfe (LB) as per composer named in the scores.

[2] Key to orchestration labelling: woodwinds (flute, clarinet, oboe, bassoon) – brass (horns, trumpet, trombone, tuba) – percussion, timpani, piano, harp, strings [violins I (vln I), violins II (vln II), violas (vla), cellos (vc), double basses (db)] – Example: 0, 0, 0, 0 – 9, 3, 4+2bass, 2 – timp, 2 perc (taiko, low toms), strings (12, 12, 18, 12, 8) means no woodwinds, 9 horns, 3 trumpets, 4 trombones + 2 bass trombones, 2 tubas – timpani, taiko, low toms – no piano, no harp, 12 violins I, 12 violins II, 18 violas, 12 cellos, 8 double basses.

Joker steals the Mob's money). The orchestration here is minimalist, performing four permutations of the Stranger motif in different registers. The fact that the score starts in bar 182 suggests that music has been playing for 181 bars that do not involve the orchestra. From bar 206, the cellos play a repeating rhythmically accented semi-quaver pattern on the notes middle C and D a step above, in equal divisi (14/14).

Cue #: 1M2 version 1
Cue title: None stated (likely "Finding the Batman")
Composer: HZ
Orchestrator: EF[3]
Instrumentation: 0, 0, 0, 0 – 8, 0, 4+2bass, 2 – 2 perc (low toms, taiko, gong, gran cassa [gc]), strings
Starting Tempo: 96bpm (steady)
Length: 44 bars (1–44)
Notes: The score states *RFK* as film title. The abbreviation stands for *Rory's First Kiss*, which was used as a code name for *TDK* during shooting.[4] No cue title is given, but this is clearly the cue "Finding the Batman."

Cue #: 1M3 v13
Cue title: Buyer Beware
Composer: HZ
Orchestrator: WF
Instrumentation: 0, 0, 0, 0 – 9, 3, 6+bass, 2 – 3 perc (taikos, toms, bass drum), hp, pno, strings
Starting Tempo: 65bpm (variable)
Length: 71 bars (1–71)
Notes: Numerous tempo meter changes. Increase in tempo (102bpm) in bar 19 with the instruction "Much Faster!" indicating that this cue was to be recorded in one continuous take, across the tempo change.

---

[3] Orchestrators key: Elizabeth Finch (EF), Walter Fowler (WF), Brad Dechter (BD), Jeff Atmajian (JA), Bruce Fowler (BF), Suzette Moriarty (SM), Randy Kerber (RK), Kevin Kaska (KK).
[4] http://www.theguardian.com/film/2007/jul/19/news (24 October 2014).

Cue #:	1M4 v7
Cue title:	Dirty Cash
Composer:	JNH
Orchestrator:	BD
Instrumentation:	1, 1, 0, 2 – 9, 3, 0, 0 – 2 perc (taiko, gc), strings (in multiple divisi)
Starting Tempo:	96bpm (steady)
Length:	22 bars (1–22)
Notes:	JNH's cues use woodwinds, whereas HZ's mostly do not. Incidentally, JNH and HZ did not share the same orchestrators. This cue was omitted from the final film. It would have been heard during the brief conversation between Gordon and Batman in the bank vault. Set in G#-minor (as oppose to D-minor, which most cues are set in), this cue is built from long held notes in the low strings and an upper strings ostinato akin to the Batman ostinato.

Cue #:	1M5 v8
Cue title:	The New DA
Composer:	JNH
Orchestrator:	BD
Instrumentation:	0, 0, 0, 1+bass – 9, 0, 0, 2 – timp, strings
Starting Tempo:	69.10bpm [sic] (var.)
Length:	19 bars (1–19)
Notes:	The cue comprises a sparse strings and piano texture. Orchestrator Brat Dechter uses the same score paper template as was used for 1M4, even though upper woodwinds and trombones remain *tacet* throughout.

Cue #:	1M6 v7
Cue title:	Hostile Witness
Composer:	JNH
Orchestrator:	BD
Instrumentation:	0, 0, 0, 0 – 9, 0, 6, 2 – 2 perc (taiko, gc), timp, pno, strings
Starting Tempo:	91bpm (steady)
Length:	44 bars (1–44)
Notes:	The cue starts with the instruction "Orch. Tacet until

m. 6." This may seem odd, but it is quite likely that the six *tacet* bars acted as placeholders for other elements that were added beforehand or later, for example, synthesizer parts.

Cue #:	1M7 v8
Cue title:	Bank Warrants
Composer:	JNH
Orchestrator:	JA
Instrumentation:	0, 0, cor, 0, 1+contra − 9, 0, 4+2bass, 2 − timp, perc (Verdi bass drum, gc), pno, strings
Starting Tempo:	Not stated
Length:	63 bars (1–61)
Notes:	Orchestrator Jeff Atmajian uses a different score template than Dechter. His template, however, is also standardized: For example, there are staves for flute and harps in the full score even though they remain *tacet* throughout this cue.

Cue #:	*1M8*
Notes:	There are a number of cues that were not orchestrated and/or recorded during the orchestral sessions. These cues comprise synthesized, electronic, and ambient elements or snippets of material recorded for other cues or from the additional effects cues (see below). In the following, cues that were not orchestrated are omitted.

Cue #:	1M9
Cue title:	Who Appointed Batman?
Composer:	JNH
Orchestrator:	BD
Instrumentation:	0, 0, 0, 0 − 0, 0, 0, 0 − hp, strings (no db)
Starting Tempo:	49bpm (steady)
Length:	22 bars (1–22)
Notes:	See 2M9 v2

Orchestrations 177

        Cue #: 2M9 v2
    Cue title: Who Appointed Batman? [*sic*]
  Composer: JNH
 Orchestrator: BD
Instrumentation: 0, 0, 0, 0 − 0, 0, 0, 0 − hp, strings (no db)
Starting Tempo: 48.5bpm (var)
     Length: 15 bars (1–15)
      Notes: It would appear that several alternative versions of this cue were orchestrated. 2M9 v2 is basically an altered version of 1M9 and is very similar in all aspects, except for small adjustments and shorter duration. Somewhat more elaborate cello divisi are used in this version (there are no divisi cellos in the above version). Dechter includes a disclaimer in boxed text, presumably addressing the composer: "This is very much like 1M9v2 which was orchestrated first. This version (2M9) included the addition of celli harmonics doubling the string pads. You may want to consider doing the same for 1M9, which I added in a 1M9Alt version." By "string pad" Dechter may be referring to pre-recorded / synthesized strings.

        Cue #: 2M10 v2
    Cue title: Move the Money
  Composer: HZ
 Orchestrator: BF
Instrumentation: Strings 24, 14, 14, 8
Starting Tempo: 105bpm (steady)
     Length: 21 bars (22–43)
      Notes: The orchestral parts of this cue were not used in the film. Ambient music design and synthesized elements were used instead.

        Cue #: 2M12 v8
    Cue title: Halfway to Hong Kong
  Composer: JNH
 Orchestrator: BD
Instrumentation: 0, 0, 0, 2 − 9, 0, 6, 2 − 2 perc (taiko, gc), timp
Starting Tempo: 94bpm (steady)
     Length: 30 bars (1–30)

178   Appendix II

Notes: This cue was not used in the film but was featured on the soundtrack album.

Cue #: 2M13 v8
Cue title: Trip to Hong Kong
Composer: HZ
Orchestrator: SM
Instrumentation: 0, 0, 0, 0 – 2, 0, 3+3bass, 2 – pnp, strings
Starting Tempo: 65bpm (steady)
Length: 26 bars (1–26)
Notes: Number of horns not specified. Unusually, the piano part is written on a single staff.

Cue #: 2M14–15 v11
Cue title: Put A Smile on That Face
Composer: HZ
Orchestrator: BF
Instrumentation: 0, 0, 0, 0 – 9, 0, 6, 2 – gc (?), pno, strings (24vln, 14vla, 14vc, 8db) + ostinato
Starting Tempo: 96bpm (steady)
Length: 49 bars (53–101)
Notes: Un-pitched percussion instrument not specified but most likely gran cassa (gc). An additional strings ostinato is slotted in between the cello and bass staves, a 4-note semi-quaver figure that goes through different pitch permutations but remains static in contour and shape. It is not specified whether this will be recorded as an overdub or provided by samples or synthesizers.

Cue #: 2M16 v19
Cue title: LSI Extraction
Composer: HZ
Orchestrator: SM
Instrumentation: 0, 0, 0, 0 – 2 (?), 0, 3+3bass, 2 cimbassi – pnp, strings
Starting Tempo: 65bpm (var.)
Length: 100bars (1–100)
Notes: The number of horns is not specified but it is likely that more than two were required to balance against

Orchestrations 179

6 trombones. Unusual use of B♭-cimbasso. Note: In the film, this cue is very percussion-heavy once Batman starts fighting the guards. None of these percussion parts are included in this version of the score.

Cue #:	2M17 v6
Cue title:	Mobsters Taken to Justice
Composer:	JNH
Orchestrator:	RK
Instrumentation:	0, 0 (1cor), 0, 2 – 9, 3, 3+3bass, 2 – 2 perc (roto toms, gong drm, odaikos), timp, strings
Starting Tempo:	94bpm (var.)
Length:	22 bars (1–22)
Notes:	Orchestrator Randy Kerber's score is more detailed and nuanced than those of his colleagues. For example, he pays attention to the tuba's breathing, recommending, "breathe at will" when they have a long held pedal note starting in bar 2. He also indicates sync points, noting that the downbeat of bar 17 should coincide with the dialogue line "Yes, I believe."

Cue #:	2M18 v7
Cue title:	Are You Up To It?
Composer:	JNH
Orchestrator:	RK
Instrumentation:	0, 0, 0, 0 – 9, 0, 3+3bass, 2 cimbassi – 2 perc (tubular bells, odaikos), timp, hp, pno, strings (16, 14, 12, 28 (!), 8)
Starting Tempo:	48bpm (var.)
Length:	22 bars (1–22)
Notes:	The cellos in this cue play divisi a 4, which means seven cellos per part. These are spelled out on four separate staves labelled A, B, C and D and further detailed as alternating "left" and "right," to instruct desk split. In the film, this cue accompanies a conversation between the mayor and Dent that gets interrupted when the corpse of a Batman imposter hits the window. This coincides with a most dissonant

and visceral musical outburst (downbeat of bar 10). For example, a low 9-note cluster in the horns, marked *ff* "a piece of lumber." The violins are instructed to play an ascending quartertone row that eerily grinds against held notes played behind the bridge on the viola and cellos behind the bridge. The players are reminded that, "this should not sound pretty."

Cue #: 3M20–21 v4
Cue title: Hero Without a Face
Composer: JNH
Orchestrator: JA
Instrumentation: 0, 0 (+1cor), 0, 0 – 9, 1, 4+2bass, 2 – timp, hp, strings (24vln, 14vla, 14vc)
Starting Tempo: 85bpm (var.)
Length: 28 bars (1–28)
Notes: The brass is instructed to play "Warm and noble. Always legato." The score also makes reference (by use of cue-sized staves) to an additional strings session in which 28 cellos and 8 basses were recorded separately and, presumably, later added to the final mix.

Cue #: 3M22 v6
Cue title: Joker Crashes Party
Composer: HZ
Orchestrator: WF
Instrumentation: 0, 1, 0, 0 – 9, 0, 4+2bass, 2cimb – 2 perc (taiko, bd, low toms), hp, 2pnos, strings
Starting Tempo: 93.63bpm (var.)
Length: 50 bars (24–74)
Notes: The scores states "audio starts bar 3," suggesting some instructions for the music editor (perhaps backing tracks?). There is an extremely busy cello part (for 1/4 of the section) from bar 43 (the 17th bar). Brass, percussion, and low strings play the syncopated Triumphant motif in bars 72–74, whereas in 1M1 it was performed without orchestral parts.

Cue #: 3M23 v2
Cue title: Panic Room
Composer: HZ
Orchestrator: KK
Instrumentation: 0, 0, 0, 0 – 9, 0, 0, 2 – 14vc, 8cb
Starting Tempo: 96bpm (steady)
Length: 14 bars (1–14)
Notes: A very brief cue, the only score typeset in portrait page layout.

Cue #: 3M24–25
Cue title: Then You're Gonna Love Me
Composer: HZ
Orchestrator: BF
Instrumentation: 0, 0, 0, 0 – 9, 0, 6, 0 (2cimb) – 3 perc ("big drum" [*sic*], toms, big taiko), pno, strings (24vln, 14vla, 14vc, 8cb)
Starting Tempo: 130bpm (steady)
Length: 36 bars (58–94)
Notes: The score states "fixes by Kevin Kaska," referring to changes made to the orchestration and/or the cue after Bruce Fowler had finished orchestrating it. Six trombones are called for. Although this is not specified further, the extremely low range of tbns 5+6 suggests bass trombones. Dissonant intervals extremely low in the instruments' range (in this case, a cluster of C, D, E-flat) result in a heavy and rough sound that is (perhaps rather suitably) ugly. To add to the dissonance, the strings are instructed to play stabs that coincide with the brass on "any note." Toms play driving triplets while the rest of the orchestra stomps accents. This cue is heard when Batman attacks the Joker in the ballroom.

Cue #: 3M26–27 v5
Cue title: Lau, Watch the World Burn
Composer: HZ
Orchestrator: BF
Instrumentation: 0, 0, 0, 0 – 9, 3, 6, 2 – strings (24, 14, 14, 8)

Starting Tempo: 80.4bpm (var.)
Length: 54 bars (1–54)
Notes: This cue comprises long held notes that create shifting textures by use of different articulations in the strings. Fowler has left a note to the copyist: "Copyist please note: We should have this available for the 28 cello line-up—just prepare the parts as they are in this score." This is the clearest indication in these orchestrations that an overdub session was held with 28 cellists.

Cue #: 3M28 v6
Cue title: Loud Enough?
Composer: HZ
Orchestrator: WF
Instrumentation: 0, 0, 0, 0 – 9, 0, 4+2bass, 2 – 2 perc (low toms, bd), strings
Starting Tempo: 65bpm (var.)
Length: 83 bars (9–92)
Notes: "Audio Start=" is marked in the score, once again indicating that backing tracks were used. In the finished mix, Batflaps is used repeatedly The strings are asked to play busy figuration in extremely quiet dynamics.

Cue #: 3M30 v4
Cue title: Speech Ambush
Composer: HZ
Orchestrator: BF
Instrumentation: Strings (24, 14, 14, 8)
Starting Tempo: 96bpm (var)
Length: 6 bars (33–38)
Notes: Mourning motif. This is a gentle ending to the noisy ambush that leads directly into the next cue (3M32B)

Cue #: 3M32B V1.03
Cue title: ?
Composer: HZ
Orchestrator: SM
Instrumentation: 0, 0, 0, 0 – 9, 0, 3+3bass, 2 – 2 perc (slapstick, odai-

Orchestrations 183

Starting Tempo:	ko), timp, pno, strings (16, 14, 28 (!), 8) 90bpm (steady)
Length:	19 bars (1–19)
Notes:	Intricate textures, aleatoric strings, low clusters in brass, resulting in an eerie overall sound. For added percussion, the scores asks to "USE PRE-RECORD: Tutti noise hits: snap pizz., col legno sul pont., col legno behind bridge."

Cue #:	4M34–35ALT
Cue title:	?
Composer:	JNH
Orchestrator:	JA
Instrumentation:	0, 0, 0, 0 – 9, 0, 2+3bass, 2 – strings (0, 0, 28, 8)
Starting Tempo:	66bpm (var.)
Length:	17 bars (1–17)
Notes:	The cue header reads "4M34–35 ALTERNATE (no midi)." There is no indication whatsoever where in the film this cue was to be used. Given the brevity of the cue, perhaps this was intended as an alternative for 3M32B? In any case, the cue numbering and naming in the third reel is somewhat inconsistent. The trombones are labelled 1, 2 (top staff), 4, 5, 6 (bottom staff, bass trombone).

Cue #:	4M37–38
Cue title:	I Don't Know Anything
Composer:	JNH
Orchestrator:	BD
Instrumentation:	0, 0, 0, 0 – 9, 3, 6, 2cimb – strings
Starting Tempo:	96bpm (steady)
Length:	71 bars (1–71)
Notes:	Bars 1–16 are *tacet*. Synthesized parts were probably added here later. These first 16 *tacet* bars would appear to be 4M37, seeing that the next cue (see below) is an overlay for 4M38 and starts in bar 17. Extensive use of aleatoric technique. For example, from bar 18 onwards, the lower trombones are instructed to play "ad-lib slow ugly glisses; soft murmur until end (breathe when needed)," meandering around the

low E and D♯. From bar 27, the strings are given different three-note cells of adjacent tones respectively (e.g., B,-B♭-A) and told to play these "randomly & rapidly repeat ad-lib." The resulting texture is dissonant and tense.

Cue #:	4M38ALT
Cue title:	Overlay
Composer:	JNH
Orchestrator:	JA
Instrumentation:	0, 0, 0, 0 – 5, 0, 3bass, 2 – strings (0, 0, 28, 8)
Starting Tempo:	96bpm (steady)
Length:	24 bars (17–41)
Notes:	Atmajian suggests an overlay for the previous cue, bars 17–41. Musically, this is very similar to 3M34–35ALT.

Cue #:	4M39
Cue title:	Blood On My Hands
Composer:	JNH
Orchestrator:	BD
Instrumentation:	0, cor, 0, 0 – 0, 0, 0, 0 – hp, pno, strings
Starting Tempo:	69.1bpm (var.)
Length:	28 bars (1–28)

Cue #:	4M39B v2
Cue title:	LB's High Strings
Composer:	HZ
Orchestrator:	BF
Instrumentation:	0, 0, 0, 0 – 9, 0, 6, 2 – strings
Starting Tempo:	105bpm (var.)
Length:	30 bars (1–30)
Notes:	Although HZ is listed as composer, the cue name strongly suggests that this cue was written by Lorne Balfe. In the context of the film, this appears to be additional music added after JNH had written 4M39.

Orchestrations

Cue #:	4M40
Cue title:	I Am the Batman
Composer:	JNH
Orchestrator:	BD
Instrumentation:	0, cor, 0, 0 – 0, 0, 0, 0 – 2 perc (gc, taiko), timp, pno, strings
Starting Tempo:	91bpm (var.)
Length:	71 bars (1–71)
Notes:	Very sparse on the page, this cue sounds much richer in the final film.

Cue #:	4M42 v4.03
Cue title:	Pod Deploys
Composer:	HZ
Orchestrator:	BF
Instrumentation:	0, 0, 0, 0 – 9, 3, 6, 2 – 2 perc (big drums, taiko), strings
Starting Tempo:	96bpm (steady)
Length:	24 bars (1–24)
Notes:	Busy pattern in the strings underneath chords in the brass. The heavy percussion is significantly processed and amplified in the final mix.

Cue #:	4M42b v2
Cue title:	Batman Down
Composer:	HZ
Orchestrator:	BF
Instrumentation:	0, 0, 0, 0 – 9, 1(2cue), 2+2bass, 2 – perc (big low drum), strings+slide strings
Starting Tempo:	98bpm (steady)
Length:	24 bars (1–24)
Notes:	Stranger motif. Three staves are dedicated to strings slides (vln, vla, vc), possibly indicating overdubs.

Cue #:	4M43 v6
Cue title:	Gotcha
Composer:	JNH
Orchestrator:	JA
Instrumentation:	0, 0, 0, 0 – 9, 0, 4+2bass, 2 – 2 perc (gc, Verdi bd), timp, strings (no vln)

Appendix II

Starting Tempo: 96bpm (steady)
Length: 29 bars (1–29)
Notes: In this cue, HD returns in the brass. The strings are asked to play extremely quietly (***ppp***).

Cue #: 4M44
Cue title: Gordon Returns Home
Composer: JNH
Orchestrator: BD
Instrumentation: 0, 1, 0, 0 – pno, strings
Starting Tempo: 52bpm (var.)
Length: 16 bars (1–16)
Notes: A sparse cue. The piano is playing a lead part and is told to play "delicately." Overdubs or synthesizer layers were used in the mix, as indicated by the use of cue notes in the lower strings in bars 4–7, followed by the instruction "*Play*" on the upbeat to bar 8.

Cue #: 5M42 [*sic*]
Cue title: BB 5M42 Backup RFK v1.0 LB
Composer: HZ (LB?)
Orchestrator: KK
Instrumentation: 0, 0, 0, 0 – 9, 3, 6(2bass?), 2 – 4 perc (huge taiko [*sic*], toms, KA rims [*sic*], doepher [*sic*]), strings
Starting Tempo: 102bpm
Length: 43 bars (1–43)
Notes: The labelling of this cue seems somewhat odd. The "LB" in the title almost certainly stands for Lorne Balfe. The label "backup" suggests that this cue was supposed to be available as an alternative version or additional support for another cue. Looking at the music more closely, it is highly likely that this is additional material for 4M42 ("Pod Deploys"). This is a continuous series of loud stabs and hits over long held notes and/or busy strings ostinato.

Cue #: 5M46–47 v9.01
Cue title: Wired [includes "Aftermath"]
Composer: HZ

Orchestrator: WF
Instrumentation: 0, 0, 0, 0 – 8, 0, 4+2bass, 2 – 1 perc (bd), strings
Starting Tempo: 162bpm (var.)
Length: 197 bars (1–197)
Notes: An extremely long cue that lasts almost seven minutes. It is noteworthy that this cue was not broken up into separate cues 5M46 and 5M47, perhaps due to the continuous dramatic arch these two cues accompany: Having previously learned that the Joker has taken Dent and Rachel hostage, Batman rushes to their rescue—and fails to save Rachel.) This long cue also includes "Aftermath," starting at bar 157 on page 23.

Cue #: 5M48–49 REVv9
Cue title: Harvey Two-Face
Composer: JNH
Orchestrator: JA
Instrumentation: 0, 0, 0, 0 – 9, 3, 5+1bass, 2 – 1 perc (gc), timp, pno, strings
Starting Tempo: 48bpm (var.)
Length: 58 bars (1–58)
Notes: The first part of this cue features a high intense drone whose source is most likely purely synthetic. The latter half contains synth drone on low D (paired with low strings) and low horns and trombones undulating between D and C♯, *ppp*, with instruction "ad lib slow 'ugly' bends."

Cue #: 5M50 v2.06
Cue title: This Is My City
Composer: HZ
Orchestrator: SM
Instrumentation: Strings
Starting Tempo: 86bpm (steady)
Length: 39 bars (1–39)
Notes: Oddly, this cue is set in 8/8 and various odd meters over 8th. The tempo is stated as 8th=192. This brief cue has a constant pedal on D in the low strings with three iterations in the high strings on b♭" and d'".

Cue #:	5M51–52 v9.01
Cue title:	Hospital Bomb Scare
Composer:	HZ?
Orchestrator:	WF
Instrumentation:	0, 0, 0, 2 (cue only) – 9, 0 (cue only), 4+2bass, 2 – 2 perc (low toms cue only, bd), strings
Starting Tempo:	94bpm (steady)
Length:	100 bars (1–100)
Notes:	Perhaps the only time woodwinds appear in one of HZ's cues. However, they are labelled "cue only," i.e., were pre-recorded. Another rather long cue. A recording of this exact cue is posted on Lorne Balfe's personal website as "Gotham Towers," where he claims credit for this piece as "additional music" for *TDK*.[5]

Cue #:	6M52b v6.05
Cue title:	Hospital Bomb Scare [*sic*]
Composer:	HZ
Orchestrator:	WF
Instrumentation:	0, 0, 0, 0 – 9, 0, 4+2bass, 2 – 1 perc (huge taiko [*sic*]), pno, strings
Starting Tempo:	96bpm (steady)
Length:	59 bars (37–96)
Notes:	Almost certainly intended as the continuation of 5M51–52, as the numbering suggests (though not the title).

Cue #:	6M55 v2.1
Cue title:	The Boats
Composer:	HZ
Orchestrator:	SM
Instrumentation:	0, 0, 0, 2contrabsn – 9 (? unspecified), 3, 3+3bass, 2 – 2 perc (tom-toms, bd), timp, hp, pno, strings
Starting Tempo:	90.4bpm (var.)
Length:	115 bars (1–115)

---

[5] http://www.lornebalfe.com/includes/mp3singleplayerhtml5.php?id=103 (26 June 2015).

Orchestrations

Notes: This is the only HZ cue with live woodwinds (double bassoons). It is remarkable how sparse this cue looks compared to the well-produced end results (during the bomb scare on the ferries).

Cue #: 6M56-57a
Cue title: Always a Catch
Composer: HZ
Orchestrator: BF, KK
Instrumentation: 0, 0, 0, 0 – 9, 0, 6, 2 – 3 perc (surdo, huge taiko, large toms), strings + 28vc
Starting Tempo: 103bpm (var.)
Length: 68 bars (1–68)
Notes: Very loud and aggressive cue, full of hits.

Cue #: 6M57
Cue title: Storming Pruitt Building
Composer: HZ
Orchestrator: KK
Instrumentation: 0, 0, 0, 0 – 9, 0, 3+3bass+3overdub, 2, 5 perc (surdo, toms, huge taiko, surdo part 2, large drum), piano, strings
Starting Tempo: 101bpm
Length: 95 bars (1–95)
Notes: The full cue title reads, "6m57 v6.00_o p7r LB," once again indicating that Lorne Balfe wrote or at least co-wrote this cue. This is another rather long cue that accompanies the action-laden and potentially confusing showdown in the Pruitt Building. An extremely loud and busy cue, full of heavy accents and hits. The cue calls for the biggest live percussion array in any of the cues. When in bar 25, the "large drum" enters, the orchestrator puts "this was 'cheese menu' patch, omit??" which appears to be a reference to the mock-up that may have contained some sample or drums pre-set considered potentially ill-suited for the final score.

190 Appendix II

Cue #: 7M58 v1.1
Cue title: Give It To Me
Composer: HZ
Orchestrator: WF
Instrumentation: 0, 0, 0, 0 – 9, 0, 4+2bass, 2 – 2 perc (low toms, bd, taiko rims, KA rims), pno, strings + 3 staves of "strings effects"
Starting Tempo: 96bpm (var.)
Length: 114 bars (1–114)
Notes: The score calls for single notes on a de-tuned piano. The strings effects are aleatoric glissandi that start in bar 56 and grow increasingly louder and denser (more notes stacked).

Cue #: 7M59 v2
Cue title: A Little Push
Composer: HZ
Orchestrator: BF
Instrumentation: 0, 0, 0, 0 – 9, 0, 0, 0 – 1 perc (bd), pno, strings (vc, cb).
Starting Tempo: 96bpm (steady)
Length: 57 bars (1–57)
Notes: A very sparse cue, supplemented by pre-recorded and synthesized elements in the final mix. The Anarchy motif is played by the piano here (in D) and the piano is de-tuned with the instruction to sound "honky-tonk." At the end of the cue, the strings shift from D to C, a step down, which is a similar, though less dramatic, gesture as the major-9th leap of the Stranger motif: The Joker is defeated.

Cue #: 7M60 v7
Cue title: An Eye For An Eye
Composer: JNH
Orchestrator: JA
Instrumentation: 0, 0, 0, 0 – 0, 0, 0, 0 – 1 perc (gc), timp, hp, strings
Starting Tempo: 88bpm (steady)
Length: 83 bars (1–83)
Notes: The strings are told to play "Alla Passacaglia quasi elegaic (sempre molto sostenuto)." Also, "All the

strings to have a darker/muted tone 1–51 then begin to brighten at 52 and be full tone by 66." The orchestrator furthermore states, "Ideally this should be done in 3 sessions: twice with full strings and once with the 28 vc/8 cb. It must at least be done once with each of the two types of sessions!!"—It is not known how these overdubs were possible with UK Musicians' Union rules stipulating punitively high additional fees for players if they are recording overdubs. This cue in its course grows increasingly terse and relies on ever-building strings and rising to a final dynamic of *fff* (Dent dies).

Cue #:	7M61 v4
Cue title:	I'm Not A Hero
Composer:	HZ
Orchestrator:	SM
Instrumentation:	0, 0, 0, 0 – 9 (? unspecified), 0, 6, 2 – hp, pno, strings
Starting Tempo:	65bpm (var.)
Length:	83 bars (1–83)
Notes:	The only cue to start with the instruction *rubato*. In bar 13, a solo cello reprises the Mourning motif.

Cue #:	7M62 v5
Cue title:	A Dark Knight
Composer:	HZ
Orchestrator:	EF
Instrumentation:	0, 0, 0, 0 – 9, 0, 4+2bass, 2 – 2 perc (snare drum, taiko), strings
Starting Tempo:	93.496bpm (steady) [*sic*]
Length:	1–14 bars
Notes:	The snare is playing straight semiquavers throughout. The whole cue is a prolonged crescendo, the strings playing spiccato figurations, getting increasingly louder, while the brass hold chords that swell and then recede. The chord progression is Dm (3 bars), F (2 bars), Dm (3bars) and, finally, in *fff*, Bb.—The author has seen a video taken during the final brass session for this film: The horns for this cue were overdubbed at Air Lyndhurst Studios in

London, playing the alternating chords in half sections from opposing balconies in the former church.

Cue #:	n/a
Cue title:	103bpm Action Ice Theme
Composer:	HZ
Orchestrator:	WF
Instrumentation:	0, 0, 0, 0 – 9, 3, 4+2bass, 2 – 2 perc (bd, low toms) – strings
Starting Tempo:	103bpm (steady)
Length:	136 bars (1–136)
Notes:	This appears to be a variation on 6m56–57a ("Always a Catch") with a lot of very similar material. Here, quite unconventionally the strings take up 12 staves, covering "solo cello," vln I, II, III, vla I, II, vc I, II, III, IV, and two staves for double bass.

Cue #:	n/a
Cue title:	DK EFX #1
Composer:	not known
Orchestrator:	BF
Instrumentation:	0, 0, 0, 0 – 9, 3, 4+2bass, 2 – 2 perc (bd, low toms) – strings
Starting Tempo:	60bpm (steady)
Length:	68 bars (1–68)
Notes:	With this score, Bruce Fowler seems to be providing a series of dissonant stacks of brass and strings (alternating), crescendoing and decrescendoing in different variations on several pitch and register permutations. Elsewhere, the brass are asked to simply hold long notes in a steady *p*. Considering the name of this cue, these chords were perhaps intended as sound snippets to be drawn upon where appropriate.

Cue #:	n/a
Cue title:	Long and Short Slides Reverse
Composer:	HZ
Orchestrator:	KK
Instrumentation:	0, 0, 0, 0 – 9, 3, 4+2bass, 2 – strings (no db)
Starting Tempo:	96bpm (steady)

Orchestrations 193

Length: 79 bars (1–79)
Notes: A series of <u>down</u>ward glissandi across the entire ensemble, in various glissando speeds (e.g., "gradual very slow gliss. Downward") and different dynamics.

Cue #: n/a
Cue title: Long and Short Slides
Composer: HZ
Orchestrator: KK
Instrumentation: 0, 0, 0, 0 – 9, 3, 4+2bass, 2 – strings (no db)
Starting Tempo: 96bpm (steady)
Length: 80 bars (1–80)
Notes: A series of <u>up</u>ward glissandi across the entire ensemble, in various glissando speeds (e.g., "gradual very slow gliss. Downward") and different dynamics.

Cue #: n/a
Cue title: New Batman Theme vSAD48 Str
Composer: HZ
Orchestrator: BF
Instrumentation: Strings (24 vln, 14 vla, 28 vc + 14 vc [!], 8 db).
Starting Tempo: 96bpm (steady)
Length: 469 bars (!) (1–469)
Notes: This extremely long cue calls for a massive strings section of 88 players. Additional staves suggest pre-recorded ostinati in violins and cellos, an overdubbed (?) cellos tremolo and a solo cello. It is not clear where exactly this material was used but it largely comprises thematic material for the Batman character.

Cue #: n/a
Cue title: RFK Slides "Seagulls and Whale Sounds"
Composer: HZ
Orchestrator: KK
Instrumentation: 28 cellos
Starting Tempo: 66bpm (steady)
Length: 10 bars (1–10)

Appendix II

Notes: This brief cue calls for "All cellos use artif. harmonics on the 4th or 5th keep hand spread locked during gliss., use the entire string. The locked hand spread is more important than the pitches. The duration of the slide is random. (a la Crumb: Voice of the Whale)." These effects would likely be added to different cues.

Cue #: n/a
Cue title: RFK: 3min Slide Reverse
Composer: HZ
Orchestrator: KK
Instrumentation: 0, 0, 0, 0 – 9, 3, 4+2bass, 2 – strings (no db)
Starting Tempo: 46bpm (steady)
Length: 43 bars (1–43)
Notes: A series of <u>down</u>ward glissandi across the entire ensemble, in various glissando speeds (e.g., "gradual very slow gliss. Downward") and different dynamics.

Cue #: n/a
Cue title: RFK: 3min Slide
Composer: HZ
Orchestrator: KK
Instrumentation: 0, 0, 0, 0 – 9, 3, 4+2bass, 2 – strings (no db)
Starting Tempo: 46bpm (steady)
Length: 47 bars (1–47)
Notes: A series of <u>up</u>ward glissandi across the entire ensemble, in various glissando speeds (e.g., "gradual very slow gliss. Downward") and different dynamics.

BIBLIOGRAPHY

Bordwell, D. "Intensified Continuity Visual Style in Contemporary American Film." *Film Quarterly* 55, no. 3 (2002): 16–28.
———. *The Way Hollywood Tells It: Story and Style in Modern Movies*. Berkeley/Los Angeles: University of California Press, 2006.
Brooker, W. *Hunting the Dark Knight: Twenty-First Century Batman*. London / New York: I. B. Tauris, 2012.
Chion, M. *Audio-Vision: Sound on Screen*. New York: Columbia University Press, 1994.
———. *The Voice in Cinema*. New York: Columbia University Press, 1999.
Collinson, G. *Holy Franchise, Batman!: Bringing the Caped Crusader to the Screen*. London: Robert Hale Ltd, 2012.
Copland, A., and V. Perlis. *Copland: 1900 Through 1942*. 2nd ed. London: Faber and Faber, 1987.
Docherty, T. "Introduction." In *Postmodernism: A Reader*, edited by T. Docherty, 1–31. London: Routledge, 1992.
Glass, P. *Words Without Music*. New York: Liveright Publishing Company (a divison of W. W. Norton & Company, Inc.), 2015.
Halfyard, J. K. *Danny Elfman's Batman: A Film Score Guide*. Lanham, MD: Scarecrow Press, 2004.
Heine, E. *James Newton Howard's Signs: A Film Score Guide*. Lanham, MD: Scarecrow Press, 2016.
Hoover, T. *Keeping Score: Interviews with Today's Top Film, Television, and Game Music Composers*. Boston: Course Technology, 2010.
Isaacs, B. *Toward a New Film Aesthetic*. New York/London: Continuum International Publishing Group Ltd., 2008.
Jess-Cooke, C. *Film Sequels: Theory and Practice from Hollywood to Bollywood*. Edinburgh: Edinburgh University Press, 2009.

Kugelberg, J. *Punk: An Aesthetic.* New York: Rizzoli International Publications, 2012.
Lack, R. *Twenty Four Frames Under: A Buried History of Film Music.* London: Quartet Books, 1997.
Lyotard, J. F. *The Postmodern Condition: A Report on Knowledge.* Minneapolis: University of Minnesota Press, 1984.
Manning, M. K., and M. Forbeck. *Batman: A Visual History.* London: Dorling Kindersley Ltd, 2014.
Manning, M. K., and R. Greenberger. *The Batman Vault: A Museum-in-a-Book with Rare Collectibles from the Batcave.* Philadelphia, PA: Running Press, 2009.
McGowan, T. "The Exceptional Darkness of The Dark Knight." *Jump Cut: A Review of Contemporary Media*, Spring 2009.
Morgan, D. *Knowing the Score: Conversations with Film Composers About the Art, Craft, Blood, Sweat, and Tears of Writing Music for Cinema.* New York: HarperCollins, 2000.
Prinz, J. "The Aesthetics of Punk Rock." *Philosophy Compass* 9, no. 9 (2014): 583–93.
Reynolds, C., and M. Brill. "On the Art and Craft of Film Music: A Conversation with James Newton Howard." *Hopkins Review* 3, no. 3 (2010): 320–51.
Reynolds, R. *Super Heroes.* London: B. T. Batsford, 1992.
Schelle, M. *The Score: Interviews with Film Composers.* Beverly Hills, CA: Silman-James Press, 2000.
Smith, S. C. *A Heart at Fire's Center: The Life and Music of Bernard Herrmann.* Berkeley/Los Angeles: University of California Press, 2002.
Sonnenschein, D. *Sound Design: The Expressive Power of Music, Voice and Sound Effects in Cinema.* Studio City, CA: Michael Wiese Productions, 2001.
Thompson, K. *Storytelling in the New Hollywood: Understanding Classical Narrative Technique.* Cambridge, MA: Harvard University Press, 1999.
Treat, S. "How America Learned to Stop Worrying and Cynically ENJOY! The Post-9/11 Superhero Zeitgeist." *Communication and Critical/Cultural Studies* 6, no. 1 (2009): 103–9.
White, M. D., R. Arp, and W. Irwin, eds. *Batman and Philosophy: The Dark Knight of the Soul.* Hoboken, NJ: John Wiley & Sons, 2008.
Wyatt, J. *High Concept: Movies and Marketing in Hollywood.* Austin: University of Texas Press, 1994.

INDEX

9/11, 24–25
Academy Awards: disqualified from, 7; Hans Zimmer nominated for, 3; Hans Zimmer winning, 5; Heath Ledger winning, 29; James Newton Howard nomitations, 11; Nelson Riddle winning, 14
additive layering: and dramatic pacing, 96; as scoring solution, 90; Hans Zimmer composing by, 45; of musical strata, 53; of synthesizer parts, 99
Air Lyndhurst Studios, 32
Akai, 32
Alfred: first appearance in compic book, 14; knows that Bruce is Batman, 85; planning trip to Hong Kong, 92; reads Rachel's letter 87; retrieving fingerprints from a bullet, 68; serving breakfast, 27; searching for Gordon's men, 95; watching Coleman Reese on television, 102
Allison, Ryeland, 7
ambient music design: in conclusion, 133–134; in the context of other soundtrack elements, 111; Mel Wesson's job title, 11; Wesson's share on cue sheet, 54; pushing boundaries and building bridges, 116–120; pushing composed musical score into realm of sound design, 113
America: accent, 72; Americana-style, 25; Captain America and U.S.-American allegiance, 24; Justice League of, 14, 15, 16; sound of Harvey Dent Theme, 81
anarchy: Joker bringing, 28; musical motif, 68, 77, 84–85, 122, 131; mutation of motif, 96; zen-like gongs of, 99

Anthony, Pete, 50
Arbeitsbeschaffungsmaß-nahme, 32
Arkham Asylum: in Batman #258, 15; Living Hell, 16
artifacts, 121
Atmajian, Jeff, 50, 61, 64, 82, 88, 89
audience: affected by music, 49; and Anarchy motif, 84; and Batflaps, 67–68, 130; and Batman Theme (BT), 69, 93, 124; appeal, 21; and Harvey Dent Theme (HD), 81; and Joker Theme (JT), 72–75, 77; can tire quickly, 96; enabled to hear dialogue, 92, 102, 103, 121; increasingly experiences incredulity towards narrative, 22; knows Batman's true identity, 28; point of audition and sound perception, 113, 119, 122; response to *TDK,* 17–18, 23–25, 60, 68, 123, 132; targeted by pop songs, 20
audio post-production, 42
audio-quantization, 117; for *Batman Begins*, 37
The Avengers, 23, 126
Backdraft, 4, 8, 35
Badami, Bob, 39
Badelt, Klaus, 41
Balfe, Lorne: at RCP, 4; additional music for *The Simpsons Movie*, 7; composing cues for *TDK*, 59; "Hospital Bomb Scare" aka "Gotham Towers" 57; royalty share on PRS cue sheet, 54; *Terminator: Genesys*, 6
Bane: in *The Dark Knight Rises*, 120; Vengeance of, 16
bangs, 7, 53, 106–108
bank robbery: action-driven vignette, 21; music cue, 6, 56, 74, 78–79, 84, 90, 97–99, 105, 107; scene, 70; sonic clarity and artifacts 120–123
basso ostinato, 88
Batflaps, 65, 67–68, 74, 94, 103, 106, 108–109, 123–124, 125, 130–131
Batman: abducts Lau, 65; and Dent, 82, 84, 132; and Gordon, 57; and Joker, 27–29, 76, 77, 79, 80, 84, 134; and Rachel, 77, 85, 87; batflaps, 67–68; Bruce Wayne is, 85; film franchise, 17–19; hero or vigilante?, 22–26; heterosexual, 27; interrogates Joker, 27, 108, 130–131; interrogates Maroni, 59, 60; kill, 15, 58; logo, 74; LSI extraction, 123–125; make-up, 27; music cues, 56, 62, 63, 75, 82, 88, 91, 92, 95, 96, 100, 101, 102, 103, 104, 105, 106, 107, 108, 109, 123; origins, 13–17; ostinato, 59; realism, 20–21; reinventing, 45; suit, 112; v. Superman, 47; Theme (BT), 69–72; truck chase, 126–129; why so serious?, 19–20;

Batman Begins: ambient music design, 117; disqualified from Academy Awards, 7; textual context, 15, 17, 20, 21, 22; music cues for, 7, 37, 67, 69, 90, 109; Zimmer and Howard collaboration on 45–46; Zimmer and Nolan partnership starting with, 8
Batman Forever, 16, 18, 20
Batman Returns, 16, 18
Batman & Robin, 16, 18, 20
Batman Theme, 63, 69–72, 76, 93, 94, 95, 103, 104, 106, 107, 125, 126, 128
Batmobile, 14, 21, 92, 128
Batpod, 21, 55, 59, 70–72, 76, 80, 92, 97, 101, 104, 108, 126–129
Bay, Michael, 4, 6, 113
Bleedings Fingers, 8
Blu-ray, 111
Boom Boom Satellites, 60
Bruckheimer, Jerry, 38
BT. *See* Batman Theme
budget: Batman franchise, 19; big-budged features, 3, 8; decreasing music, 33; overdubs, 64; *TDK* (film), 5, 17; *TDK* (music), 61
Buggles, 2
Burton, Tim, 15, 16, 18, 19, 20, 23, 45
Caped Crusader, 17, 22, 67, 68, 91. *See also* Batman
Catwoman, 13, 16
CGI. *See* computer-generated imagery
Chicago, 15, 23, 60, 126
cinéma vérité, 20, 130
click tracks, 64

collaboration, 4, 17, 39, 42, 44, 45, 46, 48, 51, 72, 115
comic book, 15, 17, 13, 14, 15, 16, 17, 18, 19, 20, 21, 22, 23, 24, 25, 28, 58, 134
commercial, 13, 15, 6, 7, 13, 15, 17, 18, 38, 44, 61, 133,
Commissioner Loeb, 99–100
computer-generated imagery, 15, 18, 21, 40, 61, 112, 128, 124
context, 13
Copland, Aaron, 63
creative control, 42
creative process: dub part of the, 43; collaborative, 36, 111, 113–116, 117, 133, 134; Zimmer's 4, 31
credit: composer 6, 7; Bob Badami, 39; Bob Kane, 15, 19; ghostwriters, 40; John Williams, 44; shared, 44; string quartet, 60; *TDK*, 54, 125; Wesson's, 11, 116, 147n19
Crimson Tide, 4, 6, 35
Cubase, 33, 34, 39, 48
cue: demo, 38, 49; Howard's, 50, 53, 61, 63, 69, 82, 83, 85, 88–89; instrumentation, 61; in *The Dark Knight Rises*, 120; Klaus Badelt, 41; omitted at dub, 42, 113; ostinato in, 91, 94, 95, 97, 104; recording, 38, 65, 83, 90, 92, 108; in *TDK*, 39, 54–59, 70–71, 72, 77, 87, 93, 96, 99–101, 105, 106, 107, 125, 131; "The Stanton Curve," 6; Zimmer's, 3, 5, 6, 7, 8, 35, 36, 39, 53, 61–62, 82, 102, 103

cue sheet, 7, 54, 58, 60, 143n1
The Da Vinci Code, 5
Daft Punk, 45
The Dark Knight Rises: Bane in, 120; Batman seen in broad daylight in, 103; dubbing of, 120; final cue of, 35; Howard not working on, 46; Nolan's, 16, 17, 23; set in New York City, 23
The Dark Knight, 6, 7, 8, 13, 43, 46, 66, 84, 103, 133–134; action sequences in 96, 126; cues in, 39, 49, 51, 90; demos and suites for, 36; Grammy for score, 11; in conclusion, 133–134; in context, 13–29; instrumentation of the score, 61–63; musical ideas for, 36, 37, 88–89; recording the score of, 63, 65; sound design, 111; soundtrack album, 44; spotting of 53–60; team involved in 41–42; themes and motifs (music), 66–88; viewing and hearing, 111, 113; Zimmer's collaborators on, 39, 45, 47, 50, 111, 115–116; Zimmer scoring, 46
Dawes, Rachel: Batman and, 71, 77, 102; Bruce and, 85–86, 87, 100; death, 21, 25, 27, 29, 59, 77, 83, 86, 87, 99, 100; Dent and, 29, 60, 71, 76, 82, 83, 85, 87, 99, 100, 101–102, 113, 132; Joker and, 27, 75, 76
DC Comics, 13–15, 74
Dechter, Brad, 50, 57, 61
demo, 33, 39, 49, 50, 66, 89, 115; and suites, 48–49
Dent, Harvey: and the Joker, 28, 75, 84, 91, 103, 127; and Rachel, 60, 71, 87, 99, 100, 101, 102, 113; becomes Two-Face, 77, 80, 81, 87, 101, 131–132; death, 22, 71; fund raiser for, 21, 60, 75; in "Batman #50," 14; kidnap, 76, 95, 102, 126–127; orchestra and, 91; role in *TDK*, 25; Wayne and, 100; white knight, 81
Detective Comics. *See* DC Comics
diegetic, 57, 58, 59, 60, 93, 121
digital: post-production, 114; sound, 40, 114, 117
director, 2, 3, 4, 6, 8, 10, 24, 35, 36, 37, 38, 40, 41, 46, 48, 49, 130, 147n1
Disney, 4
Djawadi, Ramin, 4, 144n18
Dooley, Jim, 7
drone, 36, 39, 82, 87, 94, 131
dub, 39, 40, 41, 42–44, 61, 113, 115, 116, 119
dubbing engineer, 42
Ducard, Henri, 15
dynamic, 34, 36, 37, 55, 65, 81, 87, 88, 90, 92, 97, 98, 99, 102, 103; markings, 37, 81, 83, 95, 100; processors, 65; range, 66, 73, 111, 112, 114, 117
EastWest PLAY, 48
editing: film, 5, 35, 38, 40, 41, 49, 58, 105, 114, 128; music, 31, 37–38, 39, 47,

49, 54, 64, 65, 69, 83, 87, 99, 119
editor: film, 41; music, 38, 39, 41, 54, 114, 115; sound, 113, 115
Elfman, Danny, 10, 16, 18, 20, 45, 69
emerging technology, 114
ensemble, 34, 37, 60, 62, 64, 65, 83, 88, 100
equalizers, 65
Eshkeri, Ilan, 8
executive: Disney, 4; producer, 5; studio, 4, 8, 42
experiment, 32, 35; at the dub, 44, collaborative, 5; on *TDK*, 43–44, 61, 116, 134; with electronic instruments, 2; with sound, 11, 73, 116
Fairlight, 3, 32
fan: comic book, 15, 19, 20; engagement, 19; of franchise, 18, 108, 147n1; of film music, 44, 145n18; of Wesson's methods, 50; of Zimmer, 135n3
fidelity, 20, 64
filmic narrative, 20, 89, 107, 126
Finch, Elizabeth, 61
Fowler, Bruce, 39, 61
Fowler, Walter, 39, 61
Fox: Lucius, 25, 59, 71, 85, 92, 93, 96, 104, 105; network, 16; studios, 136n12
franchise: Burton's Batman, 15; DC Comics film, 138n18; Marvel film, 138n18; Nolan's Batman, 19; Hulk, 21; *Pirates of the Caribbean*, 8, 35; superhero, 17–19; Transformers, 6

Mr. Freeze, 14, 18
frequency: high, 73, 98, 112, 121, 131; low, 67, 109, 112, 120, 123, 124, 131; of speaking voices, 121; range, 66, 98, 102, 109, 111, 114, 117, 129, 132
Gerrard, Lisa, 5, 37
Giacchino, Michael, 113
Gibson, Alex, 39, 54, 115
GigaStudio, 33, 48
Gladiator, 5, 37, 144n10
Goldenthal, Elliot, 18, 20, 69
Goldsmith, Gerry, 9
gongs, 84, 99
Gordon, 95, 102, 103, 125; and Batman, 24, 57, 68, 87, 91, 100, 103, 104, 105; and Commissioner Loeb, 99–100; and Dent, 82, 131; and his family, 83–84, 86, 87, 88; and Joker, 26, 29, 76, 87, 99, 130–131; and Ramirez, 70, 83, 91, 99; closing monologue, 71, 71; killed, 21, 58, 59, 76, 86;
Gotham City, 16, 20, 23, 25, 26, 59, 60, 67, 76, 80, 81, 87, 95, 97, 101, 103, 125
Grammy, 9, 11
Grayson, Dick, 16
Gregson-Williams, Harry, 4, 6, 8, 44, 91, 145n22
Hackford, Taylor, 9
Hamm, Sam, 15
Hanna-Barbera Productions, 14
harmony, 36, 124
Harvey Dent Theme (HD), 58, 80–84, 87, 88, 132
Hefti, Neil, 14
Helmholtz nomenclature, 53

hero: comic book, 14; definition of superhero, 22–24; in films, 17–19, 20, 21, 22, 26, 47, 63, 69, 71, 82, 85, 87, 107; or vigilante, 22; score, 25, 47, 105, 107
Herrmann, Bernard, 73
Hollywood: business model, 7, 17, 18, 20, 38, 61; conventions of, 20, 21, 22; composers, 4, 5, 9, 40; filmmaking, 38, 114, 126, 128, 133; film music 6, 31, 89, 133, 134; political outlook, 25; golden era, 7; Zimmer in, 2, 3, 35, 40
Hong Kong, 23, 25, 56, 58, 59, 92, 93, 95, 108, 123; location access in, 21; sequence, 21, 55, 107, 123–125
hospital: demolition, 29, 80, 95, 102, 103; Dent in, 27, 82, 84; evacuation, 68, 95, 103; family members in, 68; Gotham General, 80; *Hospital Bomb Scare*, 21, 57, 59, 68, 71, 95, 102–103, 104, 132
Howard, James Newton: biography, 9–11; collaborating with Zimmer, 44–47; collection at USC, 55; Harvey Dent Theme by, 80–84; instrumentation and orchestration, 61, 63; score for *TDK*, 22, 49, 53, 54, 57, 58, 59, 63, 64, 66, 85, 88–90, 108; suite and collaboration, 48–51; technical setup, 47–48, 49
Howard, Ron, 4, 8, 35

Hugo, Victor, 14
idiom: orchestral, 4, 50; pop, 3, 48, 88; preferred, 106; similar, 6; trends, 31; wide range of, 9
Illusion of Choice, 7
IMAX, 111, 112, 114, 133
Inception, closing scene of, 5; collaborating with Richard King on, 116; cue "Time" in, 5, 35; recording Johnny Marr for, 37; Zimmer and Nolan working on, 47
instrumentation, 61, 173, 174, 175, 176, 177, 178, 179, 180, 181, 182, 183, 184, 185, 186, 187, 188, 189, 190, 191, 192, 193, 194
interface: between Zimmer and Howard, 45; digital audio, 33; keyboard, 32, 34; touchscreen, 33, 34; user, 114, 117, 118; with filmmaking practice, 7; with post-production processes, 41
Interstellar, 114
interrogation: Batman and Joker, 27, 108, 130–131; Batman and Maroni, 59, 60; coercive, 25, 27; room, 23, 25, 27, 100, 101, 108, 130–131; scene, 84; torture during, 24, 109
Iron Man, 20, 21, 22, 23, 138n18
Jablonsky, Steve, 4, 6
Jackman, Henry, 4, 7, 54
John, Elton, 4, 9
Joker, the, 13, 14, 15, 26, 36, 55, 58, 71, 78, 79, 80, 81, 82, 84, 85, 87, 90, 91, 92, 96, 101, 104, 105, 107, 108, 112, 120, 122, 123, 131,

132; and Batman in *TDK*, 22, 23, 24, 25, 27, 29, 68, 69, 71, 75, 76, 79, 84, 95, 104, 106. *See also* interrogation; and Dent in *TDK*, 29, 75, 84; as chaotic antagonist, 26–29; as terrorist, 25; comparison of Batman and, 28; Heath Ledger as, 29; inspiration for, 14, 27; Jack Nicholson as, 18; kills Rachel, 25, 29; kill the 25; not crazy, 28, 29; not political, 25; representing pure evil, 26; sexual orientation, 27. *See also* bank robbery, "Stranger" (motif), "Anarchy" (motif), "Triumphant" (motif), Joker Theme

Joker Theme: 26, 58, 59, 71, 72–77, 79, 97, 98, 99, 100, 101, 102, 103, 105, 120, 122, 123, 126, 127, 129, 131; creation of, 36; sonic layers in, 37

JT. *See* Joker Theme

Julyan, David, 8

Justice League, 14, 15, 16, 17, 23

Kane, Bob, 13, 15, 19

Kane, Don, 27

Kasdan, Lawrence, 10

Kaska, Kevin, 61

Keaton, Michael, 18

Kerber, Randy, 61

King Kong, 10, 108

King, Richard, 113, 115, 116, 126

Kofsky, Steve, 4

Lau, 56, 82, 93, 124, 125; and Joker, 77; and mob bosses, 75; rendition of, 25, 65, 65, 68, 70, 82, 94, 125

Lebo M, 4, 37

Ledger, Heath, 27, 29, 72, 99, 130, 147n18

Levine, Michael A., 7

Levinson, Barry, 2–3

licensed music, 59–60

Lillie Yard Studio, 2, 11

The Lion King, 4, 37

locked picture, 35, 38, 40

Loeb, Gillian B. *See* Commissioner Loeb

London: Air Lyndhurst Studios, 32; JW Media based in, 60; London Symphony Orchestra, 37; recording in, 32; Temple Church in, 32; Wesson born in, 11; working on TDK in, 46; Zimmer in, 1–3, 32, 33, 45

Lone Ranger, 8

Los Angeles, 3, 8, 9, 55

Love Theme, 85–86; "Then You're Gonna Love Me," 56, 76, 85, 108

LSI Extraction, 21, 56, 62, 65, 68, 70, 92, 123–125

LT. *See* Love Theme

MacPro, 33, 48

madness: Batman's, 84; descend into, 16; Harvey Dent, 77, 80, 82, 88; Joker's, 80, 132; like gravity, 77, 80; stylized, 131–132

Maleficent, 9

Malick, Terence, 4, 5

Man of Steel, 34, 47, 138n18

Maroni, Sal, 25, 29, 71, 83, 104; Batman and, 59, 60
Max/MSP, 118
Media Ventures, 3, 4, 108
medium: cultural, 1; performance, 3, 32, 50, 63; physical, 55, 113; pitch range, 123
melody, 26, 36, 41, 49, 71, 81, 82
Memento, 8, 20
Metasynth, 11, 117–120
MIDI, 33–34, 50, 118
Miklosh, 60
Miller, Frank, 15
mix: -downs, 33; final, 41, 61, 62, 89, 94, 95, 98, 104, 105, 112, 114, 115, 120; re-, 42; surround, 112; temp, 115
mixer, 39; sound, 112
mixing: desk, 34; console, 48; demo, 49; digital, 40, 65, 66, 87, 114; engineer, 39–40; facilities, 8; live elements, 39, 65, 87, 89; on during dub, 43, 44, 50, 87, 89, 98, 102, 112, 117, 121, 122, 124, 125, 132; process, 64, 65; scoring by production, 99; soundtrack album, 44; takes, 31
mock up. *See* demo
Moriarty, Suzette, 61, 62, 83, 86, 94
motif, 49, 53, 66, 67, 77, 84, 97; Anarchy, 68, 77, 84–85, 122, 131; Batflaps, 65, 67–68, 74, 94, 103, 106, 108–109, 123–124, 125, 130–131; brass, 69, 70, 71, 107; four-note, 96; in Batman Theme, 69–72, 125; Joker, 72; Mourning, 86–87; mutation of motif, 96; Stranger, 75, 76, 77, 79–80, 84, 99, 123, 129; Triumphant, 75, 76, 78–79, 98, 107, 128, 145n22; two-note, 69, 71, 107;
motivic development, 36
Mourning (motif), 86–87
music editor. *See* editor
music technology, 2, 31–34, 40, 47–48, 50, 111
musical strata, 53, 90
MV. *See* Media Ventures
My Beautiful Laundrette, 2
Myers, Stanley, 2, 3
Myerson, Alan, 39–40
Native Instruments Komplete, 48
Nicholson, Jack, 18
Nightwing, 16
Nolan, Christopher: and music spotting, 97, 126, 129; at the dub, 43, 116, 124; *Batman Begins*, 8, 15, 17; Batman trilogy, 11, 13, 19, 47; *Inception*, 5; *cinéma vérité*, 130; use of digital technology, 114, 133; editing decision, 100, 105, 106; heightened realism, 20–21, 66, 70, 108, 112, 129; humor, 127; *Insterstellar*, 7, 32; interpretation of Batman, 19–20, 22, 69; interpretation of Dent, 81; interpretation of the Joker, 26–29, 72; *The Dark Knight*, 13, 16, 17, 21, 24, 25; *The Dark Knight Rises*, 16, 17, 23; version of Batmobile, 128; working

with David Julyan, 8;
working with Hans Zimmer,
35, 36, 37, 38, 45, 47, 72, 87
Nolan, Jonathan, 17, 24
Novick, Ed, 112
Omnisphere, 47
orchestra, 108; balance of the,
65, 94; for Batman and
Dent, 90–91; real, 50, 66;
recording, 32, 38, 41, 50, 64,
65, 90; recorded in stems,
41, 65; versus synthesizers,
32, 141n2; virtual, 32,
orchestration, 53, 55, 58, 61–
63, 64, 65, 66, 83, 88, 90,
92, 94, 95, 101, 102, 104,
105, 108; compared to final
score, 70, 80; cue
numbering in, 57, 59; error
in, 94; Howard providing, 9;
Lorne Balfe's, 59; Myers
teaching Zimmer, 2; of *TDK*
and USC Libraries, 11, 55;
Suzette Moriarty's, 83, 86,
94; Zimmer seeking help
with, 5
orchestrator, 6, 55, 56–57, 58,
61, 62, 64, 82, 85, 97, 116;
Brad Dechter, 50, 61; Bruce
Fowler, 61; Elizabeth Finch,
61; Jeff Atmajian, 50, 61,
64, 82, 88, 89; Kevin Kaska,
61; Patrick Russ, 40; Pete
Anthony, 50; Randy Kerber,
61; Suzette Moriarty, 61, 62;
Walter Fowler, 61
Örvarsson, Atli, 7
Oscar. *See* Academy Awards
ostinato, 53, 59, 69, 70, 71, 72,
88, 90, 91, 92, 93, 94, 95,
96, 97, 98, 99, 100, 101,
103, 104, 105, 106, 122,
123, 128
overdub, 39, 50, 63, 65, 89
palette (musical), 10, 32, 35,
43, 48, 61, 63, 92, 98, 119
pattern, 68, 82, 90–96, 97, 98,
99, 100, 103, 104, 107,121,
123,
Passacaglia, 88, 89
The Penguin, 14
performer, 5, 31, 60, 66
Pirates of the Caribbean, 8, 35
post-production: audio, 42,
112; changes to the score
during, 40, 55; decisions
made during, 111; dialogue
re-recorded during, 112;
digitally enabled, 40; team,
41, 112
Powell, John, 4, 5
The Prestige, 8, 20
Pro Tools, 33, 37, 38, 39, 48,
50
process: compositional, 31, 35,
49, 82; creative, 4, 31, 36,
43, 46, 111, 112, 113–116,
118, 133–134; collaborative,
6, 36, 46, 82, 112, 113–116,
134; demo, 49; dialectical,
36; dubbing, 42, 119;
filming, 5, 38, 134; holistic,
34; innovation, 118; mixing,
64; of orchestration, 64;
post-production, 40, 41,
112; production, 7, 48, 112;
scoring, 6, 9, 39, 41, 44, 48,
49, 134; technical, 6, 31, 65,
66, 111
processing, 31; computer
processing speed, 33
processor: dynamic, 65;
effects, 48, 73, 84, 90, 125

producer, 2, 5, 6, 8, 9, 11, 37, 38, 39, 45, 134
production: cost, 60; creatives involved in, 112; digital, 40, 89, 114; environment, 41; facilities, 8; film, 17, 18, 38, 111, 114; Hanna-Barbera Productions, 14; method, 7; music, 11, 38–39, 55, 60, 65, 66, 117; music company, 8; pre-, 34–36; phases of, 41; post-, 40, 41, 42, 44, 55, 89, 111, 112, 114, 115, 116, 134; pre-, 111, 119; process, 7, 48; re-, 117; Remote Control Productions, 4; 54; scoring by, 99; sound, 111, 112; techniques, 58; value, 7, 50
prologue, 77, 80, 97, 117
Pruitt Building, 57, 62, 69, 71, 79, 80, 95, 104, 105
Rā's al Ghūl, 15
Rachel: *See* Dawes, Rachel
Rain Man, 2, 3, 31
RCP. *See* Remote Control Productions
realism, 20, 21, 61, 108, 112, 122; heightened, 66, 112
recording, 4, 5, 6, 8, 31, 32, 34, 36, 37, 38, 39, 40, 41, 44, 47, 48, 50, 53, 58, 60, 63–66, 70, 73, 83, 86, 87, 89, 90, 105, 109, 112, 114, 117, 120, 126
reel, 55, 68, 117
Reese, Coleman, 68, 71, 92, 95, 96, 102, 103,
Remote Control Productions, 4, 5, 6, 7, 8, 34, 40, 41, 43, 47, 48, 54, 136n8
Reznor, Trent, 44

RFK. *See* Rory's First Kiss
Riddler, the, 14
Rifkin, Jay, 3, 4
Ring, The, 8
Robin, 13, 14, 16, 18, 19, 20, 138n18
Rock, The, 4, 6, 35, 39
rock: aesthetic, 72; guitar riff, 35, 78; music, 10
Rodford, Maggie, 2
Roland, 32, 33
Rona, Jeff, 4, 135n1
Rory's First Kiss, 57, 59
Ross, Atticus, 44
Ross, Diana, 9
SAM, 33, 40, 48
sample library, 7, 32, 33, 38; 5.1 surround, 33; Zimmer records his own, 32, 33
sampler, 32, 33, 34, 40, 48, 141
sampler, 32; Akai, 32; custom-built software, 34; *GigaStudio*, 33, 48; replied by computers, 33; Roland S760, 32; SAM software, 33, 40, 48
samples, 33, 34, 37, 66, 118; blended with live session recordings, 61, 108; double with synthesiser sounds, 37; -level, 117; orchestral, 32, 33; rendering live musicians redundant, 33, 66; sample-based demo, 37, 115; supplant with real instruments 32
Scarecrow, 14, 91, 94
Schubert, 60
Schumacher, Joel, 10, 16, 18, 19, 20, 23

score, 2, 3, 4, 5, 6, 7, 8, 9, 10, 11, 14, 16, 18, 20, 22, 31, 32, 34, 35, 36, 37, 38, 40, 41, 43, 44, 45, 46, 47, 49, 50, 51, 53–109; analysis, 53–109; as part of the soundscape, 111–132; close, 91, 105; conductor's, 55; crafting the, 38–39; layout, 105; Metacritic, 18; orchestrator's, 55, 56–57, 97; recording the, 63–66; session, 39, 90; under-, 54, 57, 68, 71, 71, 117; wrangler, 39; writing a, 40
scoring techniques, 53, 88–109m 154n22
Scott, Ridley, 3, 5, 11, 35
Scott, Tony, 4, 6, 145n22
script, 4, 35, 48, 133
session: changed purpose of the scoring, 40–42; dubbing, 61; musician, 9, 66; orchestral, 105; overdub, 62, 64, 89; Pro Tools, 39; score, 39, 90; scoring 6, 37, 38, 39, 41–42, 45, 61, 62, 63, 64, 66, 70, 89, 94, 108, 120, 144n11
sequel, 16, 17–19, 21, 44, 90, 138n19
Shyamalan, M. Night, 10, 48, 49
Signs, 10, 48, 49
SMPTE time code, 55
software: custom-built, 34, 40; developer, 47; glitch, 34; instrument, 7, 48; Max/MSP, 117; Metasynth, 11, 117–119; recording, 48, 64; sampler, 33, 34, 40, 48; sequencing, 33, 48, 117;

specialist, 6; synthesizer, 33; Vienna Ensemble Pro, 34
sonic, 31, 69, 73, 112–113, 115, 118, 127; clarity, 120–123, 149; competition, 40; continuity, 90; distractions, 130; duration, 130; elements, 120; extension, 109; experience, 115; heft, 130; identity, 67–68, 129; impact, 78, 126; interplay, 111; layers, 37; logo, 130; palette, 61, 118; parallel, 130; possibilities, 114, 118; qualities, 37, 117, 118; slap in the face, 78, 145n19; sonically conceived music, 116; sphere, 114; territory, 111, 113–114, 118; texture, 73; vector, 74
sound design, 11, 40, 41, 51, 90, 94, 97, 98, 111, 112, 113–116, 117, 118, 119, 120–132, 133–134, 135–136n3, 146n12
soundscape, 98, 111–132
spectacle, 20, 21, 78, 96, 108, 112, 133, 146n12
Spectrasonic, 47
speculative, 16, 41, 116
Spider-Man, 17, 23, 47, 138n18
Spielberg, Steven, 5
spotting, 40, 53, 54–60, 144n4, 149–177
stems, 33, 41, 42, 49, 65, 102, 120
stripes. *See* stems
Storming Pruitt Building, 57, 62, 71, 95, 104–106
storytelling, 20, 67, 134

Stranger (motif), 75, 76, 77, 79–80, 84, 99, 123, 129
studio: Air Lyndhurst, 32; executives, 4, 42; facilities, 6, 7, 48; film, 17, 18, 19, 135n3, 136n12, 147n1; furniture, 48; Lillie Yard, 2, 11; London, 33; music, 8, 48, 62; recording, 47; session, 38; setup. 32, 33
style: Americana-, 25; and idiom, 6, 9; *cinéma vérité*- 130; comic book, 14, 17; compositional, 3; developmental, 45, 88; musical, 41, 45, 88; non-Western, 10; of Nolan's Batman, 22; pseudo-realistic, 15; range of, 50; reinvent, 7; surf music, 14; symphonic, 60
suites, 8, 36–38, 39, 48–49
superhero. See hero
superimposition, 90
Superman, 14, 16, 18, 22, 23, 24, 25, 47, 138n18
surround sound, 33, 34, 40, 112, 114
swells, 53, 97, 102, 104–107, 124, 125
synchronization, 54, 58, 64
synthesizer, 2, 3, 4, 5, 7, 10, 11, 32, 33, 35, 37, 47, 50, 65, 69, 70, 78, 86, 90, 91, 92, 97, 99, 100, 104, 105, 120, 132, 141n2
TDK. See *The Dark Knight*
television, 1, 2, 7, 11, 13, 14, 16, 19, 33, 102
terror, 24, 29, 73
texture, 60, 62, 65, 73, 78, 89, 90, 91, 93, 97, 98, 99, 100, 101, 102, 103, 104, 105, 106, 108, 120, 121, 122, 123, 124
The Power of One, 4, 34
The Sixth Sense, 10, 49
theme. See Batman Theme, Harvey Dent Theme, Joker Theme
Thin Red Line, A, 4, 5, 35
thud, 53, 74, 106–109, 120, 127
Total Soundtrack Composition, 111, 113–116
Transformers, 6, 113
Trank, Josh, 147n1
triumphant, 80, 105, 125, 127; Triumphant (motif), 75, 76, 78–79, 98, 107, 128, 145n22;
truck, 21, 27, 55, 59, 68, 71, 76, 97, 125, 126–129, 133
Tumbler, 91, 127–129
Two-Face, 15, 14, 25, 27, 29, 57, 83, 84, 88; Dent becomes 77, 80, 81, 87, 101, 131–132;
Tykwer, Tom, 45, 146n11
University of Southern California, 9, 11, 55
Unstoppable, 6, 145n22
Verbinski, Gore, 8
vigilante, 22, 23, 24
villain, 14, 16, 26, 27, 28
Waldorf, 33
War on Terror, 24–26
Warner Bros. Pictures, 9, 17, 19, 29, 43, 67, 74
Wayne, Bruce, 14, 15, 16, 17, 20, 21, 27, 58, 59, 92, 100, 123; allies, 16; and Alfred, 92, 95; blackmail, 92; death, 15; Enterprises, 96; Fox and,

59, 93; fund raiser, 21, 58, 60, 78, 99; is Batman, 22, 45, 107, 123; Manor, 14; mourns Rachel, 59; penthouse, 79, 95; restaurant, 57, 60; yacht, 92 weight, 68, 69, 72, 105, 109, 123–125, 129
Wesson, Mel, 11, 37, 39, 40, 42, 43, 45, 46, 47, 49, 54, 61, 67, 111, 116–120, 122, 123, 134
Wired, 57, 77, 87, 100–102, 104, 131
Wuertz, 70, 83, 144n4
X-Men, 22, 23, 138n18
Yamaha, 2, 47, 48; C6 grand piano, 48; DX7, 2, 47; GS-1, 9
Zebra2, 7

Zimmer, Hans, biographical overview, 1–9; collaborators, 39–40, 115, 116, 133; score for *TDK*, 11, 26, 36, 41–42, 53, 54, 61, 62, 63, 66, 67, 72–74, 80, 82, 85, 87, 88, 89, 90–109, 115, 116; style and technique, 2, 3, 4, 5, 6, 7, 8, 9, 20, 31, 32, 34–36, 37–38, 41, 42–44, 45, 47, 48, 55, 61, 66, 80, 90–109, 115, 120; technical setup, 31–34, 37–38, 38–39; working with Howard, 11, 20, 22, 44–47, 50, 51, 61, 62, 63, 66, 134; working with Nolan, 7, 8–9, 69, 87; working with Wesson, 11, 40, 67, 116, 119, 134

ABOUT THE AUTHOR

Vasco Hexel leads the Masters Programme in Composition for Screen at the Royal College of Music, London, and is visiting lecturer at the Faculty of Music, University of Cambridge. He is consultant at the Film and Television Music Research Center, Beijing Normal University. He earned his Bachelor of Music degree in Film Scoring and Vocal Performance at the Berklee College of Music, Boston. He earned his Masters degree in Composition for Screen at the Royal College of Music, where he also submitted his Ph.D. thesis "Understanding Contextual Agents and their Impact on Recent Hollywood Film Music Practice." His ongoing research interests include practice-lead investigations of the influence of technology on media music composition and production as well as musical creativity and originality in competitive and collaborative environments. He has composed music for award-winning animations, documentaries, commercials, and feature films. His music has featured in numerous broadcasts internationally and his clients include the BBC, Channel 4, ZDF, France 2, the Discovery Channel, ABC Television, and Universal Production Music. He is a member of the British Academy for Film and Television Arts and the Royal Television Society.

www.hexelproductions.com

Printed in France by Amazon
Brétigny-sur-Orge, FR